THE ETHICS AND POLITICS OF
HUMAN EXPERIMENTATION

THE ETHICS AND POLITICS OF HUMAN EXPERIMENTATION

PAUL M. McNEILL

School of Community Medicine, University of New South Wales

Published by the Press Syndicate of the University of Cambridge
The Pitt Building, Trumpington Street, Cambridge CB2 1RP, UK
40 West 20th Street, New York, NY 10011-4211, USA
10 Stamford Road, Oakleigh, Melbourne 3166, Australia

Printed in Hong Kong by Colorcraft

National Library of Australia cataloguing in publication data
McNeill, Paul M.
The ethics and politics of human experimentation
Bibliography.
Includes index.
ISBN 0 521 41627 2.
1. Human experimentation in medicine – Moral and ethical
aspects. 2. Medical ethics. I. Title.
174.28

Library of Congress cataloguing in publication data
McNeill, Paul M. (Paul Murray), 1946–
The ethics and politics of human experimentation/Paul M. McNeill.
Includes bibliographical references and index.
ISBN 0-521-41627-2
1. Human experimentation in medicine – Moral and ethical aspects.
2. Human experimentation in medicine – Political aspects. I. Title.
R853.H8M35 1993
174′.28--dc20   92-32322
                                                          CIP

A catalogue record for this book is available from the British Library

ISBN 0 521 41627 2 hardback

To Deanne

Contents

Tables

Preface

Since the mid-1960s most Anglo-American countries, and many European countries, have adopted a system of review by committee to ensure that human subjects of experiments are treated ethically. Two things struck me when I began to investigate the workings of these committees: first, the lack of easily accessible empirical and descriptive material on these committees; and second, the lack of a theoretical model on which their work should be based. On the first issue, I have collected all the material that I could find – from the literature (some of it now out of print), from an empirical study of committees in Australia, and from interviews of relevant people in the United States, Canada, New Zealand, Europe and India. This material is presented in Chapters 3 and 4 of the book and in Appendix 1.

On the second issue – the underlying theory of review by committee – I have puzzled long and hard over the appropriate model for committee review. I came to see human experimentation itself, and the review of experimentation by committees, as a political process. I mean this in the broadest sense – as a balancing of different priorities in the community as a whole. Recognising the political dimension makes it apparent that the appropriate mechanism for resolution of ethical issues in experimentation will also involve political considerations. This is the issue that I develop in later chapters in this book. The early chapters establish the need for restraint on researchers who experiment on human subjects by reporting accounts of unethical experimentation. They also outline the development of rules of law and ethics.

The book is the result of a substantial re-working of my doctoral dissertation, 'Science, Society and the Subject', which was written in history and philosophy of science for the University of New South Wales. However, whereas the thesis focussed on Australian research ethics review, this book is international in its focus. The book is half as long as the thesis and has been brought up to date so as to include recent developments.

During 1987–88 I took study leave and met many people who have written about research ethics review in the United States, Canada, Britain and Europe. Those who were particularly helpful include Professor George J. Annas of the Center for Law and Medicine in the Boston School of Public Health (where I spent most of my sabbatical); Professor Jay Katz of Yale, one of the early and comprehensive writers in the field; Professor Robert J. Levine, also from Yale, author of a definitive book on ethics review in the United States; Professor Povl Riis from Denmark, one of the authors of the Helsinki Declaration II; Professor Margaret A. Somerville from the McGill Centre for Medicine Ethics and Law; and Judith N. Miller who was, at the time, with the Canadian Medical Research Council.

On my return from study leave I began an empirical study of research ethics review in Australia, which was funded by the Australian National Health and Medical Research Council (NHMRC). This was a three-year project that coincided with the historical and theoretical exploration I was conducting for the thesis. It was rewarding to be able to undertake the historical and theoretical study while simultaneously having the support of the grant to collect empirical data on the current practice of ethics review in Australia. I believe the empirical and the theoretical approaches complement each other well.

The book is necessarily cross-disciplinary. It touches on a number of fields including philosophy, history, law, bioethics, philosophy of science, sociology of science, and scientific questions concerning the validity of scientific research. I make no pretence of having expertise in all these areas and acknowledge that I may not have done justice to all of them. I would defend this approach however as an attempt to bring together the many fields of enquiry that are relevant to the ethics of experimentation on human subjects. Indeed, like Weisbard (1987), I consider that a multi-disciplinary approach is necessary for informed and sensible public policy.

I have been supported by many people – too many for me to acknowledge them all by name. However, I particularly thank those who helped me with the original thesis, especially my supervisor Professor Randall Albury. Other friends who gave me considerable assistance include Dr Frank Clarke (from the Department of History,

Philosophy and Politics at Macquarie University) and Jo Gaha (from Social Work at the University of Newcastle). I am very grateful to them for their many helpful suggestions and the detailed and painstaking work that they put into reviewing early drafts of the thesis. My colleague Brian Bromberger from the Faculty of Law at the University of New South Wales was helpful with the chapter on the law (Chapter 5).

One of the advantages of re-working a thesis is that I had the benefit of my examiners' reports as well as the reports of readers for Cambridge University Press. All of my examiners and readers subsequently made themselves known to me and I am pleased to be able to acknowledge their careful, detailed and encouraging comments. This includes Professor Peter Singer of the Centre for Human Bioethics, Monash University; Professor George J. Annas from Boston University School of Public Health (also mentioned above); Dr Richard Gillespie, previously of the Department of History and Philosophy of Science at the University of Melbourne; Professor Hiram Caton, of the Division of Humanities, Griffith University; and Professor Max Charlesworth, previously of the Department of Humanities, Deakin University.

I also wish to thank Emeritus Professor Richard Lovell, Chairman (until 1991) of the Medical Research Ethics Committee of the NHMRC, for his gracious encouragement of the empirical work. On particular issues, I wish to thank Professor George Annas for directing me to the material on the World Medical Foundation (Chapter 2), and, in Chapter 9, I am grateful to Gerry Harlos of Harlos Australia Pty Ltd for pointing out the importance of group leadership, consensual decision-making and training, and for drawing my attention to the relevant literature; and to Amanda Adrian for pointing out the parallel between my ideas on representation on research ethics committees and representation of management and employees on occupational health and safety committees.

I am very appreciative of the contribution of Catherine Berglund and Julie Walters who have been research assistants with me on consecutive NHMRC projects; and Susanna Davis, research assistant with me on another project. All three have extended themselves beyond their roles in helping with research material and reading critically early drafts of this book. I am very appreciative too of the support from Professor Ian Webster, previous Head of the

School of Community Medicine at the University of New South Wales, who has collaborated with me on a number of research projects. I am grateful to Professor Peter Baume, Head of the School of Community Medicine, for his encouragement and thankful for the practical support from Pam Brown and Gallia Therin.

I appreciate the friendship of my colleague Dr Debbie Saltman in urging me some time ago to develop my interest in health law and medical ethics, and also the helpfulness of Peter Drahos in suggesting that I make an empirical study of Australian research ethics committees. I wish also to express my gratitude for the inspiration of Swami Chidvilasananda who continues to show me by example what it means to be an ethical, compassionate and loving human being.

Lastly, I gratefully acknowledge the support of my wife Deanne who has reviewed many of these chapters and given me welcome advice on the construction both of my thesis and subsequently of this book. She has put up with an absent and distracted husband for four years now and continued to sustain me emotionally and physically. I know I speak for both of us in saying that we look forward to exploring the world that (I'm told) exists beyond the blue screen of my computer.

Sydney   PAUL M. McNEILL

Abbreviations

AHEC	Australian Health Ethics Committee
CIOMS	Council for International Organizations of Medical Sciences
FDA	Food and Drug Administration (United States)
IEC	institutional ethics committee (Australia)
IRB	institutional review board (United States)
LREC	local research ethics committee (Britain)
MRC	Medical Research Council (Britain and Canada)
MREC	Medical Research Ethics Committee (Australia)
NBCC	National Bioethics Consultative Committee (Australia)
NHMRC	National Health and Medical Research Council (Australia)
NHS	National Health Service (Britain)
OPRR	Office of Protection from Research Risks (United States)
PHS	Public Health Service (United States)
PRIM&R	Public Responsibility in Medicine and Research (United States)
RCP	Royal College of Physicians (Britain)
REB	research ethics board (Canada)
REC	research ethics committee
SAMS	Swiss Academy of Medical Sciences
SSHRC	Social Sciences and Humanities Research Council (Canada)
WHO	World Health Organization

Introduction: The Ethics and Politics
of Human Experimentation

The words 'human experimentation' in the title of this book refer
to experimentation which is conducted on human beings to test an
idea or hypothesis. The human beings on whom the experiments
are conducted are known as 'participants' or, more commonly, as
'subjects' of experimentation. The principal method for ensuring
that human experimentation is ethical is to require researchers to
have their proposals for experimentation on human subjects
approved by a research ethics committee.

THE POLITICS OF REVIEW

I will argue that review of experimentation on human subjects by
a research ethics committee is a political process as much as it is
an ethical process. This is politics in the broadest sense. It is about
balancing one set of interests in the community against another set
of interests: the interests of science and scientists (principally) on the
one hand and the interests of the human subjects of experimentation
on the other.

It is believed that 'the most vigorous science is unfettered science'
(Cheston and McFate 1980: 7–8). In other words, science will be most
effective when scientists are free to determine their own research
directions and agenda. Consequently, scientists decide on the aims
of their research, the methods, and the research materials. In the case
of human experimentation, these materials are the human subjects
from the particular subject population being investigated. Scientists
also assess the evidence and interpret it within their preferred
theoretical framework.

However, this freedom to experiment is not absolute. As Cheston
and McFate (1980) pointed out, it is also accepted that society has a
duty to protect its citizens from potential harm. Atrocities committed

1

by doctors and researchers on prisoners during the Second World War, and experiments conducted at other times, in the name of science, have shown that some researchers are capable of a callous disregard for the welfare of their human subjects. As a result, the freedom of scientists to experiment on human subjects has been limited by the need to justify their research on ethical grounds. There are now national and international codes of ethics which set out some parameters for what constitutes ethical research.

RESEARCH ETHICS COMMITTEES

Most countries have adopted a system of review of proposals for research by a research ethics committee to consider whether those proposals are ethical in terms of national and international codes of ethics. In many countries the requirement for review must be satisfied before research is eligible for funding and for publication in reputable scientific journals. Some countries have also made it a requirement of law that all research on human subjects must have gained the approval of an ethics committee.

Research ethics committees have a discretion to decide whether the proposals are reasonable and can be supported, whether they are so unreasonable that they should be rejected, or whether there is some modification that could be made to satisfy the requirements for ethical research and allow the study to go ahead. Given this reliance on committees it is important to examine research ethics committees to see whether they are appropriately equipped to carry out this discretionary function. This is one of the objectives of this book.

Research ethics committees are typically composed of members from a research institution with the addition of one or two members from the community. Some of the institutional members will be experienced researchers. In addition, committees usually include practising doctors of medicine, an administrator and other health professionals such as a nurse or psychologist. Many committees also include a lawyer and a minister of religion. The research institution sponsoring the committee might be a hospital, a university or a dedicated research institute. In some countries, rather than an institutional base, committees are formed on a regional basis and research proposals are referred to the committee for consideration, by various research institutions within that region. However, the requirements for membership, and the method of operation of research ethics committees, differ from one country to another as is outlined in Chapters 3 and 4.

ADEQUACY OF REVIEW

The development of protective mechanisms for the subjects of experiments is very recent. It is only in the last few decades that most countries have adopted a system of review by ethics committees. The question asked in this book is whether these systems of review are adequate. Research ethics committees exercise wide discretion to approve research or reject research proposals or to require modification to the overall design before giving their approval. In practice, most committees approve more than 95 per cent of the research proposals they are asked to consider. Often this is after minor modifications have been made at the request of the committee.

This does not necessarily reflect on the adequacy of review. It may well mean that a *requirement* for review, along with clear criteria for what constitutes ethical experimentation, is sufficient for 95 per cent of researchers to modify their research proposals to meet the requirements for ethical research. This is understandable in that researchers who do not conform to the guidelines risk having their research proposals rejected. However, it is also possible that the high rate of approval could result from a less than demanding standard by research ethics committees.

At first sight, the review of experimentation on human subjects by ethics committees appears to be thorough in most industrial countries. It is apparent that a great deal of thought has been given to ethics review. At the local level, many people give of their time, as members of ethics review committees, to examine research proposals for potentially harmful consequences. Because of this scrutiny, it may seem unreasonable to challenge these committees. There is little evidence to suggest that unethical experimentation has been conducted on human subjects as a part of research approved by an ethics committee. Chapters 1 and 3 of this book contain accounts of grossly unethical experiments on human subjects but none of these was adequately reviewed by an ethics committee prior to commencement of the research studies in question. Most of the evidence for such cases of abuse is from experimentation that was conducted before a system for research ethics review had been established or properly instituted. The claim has been made that there have been no major abuses of research subjects since the requirement for review was instituted,[1] and that injuries to subjects of experimentation are rare (Veatch, 1979; Cardon, Dommel and Trumble, 1976). This claim is disputed however, by Annas (1980).

Some cases of review by research ethics committees have raised concerns. On at least two occasions, research ethics committees in the United States (known as institutional review boards or IRBs) have given approval to experimental operations that were ethically dubious at best. One of these cases concerned approval given by the Linda Loma Institutional Review Board for the implantation of a baboon's heart into 'Baby Fae', an infant girl with a fatal heart condition, who was born to an impoverished mother. The experimental operation was poorly conceived and was hastily conducted without even matching the baboon's blood type with that of the infant's. It has been described by Professor Annas, a leading commentator on law and medicine in the United States, as a 'gross exploitation of the terminally ill' and as 'ruthless experimentation in which her [Baby Fae's] only role was that of victim' (Annas, 1985: 15–16). Another case involved an approval given by the Utah IRB for the implantation of an artificial heart into a patient deemed unsuitable for a heart transplant. Annas concluded that the IRBs in these cases were ill-equipped for deciding the issues raised by surgical innovation (1983, 1985). He also suggested that both of these research ethics committees were more interested in promoting their own institutional concerns than in protecting subjects. This is a point to which I will return later, namely that committee members are caught between a need to protect subjects and a desire to promote the interests of the institution by supporting innovative medical practices and research.

In New Zealand the ethics committee in the National Women's Hospital in Auckland approved a study in which women diagnosed with carcinoma *in situ* were left untreated in order to observe whether or not their condition would develop into invasive cancer. The women were not told of their diagnosis nor were they told that they were the subjects of research. They were repeatedly brought back to the hospital for observation. Many of these women died when timely

1. Charles R. McCarthy, Director of the Office of Protection from Research Risks (OPRR), National Institute of Health, United States, in an interview with author, 30 November 1987.

treatment would almost certainly have saved their lives (McNeill, 1989b; Paul and Holloway, 1990). This study is discussed in more detail in Chapter 3. The point I wish to make here, however, is that all the members of the ethics review committee were staff of the National Women's Hospital. This was a factor in both of the United States cases also. The majority of members on the Linda Loma IRB and the Utah IRB were salaried members of staff of the relevant hospitals. All three cases illustrate an intrinsic difficulty for members of institutional committees: they have to find an equitable balance between promoting research, which may benefit the institution (and colleagues within the institution), and protecting the interests of subjects. This is not a task which can be performed with equanimity by committees with a predominance of members who have institutional allegiances.

In both Britain and New Zealand the purposes stated for research ethics committees include: (1) the protection of the human subjects of research; (2) promoting research; and (3) reassurance of the public.[2] The guidelines in other countries do not explicitly include promotion of research. Nevertheless the dilemma between promotion of research and protection of the interests of subjects is inherent in the review process. On the one hand research is promoted by research institutions and accepted as a public good. On the other hand any experimentation on human subjects involves unknown consequences for the subjects and the possibility of harm. There is a conflict between protection of subjects and promotion of research in that protection may mean calling a halt to some research. In some institutions that could also mean a reduction in funding. Balancing these objectives necessarily requires impartial decision-makers. However, on many committees the majority of members are staff of the institution who are likely to have commitments to colleagues and to promoting the institution and its research enterprise.

In all three cases discussed above, the fact of approval by an ethics committee was used in defence of the innovative programs. Once a study is given approval by an ethics committee it is assumed by others that the ethics of a study have been examined thoroughly and

---

2. For example, the Royal College of Physicians of London 'Guidelines' (1990a) state that research ethics committees are to 'preserve the subjects' rights'; 'provide reassurance to the public' and 'facilitate good research'. The New Zealand Department of Health 'Standard' (1991) include 'protection of participants', the encouragement of 'public confidence', and the extension of 'the frontiers of medical knowledge'.

that there is no need for further critical analysis. Researchers are also given some protection from legal liability and from charges of unethical experimentation by receiving ethics committee approval. It is very important therefore that the body evaluating the ethics of a research study is appropriately constituted and competent to decide the issue. Otherwise, ethics committees could do the opposite of what they are intended to do and, in effect, act as sponsors of unethical experimentation.

THE INFLUENCE OF RESEARCHERS

Another factor that constrains an objective evaluation of the ethics of research is the dependence of research ethics committees on those with research expertise. Members of committees without that expertise depend on researchers to help them understand research proposals and to grasp clearly the implications for human subjects. The non-research members of committees are also dependent on their research members for information about current research practices and the likely effect of the particular experimental interventions proposed. Research expertise is therefore needed in the review process. The difficulty is that members with this expertise have a particular perspective that could bias them in weighing the relative concerns for scientific research and the well-being of subjects. By their training and commitment to the scientific process, they have a unique commitment to research. Their priorities and values will not necessarily be shared by the rest of the community. Furthermore, the experts have a stake in the outcome. They are personally and institutionally interested in the success of scientific research. Involving them in a review of the ethics of research, when the essential issue is balancing the value of research against protection of the interests of subjects of research, is problematic. This is a part of a broader problem concerning power and expertise in a democratic society.

Given the potential bias, it should not be taken for granted that review systems are adequate or effective. Researchers stand to gain considerable benefits from the experiments they conduct. They are well represented in the review system: both on national and international panels which have discussed research ethics and formulated ethical guidelines, and on individual ethics review committees. The question of whether systems of review are sufficiently balanced between their interests and the interests of subjects is valid and worthy of exploration. Although codes of ethics state that priority should be given to protecting human subjects of experiments, it is not clear that, in practice, this is the priority. It may be that interests of the researchers and research institutions predominate over the interests of subjects.

REPRESENTATION OF SUBJECTS

The people on whom research is conducted, the 'subjects of research', are not represented on research ethics committees as presently constituted. Yet these are the people who are most affected by the research – especially if something untoward occurs. I argue that subjects should be represented. I base this argument on the democratic principle that we should all have some means for influencing decisions that affect our lives. Many guidelines on committee membership specifically exclude community members who might be representative of subjects or any group in the community.[3] Lay members and community representatives are chosen as people without affiliations to any relevant organisation.

Originally, research ethics committees were composed entirely of researchers or members of the research institution. As is indicated above however, most committees now include members of the community. This is part of a growing movement toward including representatives of the community on boards and committees which make many of the important policy decisions about science. These people are included as representatives of the 'common view'. It is understood that specialised groups and committees of experts can become narrow in their views and lose sight of a common perspective. For this reason community members are included to restore a balance to these proceedings. It is assumed that these members will look at proposals from a lay perspective and will be interested in protecting the interests of the vulnerable, including the human subjects of experimentation.

3. For example, the Royal College of Physicians of London, 'Guidelines' (1990) state that 'members should serve on the Committee as individuals and not as delegates taking instruction from other bodies or reporting to them'. The New Zealand Department of Health 'Standard' (1991) states that members should not be representative of 'any single profession or group'. The UK Department of Health (1991), 'Local Research Ethics Committees' states that 'LREC members are not in any way the representatives of [various] groups'.

While it is probably true that most lay members are concerned about the welfare of volunteers who participate in research, they are in a difficult position in weighing that concern against persuasive arguments in favour of research. In this situation they tend to sit back and leave it to the experts. The evidence (from studies outlined in Chapter 4) is that lay members of research ethics committees are less active on committees than other members and they are seen as being less important to committees in reaching their decisions. This brings us back to the difficulty discussed earlier, that most of the influential members have a commitment to research either because they are researchers themselves or because they are staff of the institution and are committed to furthering the institution's goals (which include research). The effect is that committees, as presently constituted in most countries, are balanced in favour of the interests of research.

AN ALTERNATIVE MODEL

In response to this situation I propose a radically different rationale and model for committee review. It is based on a recognition that research ethics committees are endeavouring to reconcile different values. These are the values of research, both to the researchers and to other possible beneficiaries in the community, and the value that should be given to protecting the interests of the subjects. I will argue first that both these perspectives need representation; and secondly, that the representatives of each perspective need to be people with equal support and influence. In other words, they need to be on an equal footing in terms of their relative strength and influence within committees and on national and international panels that consider research ethics.

The research perspective should be represented by appropriately qualified researchers. Almost invariably these will be people with professional affiliations and positions of responsibility in research institutes. They have the support of those institutions. So, while they may appear to be on committees as individuals, they inevitably represent the interests of research. Furthermore they are accountable, at least informally, to their colleagues. Research representatives can expect to be challenged when colleagues disagree with a decision taken by the committee.

Representatives of subjects should also be properly qualified for their role and they too need adequate support. Subject representatives can gain this support with the backing of an appropriate community group. My argument draws on a distinction between 'lay' or 'community' members and 'subject representatives'. The difference is that lay members are included on committees as individuals from the community whereas subject representatives are nominated by an appropriate community group with an interest in the welfare of subjects of human experimentation. Subject representatives, like the research representatives, are not present as individuals. Their role is to represent the concerns of subjects of experimentation generally. Furthermore, subject representatives are accountable to the community through the relevant organisation.

Related to the recognition of the need for representation in the review of human experimentation is a shift in paradigm from *protectionism* to *consultation* and *consensus*. The guidelines on research ethics in most countries require committees to protect subjects of experimentation. The difficulty is that there is no process established for consultation between committee members and subjects to discover what the subjects wish to be protected from. It is assumed that they would wish to be protected from harm of various kinds. It is also assumed that they would wish to have their rights to privacy and confidentiality preserved.

Part of my concern is that protection may have become 'over-protection'. A model based on protectionism has led to the exclusion of some potential classes of people from participation in research. For example, women are typically excluded from medical research. Dresser (1992) suggests that this is from concern not to harm the 'weaker sex' although the exclusion of women from studies may also be based on a concern not to cause a miscarriage or damage to a fetus. There is also a concern that the menstrual cycle in women means greater hormonal fluctuation than in men and could complicate studies. The pitfall is, however, that excluding women from research denies them the benefit of research. It also means that the effect of drugs and other medical treatment is almost entirely judged by the effects on male subjects. As Dresser (1992) concludes, this is not a suitable basis for predicting the outcome of treatment for women.

What I am suggesting is that potential subjects themselves may view the balance between risks and benefits differently from others who are supposedly acting on their behalf. It needs to be recognised that the subjects themselves have an important stake in the research and they ought to have a say. Committee review is not adequate if it is the research establishment acting magnanimously to protect the subjects of its experiments. Protection of physical well-being may not be their major concern and I illustrate this in Chapter 7 by reference to persons with HIV/AIDS. These people are understandably more interested in supporting research, even risky research, in the hope of finding an effective treatment than they are in protecting themselves against the possible toxic effect of new drugs.

Additional concerns about the adequacy of the system stem from the finding that review of research and experimentation is almost entirely focussed on research proposals prior to their implementation and not on research as it is conducted. Chapter 4 includes reports from various countries indicating that there is almost no surveillance of research by independent assessors after initial approval of research by an ethics committee. I argue that this places too much emphasis on researchers' intentions and not enough emphasis on researchers' practice. In Chapter 9 a number of practical suggestions are made for on-site monitoring of research in progress to overcome this inadequacy.

Although the book contains accounts of gross harm which appear to have been inflicted deliberately, I believe that most harms are the result of inadequate consideration given to the effect of research procedures on subjects. Patients (in particular) are trusting of medical researchers and will volunteer for experiments without understanding the likely impact of a study on their lives. Consequently there is a need for careful oversight by a group of people who weigh the relative merits and potential problems of research with impartiality. The difficulty (as is outlined above) is that researchers and staff of the research institution cannot be regarded as impartial. For this reason I advocate that the research ethics committee members should collectively create a balance between the interests of science and the interests of subjects. The members also need to be sufficiently independent to challenge and, if necessary, halt research which asks too much of its subjects. This book considers the extent to which this need to oversee human experimentation is satisfied by systems of review, as they are presently constituted. It goes further and suggests changes which could strengthen the review process to make it more effective and equitable for both researchers and the human subjects of experimentation.

TERMINOLOGY: RESEARCH ETHICS COMMITTEES

Committees of review are referred to by various names. In the United States (as already noted) they are referred to collectively as 'institutional review boards' or IRBs (Levine, 1986), although there are also 'non-institutional review boards' dealing with review of research (Herman, 1984, 1989). In Great Britain these committees are referred to as 'local research ethics committees' and as 'ethics committees' (UK Department of Health, 1991; Royal College of Physicians, 1990a: 3, 9) although academic commentators have referred to them as 'research ethical committees' (Thompson, French, Melia et al., 1980). In Canada they are known as 'research ethics boards' (REBs), although they were previously called 'ethics review committees' in the Medical Research Council of Canada 'Guidelines' of 1978. I warn the reader that there is some confusion between terms used in Australia and the United States. The term 'institutional ethics committees' in the United States describes committees that are concerned with clinical ethics and not with research (Cranford and Doudera, 1984). Australian research ethics committees are called 'institutional ethics committees' (IECs) by the Australian National Health and Medical Research Council (1983a). Prior to 1982 however, Australian committees were known as 'medical ethics review committees'.[4] It should also be noted that, as well as these generic names, various institutions within all countries have given their research ethics committees names which are particular to each institution. For simplicity I refer to all committees that review the ethics of human experimentation as 'research ethics committees' or as 'committees of review' throughout this book.

'EXPERIMENTATION' MORE INCLUSIVE THAN 'RESEARCH'

The choice of the word 'experimentation' rather than 'research' in the title of this book was deliberate. Professor Levine, a prominent commentator on IRBs in the United States, considered that 'experimentation' was an unacceptable term because it was loose and described a range of activities which might not amount to research (1986). He considered that much of medical practice was experimental

---

4. Minutes of the NHMRC Ethics in Clinical Research Subcommittee Meeting of 27 March 1973. They were referred to as 'medical ethics review committees' in the NHMRC (1976) Revised Statement on Human Experimentation.

in the sense of trying out new procedures in diagnosis and treatment. In his view, all non-validated medical practices should be reviewed by an IRB as part of properly designed research trials. In other words, he argued that experimentation should be conducted within proper research programs so that a conclusive result could be found and the relevant practice would either be validated or not. While I accept that as an ideal, I would not restrict ethics review to properly conducted research trials. I believe that all experiments which are conducted on human subjects, for the purpose of obtaining new knowledge or for testing innovative procedures, should be included in the review process. I do not accept the argument that much of medical practice is experimental and that therefore only properly conducted research should be reviewed. Most medical practice relies on known and accepted practices. The fact that the results are variable from one patient to another should not be allowed to obscure a reasonably workable distinction between known and accepted practices and experimental or innovative practices. I would include for review, experimentation in medical research and the use of innovative medical procedures such as innovations in surgery. This is the position in New Zealand where proposals for new, untried or unorthodox medical treatments need to be approved before being adopted (New Zealand Department of Health, 1991).

My reason for arguing that experimentation rather than research is the appropriate term is that the emphasis of review should be on the protection of the interests of the subjects of experiments. The distinguishing feature of experimentation is that something new is being tried. Experiments necessarily carry with them unknown consequences. Once the consequences are known, they are no longer experiments. All experiments on human subjects should be included in the review process. There may be a greater element of risk of unexpected consequences in haphazard and scientifically invalid experiments than in properly conducted scientific experimentation. This is a good reason for encouraging properly validated studies. It is not a good reason for restricting review to scientifically valid studies.

The major concern of volunteers for experimentation is not whether the study is scientifically well grounded. Rather, it is whether there is inconvenience, or economic loss, or a risk of physical or psychological harm. Included in psychological harms are obvious damage to the psyche as well as 'loss of dignity and self-esteem, guilt and remorse, or feelings of exploitation and degradation' (Medical Research Council of Canada, 'Guidelines', 1987: 7). As all experiments have the potential to harm subjects, I maintain that all experiments on human subjects ought to be registered with a research ethics committee and all studies, other than those eligible for expedited review, should be thoroughly examined before being allowed to proceed. The criterion for minimal (expedited) review (as discussed in Chapter 9) is that the probability and magnitude of harm is no more than that encountered in daily life.

I accept the need for review of research in other areas also. Psychology, education, anthropology, sociology and even economics require the testing of ideas on humans as individuals or as communities. This experimentation should be included in the review process and be registered with a committee. Some of the research may well be eligible for expedited review. However, it should be registered so that there is some overseeing of all human experimentation.

OUTLINE OF THE BOOK

In summary, this book is concerned with finding an appropriate balance between the major interests in human experimentation: the interests of science and the interests of subjects. The history of human experimentation is one of imbalance in favour of the interests of researchers. The early chapters (Part I) trace the history of unethical experimentation and the development of codes of ethics to protect subjects of experimentation. Chapter 1 contains an historical account of unethical experiments on human beings from early records through to accounts of 'scientific atrocities' in this century. Chapter 2 details the resulting development of national and international codes of ethics. Chapters 3 and 4 (Part II) outline the research ethics committee review system including its inception in the United States and its development there and elsewhere. I have given particular attention to the United States because the development of the committee review system there was seminal in the development of review systems elsewhere. Chapter 4 contains an account of empirical studies of research ethics committees throughout the world.

In Part III, I consider legal and ethical principles and rules as a basis for ethics review. The extent of discretion that should be left to individual ethics committees is also considered. Chapter 5 outlines the law in this respect, and Chapter 6 explores ethical principles and the necessity for discretion in the application of ethical principles and rules to particular research studies. Finally, Part IV focusses on the politics of review by research ethics committees. It contains a theoretical analysis of the assumptions behind committee review and the issue of power between professional and non-professional members. Chapter 7 examines the three main interests at stake in experimentation on human subjects: those of science, society and the subject. Chapter 8 examines the power of researchers and their institutions from a political perspective. I suggest that subjects of experimentation should be represented within committees of review and that their interests would be more effectively protected by requiring monitoring of research in progress and compensation for injured subjects. Finally, Chapter 9 outlines practical measures for effectively representing both the interests of science and the interests of subjects. The Conclusion, complementing this Introduction, summarises the main arguments and recommendations raised throughout the book.

PART ONE

A History of Experimentation and Codes of Ethics

CHAPTER 1

A History of Unethical Experimentation on Human Subjects

EARLY RECORDS OF UNETHICAL EXPERIMENTATION

Experimentation in medicine is claimed to be as old as medicine itself (Brieger, 1978). Hippocrates, for example, while removing splinters of bone from the exposed cortex of a boy, is said to have 'gently scratched the surface of the cortex with his fingernail' and observed corresponding movements on the opposite side of the boy's body (Katz, 1969: 481). During the time of the Ptolemies in Egypt condemned prisoners were used for experimental purposes (Beecher, 1970: 5) and their rights were not considered to be of any account. Prisoners were part of a wider class of subjects who were more frequently experimented on in the name of science. As Gillespie (1988) states, throughout history 'it is the socially powerless and disadvantaged who are most likely to be subjected to unethical research'. Early records suggest that this has always been the case. A Persian prince, in the second century A.D., is said to have advised a medical student to 'experiment freely' but not on 'people of high rank or political importance' (Platt, 1966: 149). This dictum appears to have been followed throughout history. Abuses of the rights of experimental subjects seldom happen to 'people of high rank or political importance'.

Lower class people are still at greater risk of being used in unethical experimentation. The New Zealand cervical cancer case, in which treatment was withheld from women with carcinoma *in situ* as part of an experiment, is a relatively recent example. Both Coney (1988: 103–4) and McNeill (1989b: 268) have identified the low social status of many of these women as a factor in the disregard shown by doctors for the welfare of the women. Leslie Brown, the first mother of a 'test-tube' baby, was a 'factory floor' worker. She had not even been told that she was the subject of

17

an experiment. Scutt (1988: 1–11) has argued that it is lower class women who have been experimented on for the development of new reproductive technologies and new contraceptive measures because they were less likely to complain if something went wrong. Yet women at this socio-economic level, having been subjected to the risks, were unlikely to benefit from new and expensive reproductive technologies.

The development of modern medicine in the hospitals of Paris in the eighteenth century depended on large numbers of poor and working class patients who provided a ready pool of experimental subjects for middle class physicians and surgeons. It was the use of human subjects for systematic experimentation to establish systems of classification of disease (nosology) that eventually led to modern concerns about the ethics of research on human subjects. By the end of the eighteenth century, nosology was based on a relationship between symptoms in patients and pathology revealed in post-mortem examinations. As a result, doctors began to see disease in terms of pathological entities within specific organs and tissues in the body rather than as a general imbalance of the humours.

There is evidence that experiments at this time were conducted on human beings to test the effects of various disease organisms without regard for the welfare of the subjects. To draw attention to these unethical studies, a Russian physician (by the name of Smidovich) reported studies by numerous researchers throughout the 1800s that involved infecting experimental subjects with syphilis or gonorrhea. It was apparent that the researchers were fully aware of both the infective capacity of the material they introduced to unwitting patients and the seriousness and painfulness of the disease. Some of these patients were suffering from other diseases and near death. They died suffering from both the original condition and the symptoms of the venereal disease (Katz, 1972: 284–91).

The experiments were not confined to hospital patients. A Dublin physician deliberately infected healthy subjects with syphilis to prove the contagiousness of the disease. Another doctor injected a medical orderly under his control with syphilitic material. Three girls (said to be prostitutes) aged between 13 and 16 years were injected with the milk from a woman with syphilis to demonstrate that the milk was infectious. In another study, the eyes of infants were infected with gonococcus. In other unethical studies, the blood of typhoid patients was injected into 17 healthy soldiers; and the exposed cortex of a woman was subjected to repeated stimulation with electrodes resulting in convulsions, coma and paralysis (Katz, 1972: 284–91).

There are also records of unethical experiments conducted in the nineteenth century. In the United States, physicians put slaves into pit ovens to study heat stroke, and poured scalding water over them as an experimental cure for typhoid fever. One slave had two fingers amputated in a 'controlled trial', one finger with anaesthesia and one without, to test the effectiveness of anaesthesia. Slaves were also used for experimenting with internal surgery (Pernick, 1982: 19–20), and there are other accounts of slaves being used for experimentation, surgical practice and medical education during the nineteenth century (Savitt, 1982).

However, Rothman (1987) has concluded that unethical experiments were 'highly exceptional' before the 1940s and that 'research ethics was not a subject of widespread concern'. His conclusion was based on the observation that experimentation was still conducted on a relatively small scale. It is a surprising conclusion and somewhat misleading in that there were large numbers of subjects involved in some of the experiments discussed above, including the experiments referred to by Rothman himself. It may be true that before the Second World War, experimentation on human subjects was conducted on a relatively small scale. It is also apparently true that 'research ethics was not a subject of widespread concern'. However, there is enough evidence to suggest that there was considerable abuse of the subjects of experiments in the nineteenth and early twentieth centuries. And because there is very little evidence of concern for the subjects of experiments, it is likely that many other such studies occurred without being remarked upon.

The important issue in all of these cases was the lack of therapeutic intent and a callous disregard for the welfare of the subjects. The interests of science were seldom restrained by a concern for the interests of the subject and rarely did the subjects gain any benefit. One of the exceptions was the curing of vesico-vaginal fistula in slave women who served as subjects in experimental operations. However, some of these women were operated on experimentally up to 30 times (Savitt, 1982: 344–6). Clearly, without supervision, there was a tendency for scientific research to 'take on a life of its own, independent of – and often morally antithetical to – its social and cultural milieu' (Reams and Gray, 1985: 35).

Few in society expressed any humanitarian concern for subjects of experiments. One notable exception was Smidovich (mentioned earlier), who published a book in 1901 describing these experiments. He appealed to society as the protector of the subjects and portrayed experimenters as 'bizarre disciples of science' and as scientific 'zealots'. He was apparently aware of the possible adverse consequences to himself of drawing attention to these 'criminal experiments' and therefore wrote under a pseudonym.[1]

THE SECOND WORLD WAR AND ATTITUDES TO HUMAN EXPERIMENTATION

The Second World War represented a turning point in experimentation on human subjects. Funding of research increased significantly and an associated bureaucratic framework developed. Clinical research became centrally funded, increasingly well co-ordinated and extensive, and involved large research teams. Many of the investigations were designed to benefit soldiers coping with diseases, especially malaria, on the battle fronts. In the United States, the Committee on Medical Research distributed $25 million to universities, hospitals, institutes and companies to find antidotes to dysentery, influenza, and malaria (Rothman, 1987: 1196).

The effect of this association between the war and medical research, however, was to further undermine any concern for the welfare of research subjects. It was considered valid to put research subjects at considerable risk in experiments that had no possible therapeutic advantage for them. The needs of the war effort predominated. Research subjects drawn from mental asylums and state penitentiaries were infected with malaria and given experimental antidotes to test the therapeutic effectiveness of the antidote, the relapse rate and the severity of side-effects. The public reaction was to congratulate the subjects for repaying their debt to society and for contributing to the war effort. In 1945, the *New York Times* wrote of prisoner 'volunteers' for experimentation that 'these one-time enemies to society' had demonstrated 'to the fullest extent just how completely this is everybody's war' (quoted in Rothman, 1987: 1197). The propriety of this research on incarcerated subjects was not questioned.

---

1. 'Veressayev' and also 'Veresaeff' were pseudonyms for the Russian physician V. Smidovich (see Veressayev, 1916; and Faden and Beauchamp, 1986: 152, 189, note 6).

Soldiers were being drafted into the army to risk their lives; by extension, it was considered reasonable that the institutionalised, retarded or mentally ill should contribute and accept some of the risks involved in research designed to alleviate the diseases of soldiers – whether or not they were capable of consent. Consent was not considered important as the research was justified by the greater good that was served. As Rothman put it 'the ethics of American research during World War II were frankly and unashamedly utilitarian'.

In the United States after the war, members of the bureaucracy (established to support medical research in the interests of the war effort) argued for the continuation of funding by pointing to the success of the research programs conducted during the war (Swain, 1962: 1235). Although the wartime Committee on Medical Research ceased to function, its philosophy continued. The National Institutes of Health inherited both its contracts and the Committee's organisational framework and ethos. At this time there was a dramatic increase in funds distributed through large grants for medical research. The war image continued to be employed in the metaphorical sense of a war against disease. This metaphor helped to perpetuate the public's perception of science in the service of society and was successfully employed to argue for increased funding. It also perpetuated an ethic that subordinated subjects' interests to those of science on the implicit assumption that this was also in the interest of society.

Research practices which had been established during the war 'profoundly influenced researchers' behavior in the postwar era' and their attitude to subjects (Rothman, 1987: 1196). This was in part because of the precedent established during the war, in part because of the belief that the benefits of research justified the risk of harm to subjects, and in part because of a lack of any opposition to this program. It was not until the 1960s that an effective challenge to this ethos was mounted. In subsequent chapters I will return to discuss the challenge to this ethos.

GERMAN AND JAPANESE ATROCITIES DURING THE WAR

The most abhorrent medical experimentation on human subjects was conducted during the Second World War by German and Japanese doctors and researchers. The German experiments are relatively well known.

Experimentation in Nazi Germany

The atrocities committed by the German doctors and scientists gained publicity as a result of the trial conducted by the Allied Forces after the Second World War. This case was known as *United States v. Karl Brandt*. The Court was established by the Allied Control Council of Germany which exercised its authority through the Military Governor of the American Zone. The judges, all American attorneys, were appointed by the Governor and their opinions were issued as international criminal law (Annas, Glantz and Katz, 1977: 8).

This case was a trial of 23 German doctors and scientists for war crimes and crimes against humanity. Of the 23 accused, 20 were doctors and all but one of the doctors held positions in the medical services of the Third Reich. These included Karl Brandt who was Hitler's personal physician. Of the 23 defendants, 16 were found guilty and seven of these (including Karl Brandt) were hanged. They were found guilty of various crimes including placing prisoners in low pressure chambers and observing their deaths; exposing prisoners to freezing air and water; infecting prisoners with typhus and malaria to test various drugs; sterilisation and castration by various means; and murdering prisoners (including children) for specimens of their anatomy (Alexander, 1949). Many of the experiments were related to goals of the military. The tests at low pressure, for example, gave information on the extent to which humans could withstand low pressure during high altitude flying; the infliction of various diseases was part of a program to combat diseases experienced by the German occupation forces; and the exposure of prisoners to freezing water and air were to test methods for reviving pilots rescued from the sea. There was also a more sinister objective. The prosecutor coined the word 'thanatology' to denote the science of producing death rapidly and argued that these doctors and scientists were involved in research to develop methods of mass extermination. The various means of 'medical killing' and 'euthanasia' were developed as a part of the Third Reich's program for 'racial hygiene': the extermination of unwanted groups (Lifton, 1986).

In defence of the German doctors and scientists it was argued that the sacrifice of a few lives was necessary to save the lives of many; that they had acted under superior orders; that many famous medical pioneers throughout history, including Nobel Prize winners, had conducted ethically dubious experiments on human subjects; and that throughout the literature on medical experimentation (including experiments with cholera, plague, and syphilis) the word 'volunteer' was used to disguise 'compulsion'. A more general defence was that the German experimenters were accused of being in breach of an absolute requirement for consent that was seldom satisfied by medical researchers (Katz, 1972: 300–5). It is disconcerting to recognise that many of these defences were valid. Even the recent history of experimentation on human subjects reveals a continuing disregard for their well-being. The main difference between the experiments in the German concentration camps and experimentation on human subjects elsewhere was in the extent of the atrocities committed by German doctors and scientists and the deliberate intention to inflict brutal injury and death. Yet this distinction should not blind us to the overlap with experiments conducted on human subjects elsewhere. The difference may be more of degree than of type.

The Nuremberg judges measured the culpability of the accused against a set of ten principles that included an absolute requirement for consent and found that the principles 'were more frequently honored in their breach than in their observance' (Katz, 1972: 305–6). The claim from the defence that these principles were breached by other medical researchers was not acknowledged. The set of ten principles, which were included in the judgment, became known as the Nuremberg Code. The Code, and the subsequent resistance of the medical profession to that Code, is discussed in Chapter 2.

Japanese experimentation

Whereas the atrocities committed by German doctors and scientists are well known as a result of the Nuremberg trials, similar atrocities committed by Japanese doctors and scientists during the Second World War have only recently been given any publicity. Capron (1986: 229) has referred to them as 'the hidden Japanese experiments' and Williams and Wallace (1989) as 'Japan's secret biological warfare'. Between 1930 and 1945, Japan conducted trials of biological warfare through the use of various diseases including anthrax, cholera, typhoid and typhus. The principal testing site, Unit 731, was on mainland China where there were installations for germ-warfare, a prison for the human experimental subjects, and a crematorium for the human victims. There was also an airfield and special planes for dropping germ-bombs. At least 11 Chinese cities were subjected to biological warfare attacks. In one incident, a Japanese plane dropped fleas carrying bubonic plague on a city leading to the deaths of almost a hundred people.

The prisoners at Unit 731 were known as *maruta*, which means 'log of wood', and they were treated with as little dignity (Williams and Wallace, 1989: 36). They were murdered in bizarre surgical experiments including the connection of different parts of the body. Some were dehydrated to the point of death. Some had their arms frozen to test various methods of thawing with the result that the flesh became rotten and simply dropped off. Other experiments included prolonged exposure of the liver to X-rays; syphoning off their blood and replacing it with horse blood; the deliberate infection of Chinese women with syphilis to test methods of preventing the disease; and the explosion of fragmentation bombs beside the exposed legs and buttocks of prisoners to test the effectiveness of the bombs as a means for infecting humans with gas gangrene (a wound infection caused by the anaerobic bacteria *Clostridia*). More than 3,000 people were reported to have been killed at Unit 731. As Powell (1981), Gomer, Powell and Roling (1981) and Williams and Wallace (1989) have documented, these human guinea-pigs either died during the experiments or were executed when they were 'no longer fit for further germ tests'. This Unit was claimed to have infected British, American, Australian and New Zealand prisoners-of-war with various diseases to test whether they had the same effect on Anglo-Saxons as on Asians. More recently, the finding of 35 skulls on a construction site in Shinjukyu, Tokyo, previously the site of the headquarters of the 'Epidemic Prevention Research Laboratory' at the Tokyo Army Medical College, drew public attention in Japan to this shrouded corner of Japanese history (Hartcher, 1989; Williams and Wallace, 1989: 235–43).

Documents obtained by freedom of information applications revealed that the United States agreed to give the Japanese experimenters immunity from prosecution in exchange for information about biological warfare. One of the American government documents acknowledged that 'because of scruples attached to human experimentation' it was not possible to conduct such experiments in the United States. It went on to express the hope that the individuals involved would be 'spared embarrassment'. It was a delicate show of concern considering that they had used humans as guinea-pigs in lethal experiments and executed any that survived (Powell, 1981: 47). Far from being embarrassed, many of them have become influential and respected figures in modern Japan. Some have held positions that apparently drew on their knowledge and experience from experiments they had conducted on humans in Unit 731. For example, it is alleged by Hartcher and by Williams and Wallace that the doctor who supervised the freezing of people to their deaths served as an adviser to the Japanese Antarctic Expedition and a consultant to the frozen food and fisheries industry before going into important posts in academia. Another senior officer from Unit 731, associated with the transfusing of animal blood into humans, is alleged to have become a founder and chairman of a multi-national company specialising in artificial blood and blood plasma. Williams and Wallace list 15 Japanese doctors who took part in fatal experiments on human subjects and subsequently went on to develop their specialties, becoming professors within (and in some cases directors of) university medical schools and research facilities. Other medical officers and staff from Unit 731 were given elevated positions in Japanese institutions and companies. Many of these men received high honours and awards for their contribution to society (Williams and Wallace, 1989: 235–43).

The Command of the American Occupation Forces in Japan gave great weight to the fact that the Japanese experiments were 'the only known source of scientifically controlled experiments' showing the direct effect of biological warfare techniques on humans. The information was valued for its potential to put the United States ahead in the development of its own biological warfare program and the potential deployment of this method of warfare. The American Forces Command decided that this value was higher than the value of prosecuting the experimenters. It was argued that trials of these Japanese for war crimes would have led to this information becoming available to other countries. The United States officials therefore offered immunity from prosecution to the Japanese experimenters and justified this decision on the grounds of national security (Powell, 1981).

There is a stark contrast between the Americans' treatment of German and Japanese experimenters. The Germans were tried for war crimes and hanged for being criminally culpable and in breach of a universal standard of ethics. The Japanese were protected by secrecy and allowed to establish themselves as pillars of Japanese society. The only possible explanation for this difference was political expediency.

Unlike the Americans, the USSR (Soviet Russia) prosecuted some of the Japanese involved. In December 1949, a Soviet military tribunal in Khabarovsk, Siberia, charged twelve Japanese army personnel from Unit 731 with manufacturing and employing bacteriological weapons. Evidence was produced concerning the activities of the Unit but the tribunal was apparently unaware of the information held by the Americans (Powell, 1981). It appears that this tribunal had proposed rules, which embodied an ethics code on human experimentation, in the same manner as the Nuremberg Court.[2] Russian attempts to give publicity to the findings of the Khabarovsk trial in the West were unsuccessful (Williams and Wallace, 1989: 231–2).

TESTING OF MILITARY WEAPONS IN AUSTRALIA

War, it seems, justifies all sorts of inhumane treatment of human beings. The Japanese conducted their experiments on 'foreigners' as part of their war in China and their involvement in the Second World War. Similarly, the Germans experimented on human subjects from stigmatised minority groups within Germany and in bordering countries as part of their war effort. In the same war the Australian Armed Forces Command conducted harmful experiments with mustard gas on their own nationals and, after the war, the British tested nuclear weapons with a callous disregard for Aborigines in the Australian desert.

Mustard gas experiments on human subjects

In the late stages of the Second World War, a series of experiments using mustard gas were carried out on approximately one thousand human subjects in Australia. The subjects had little idea what they were volunteering for. They had been recruited to the study through a letter that simply asked if they would 'volunteer' for a 'gas school'

2. These were known as the 'Khabarovsk Rules' although the authors of a WHO paper reported that they had not seen any documents relating to them (World Health Organization, 1987).

to assist in the war effort. Some of them were to suffer long-lasting damage to their health (Goodwin, 1989).

The trials were conducted by an agency of the Australian Department of Defence. The investigations were mainly into mustard gas, although some work was done with phosgene. It had been discovered early in the experiments with mustard gas in Australia that the gas was at least four times more effective in tropical conditions than in temperate climates. The damaging effects of the gas at temperatures above 32° Celsius and in humidities of more than 80 per cent were much more extreme. Sensitive areas of the body exposed to the gas were seriously burnt within a minute of exposure to the gas vapour in these conditions. The gas was also found to disperse easily in rainforests and therefore appeared to be a more effective weapon than explosives for action against the enemy in tropical rainforest conditions (Mellor, 1958: 367–80).

It was believed that information was needed from systematic trials. The intention was to investigate mustard gas as an offensive weapon for chemical warfare and to develop protective measures by testing respirators and protective clothing. The first volunteers were Melbourne University students. Then, physiologists working for the Defence Board became their own guinea-pigs. Later, when the vesicant nature of these gases had to be experienced in the tropics, the 'volunteers' were drawn from the infantry (Mellor, 1958).

An experimental unit was established at Innisfail, North Queensland. Personnel volunteering were exposed to gas in a number of different situations, in the open and in a gas chamber. In the gas chamber experiments, mustard gas was released and soldiers, wearing gas masks and army clothing, were asked to move bags of sand from one corner of the chamber to another. The gas burnt their bodies especially in areas where they had been sweating. One participant described how small blisters broke out initially and over a period of days the blisters enlarged to become one sheet of blisters. In his case, the burns covered 95 per cent of his body. In the days following their exposure to the gas, the soldiers were asked to run an assault course to determine the extent to which their injuries would reduce their combat abilities.[3]

3. From an interview with Bridget Goodwin, producer of the video 'Keen as Mustard' (1989), 20 March 1990.

There were also trials of the gas on a beach. In one of these, soldiers were ordered to enter the water while bombers dropped gas bombs on the beach itself. The subjects then came out of the water wearing gas masks and army clothing and into the mustard gas vapour. In another trial 'assault', personnel were landed on a tropical island immediately after it had been bombed with mustard gas. Many of these troops 'carried out manoeuvres for several hours' with a minimum of protective clothing (Mellor, 1958: 378). They were taken off the island the following morning. In a television documentary made some 40 years later, one of these men described how he and a companion were left over night on the island with no gas masks, in the vicinity of gas canisters that were still giving off gas, among goats that were clearly suffering. He had suffered continuing and serious lung problems since that exposure (Goodwin, 1989).

All 'volunteers' were subsequently 'awarded commendation cards in recognition of their loyal and unselfish services' (Mellor, 1958: 378). There was no follow-up of the effects of the gas on the health of these men. One of the victims, who appeared in the television documentary, brought an action against the Commonwealth for compensation for damages to his health. The claim was settled out of court.[4] No information is available on the total number of subjects who suffered long term effects.

The damage done to the physiologists and the Melbourne University students assisting them early in the testing program could be partially excused by the lack of knowledge of the effectiveness of mustard gas in tropical conditions. However, by the time of the main trials, it was already known how damaging the gas could be in tropical conditions. After the injuries sustained in the First World War, mustard gas was thought to be 'more horrifying than the time-honoured missile weapons' and there was a reluctance to use it even on the enemy (Mellor, 1958: 380). Yet the Australian High Command was willing to experiment on its own troops with an inhumane disregard for the life-long suffering they were imposing. The 'volunteers' had insufficient knowledge of what they were volunteering for and were asked to volunteer under conditions that amounted to coercion. The experiments were designed to test

4. *Sydney Morning Herald* (12 October 1988: 14) 'I was gas guinea-pig: Digger'. The case was *Thomas W. F. Mitchell* v. *Commonwealth of Australia*. Thanks to Laurence W. Maher of Melbourne solicitors Howie and Maher for this information.

chemical weapons on human subjects and were no different, in principle, to the testing of other weapons. It is unlikely that the Australian command would consider testing the effectiveness of bombs, or shrapnel, or new bullets on its own troops. Yet it was apparently prepared to test the effectiveness of mustard gas as a weapon on its own men.

The trials were supervised throughout by doctors and physiologists who were under an ethical obligation to do no harm. The principle of nonmaleficence, as expressed by the maxim *primum non nocere* – 'above all do no harm', has long been regarded as a fundamental principle of medical ethics. Yet this principle was flouted without adequate justification. Australia was thought to have been free of any major scandal of experimentation on human subjects. However, this case, while falling short of the extremes of the German and Japanese experiments conducted during the war, ranks with the worst cases of abuse of human subjects in experiments conducted elsewhere in the world.

British nuclear tests in Australia[5]

From 1952 until 1963 the British government conducted a series of tests of atomic weapons within Australia. In 1984 the Australian federal government established a Royal Commission to inquire into the effects of the nuclear tests and the measures that had been taken to protect people.

The Commission found that the tests were conducted as a result of the intention of the British Government to join the United States and Soviet Russia as a nuclear power. The United States had been reluctant to share its nuclear information with Britain and the British Government decided to develop its own weapons. British Prime Minister Attlee sought permission from Australian Prime Minister Menzies to use the Monte Bello group of islands off the north-west coast of Australia as a testing site. Menzies, on the basis of minimal information and assurances, accepted the British request without reference to his Cabinet. He subsequently gave permission for further testing on the mainland – initially at Emu Fields and then at the Maralinga Range.

5. This section draws heavily on the *Report of the Royal Commission into British Nuclear Tests in Australia* (McClelland, Fitch and Jonas, 1985). (Page numbers given in the text refer to this report.)

The British nuclear tests in Australia were tests of weapons and ancillary equipment and were not designed as experiments on human subjects as such. There had been suggestions made to the Commission that various people were deliberately exposed to radiation but the Commission found that there was insufficient evidence to substantiate this claim. Even so, I have included this case because of the obvious risk of harm to humans and the commonality of many of the ethical issues in nuclear testing and experimentation on human subjects.

The Commission identified a number of omissions in the application of safety procedures (by the accepted standards of the time) affecting the armed forces personnel involved. Royal Australian Air Force personnel, for example, were exposed to radiation by flying through radioactive contaminated cloud in air sampling operations.

The main inadequacy identified by the Commission however, was a lack of regard for the risks of harm to Aboriginal people in the test areas. In none of the tests were adequate measures taken to identify the number of Aborigines who might be affected or to take adequate precautions to protect them. From the initial trials in the Monte Bello Islands, to the trials at Emu Field and the trials at Maralinga, there were insufficient attempts to identify the likely presence of Aborigines in the vicinity prior to the tests. These people were at greater risk than Europeans and required greater protection because their way of living left them more exposed to atomic fall-out.

Evidence that Aborigines had indeed been exposed to radiation was presented to the Commission. The Milpuddie family, for example, was found in 1957 within an area of craters formed by nuclear explosions detonated only eight months previously. This incident was treated as a 'political embarrassment' and kept secret. Nothing further was done to check on possible harmful effects to these people – nor was security tightened in the area. A group of 14 were found there in 1960. In 1963, another group of Aborigines was identified when a party of six or more attempted to walk out of the Maralinga Range area. There were accounts of Aborigines hiding from surveillance aircraft. Given the difficulty of identifying Aborigines within restricted areas and their isolation from white culture it is likely that a great many more Aborigines were within the danger zones and suffered the effects of radiation exposure.

From this evidence it appears that the authorities were aware, or could easily have become aware, of the likely presence of

Aborigines within danger areas. While some efforts were made to keep Aborigines away from test sites and from contamination, these efforts were both inadequate and conducted in a manner that was insensitive to the Aborigines' way of life and to their traditional use of the land. Many of the 'protective' measures appeared to be prompted by a cynical concern for the effects of adverse publicity on the testing program rather than a genuine humanitarian concern for the well-being of the Aborigines.

One patrolman had warned his superiors of an apparent disregard for the Aborigines. His superior, while acknowledging the patrolman's 'sincere desire to protect the welfare of aborigines', rebuked him for his 'lamentable lack of balance in outlook'. The patrolman was accused of 'apparently placing the affairs of a handful of natives above those of the British Commonwealth of Nations' (McClelland, Fitch and Jonas, 1985: 309–11). The 'lamentable lack of balance' was attributable to the whole enterprise rather than the maligned patrolman.

It became increasingly apparent that the British and Australian authorities responsible for the conduct of the test gave greater importance to the testing program than to the safety of Aborigines. The fundamental issue here is the same basic ethical issue in experimentation on human subjects, namely that researchers' commitment to their research can override any humanitarian concern for those who may suffer as a result of their experiments.

Committee review: the Atomic Weapons Tests Safety Committee
Another issue, common to both the atomic testing and to experimentation on human subjects, is, that committees have been relied on to ensure the safety of people exposed to risk. Given that those involved in experiments might be biased, the members of such committees needed to be disinterested. The relevant safety committee for the atomic tests was the 'Atomic Weapons Tests Safety Committee' which was formed to ensure that 'the tests were carried out with full regard for the safety of the Australian mainland and population' (p. 17).

Australian Prime Minister Menzies had stated that members of the Safety Committee should 'not in any way be identified as having an interest in the success of defence atomic experiments'. Yet, one of the Committee members clearly had such an interest. Dr Ernest Titterton had previously been a member of the British scientific mission to the United States which had taken part in the development of the first nuclear weapon. The Commission found that Titterton, as a member and subsequently as Chairman of the Safety Committee, had clearly played a political role and concealed information from the Australian Government and his fellow committee members to support the British interests and the testing program. He 'was from first to last, "their man" ' (pp. 16–18, 526).

In 1957, Sir Macfarlane Burnet, a Nobel Prize winner and one of Australia's most respected medical researchers and scientists, commented on the nuclear trials. He recognised that there was an inevitable tendency for those involved to play down the risks of the experiments to others. In his view there needed to be an impartial committee to oversee the operation:

> There must always be a public suspicion – sometimes not without foundation – that any group of men directly concerned in the success of an enterprise will be inclined to minimise danger and to resent any safety precautions which will impede the enterprise. The political requirement is therefore for an uninvolved body to be available to satisfy itself that precautions for the public safety are adequate and to report this to Government and people. (Quoted in McClelland, Fitch and Jonas, 1985: 17)

This statement could be taken as a model for research ethics committees also. Medical research creates a similar situation in that expertise is required to understand the technical information and determine what is reasonably safe. Yet those experts need to be impartial. Burnet's statement is a simple recognition that the experts need to be independent of the enterprise. Otherwise there is a potential for them to act simply as apologists.

NUCLEAR TESTS ON HUMANS IN THE UNITED STATES

In October 1986, a report entitled *American Nuclear Guinea Pigs: Three Decades of Radiation Experiments on U.S. Citizens* was issued by a committee of the United States House of Representatives.[6] This was a result of an investigation into the health and safety policy of the Department of Energy and its two predecessors, the Atomic Energy Commission and the Energy Research and Development Administration. The report described 31 experiments conducted on

6. This section draws extensively from this report (Markey, 1986) and page numbers given in the text refer to it.

a total of 695 human subjects in the period from the mid-1940s until the early 1970s. The intention of these experiments was to test the effects of nuclear radiation on humans.

Many of the experiments were *intended* to cause harm to the subjects. There was no positive potential outcome for these subjects. Although some of these experiments were conducted to test radiation as a therapy, most of them were intended to measure the harmful effects of radiation. As the Chairman of the Committee, Edward Markey, put it 'American citizens thus became nuclear calibration devices for experimenters run amok'.[7] The subjects included elderly patients, prisoners, and hospital patients suffering from terminal diseases. Many of them were incapable of informed consent.

In one study conducted in 1946 and 1947 by the Atomic Energy Project at the University of Rochester, six hospital patients with normal kidney function were injected with uranium nitrate 'to determine the concentration which would produce renal injury'. At least two of those patients were given doses of uranium nitrate enriched with U-234 and U-235 that resulted in immediate symptoms of kidney damage (pp. 27–9).

In a study conducted from 1961 to 1965 at the Massachusetts Institute of Technology, twenty elderly subjects were injected or fed radium or thorium and they were monitored for radioactive intake. A few were retired Massachusetts Institute of Technology employees and the majority were from the Age Center of New England in Boston. The Center's pool of subjects consisted of 'apparently healthy men and women' who were over 50 years old and were willing to take part in research projects on ageing. The study was unrelated to aging. No follow-up of the health of these subjects had been conducted (pp. 24–5).

In another study conducted from 1945 to 1947 at the Manhatten District Hospital, 18 patients believed to have limited life spans were injected with plutonium. Most of the subjects in this experiment were over 45 years of age although one was 5 years old and another was 18. There was no informed consent and the word 'plutonium' was never used with these patients. Relatives of deceased patients were informed that exhumation of the bodies was necessary 'to determine the composition of an "unknown" mixture of injected radioactive isotopes' (pp. 22–3).

7. In a letter to John S. Herrington, Secretary, Department of Energy, 24 October 1986.

A total of 131 prisoners from two state prisons had their testes exposed to X-rays to examine the effects of radiation on human fertility and testicular function in studies conducted from 1963 to 1971. The doses given to different subjects in a single session ranged from 1.6 to 120 times the safe occupational limit per year for exposure of reproductive organs to radiation. The prisoners were between 25 and 52 years old.

One of the few praiseworthy outcomes from all these studies was that the University of Washington Subjects Review Board (the relevant research ethics committee) refused to authorise further irradiation of prisoners at Washington State Prison. This action resulted in the termination of the study.

There were many other unethical studies included in the Nuclear Radiation Report. In one experiment, seven human subjects drank milk from cows which had grazed on iodine-contaminated land. In another, seven human subjects were left unprotected in an already contaminated field while one curie of radioactive iodine was released. The purpose was to measure their intake of radioactive material from inhalation. There was no follow-up of the health effects on any of these subjects. Other subjects were fed simulated fall-out particles containing radioactive material, or solutions of radioactive caesium and strontium. From 1963 to 1965, radioactive iodine was purposely released on seven separate occasions by the Atomic Energy Commission's National Reactor Testing Station in Idaho to test its direct and indirect affects on humans. From 1961 to 1963, human subjects, including university students and members of the researchers' staff, were fed actual fall-out material from the Nevada Test Site (pp. 32–48, 412).

While many of the subjects in these experiments were at risk of extreme harm and death, the scientists prospered. The studies resulted in the publication of a number of scientific papers. However, the Chairman of the Committee was outraged. He asked whether their 'intense desire to know' had led 'American scientists to mimic the kind of demented human experiments conducted by the Nazis'.[8] The reference to 'the Nazis' was not misplaced. The utter disregard for the welfare of these subjects is hard to believe. What is even more disturbing was that these studies were conducted in so many different locations by so many different researchers. History had again

8. In a letter from Markey to Herrington (Markey, 1986).

repeated itself and reaffirmed the statement quoted earlier that there is a tendency for scientists to act independently of, and morally antithetically to, their social and cultural milieu (Reams and Gray, 1985: 35).

CONCLUSION

The history of unethical experimentation is an appalling account of 'man's inhumanity to man'. One of the commonalities, across many of the experiments recounted in this chapter, is an attitude of superiority in the experimenters toward their human subjects. This is apparent from earliest times in the treatment by doctors of patients with syphilis and gonorrhea, and their cruelty to slaves. Before and during the Second World War, German and Japanese doctors and scientists treated their prisoners as less than human. I believe that a similar attitude of British and Australian scientists towards Aborigines was the major factor in their failure to adequately protect them. The chairman of the committee investigating the American nuclear radiation studies stated that many of the subjects were from 'captive audiences or populations that some experimenters frighteningly perhaps might have considered "expendable" '.[9] The statement quoted earlier that 'it is the socially powerless and disadvantaged who are most likely to be subjected to unethical research' has been underscored by these accounts.

It could be argued that the wartime conditions of some of these experiments was a major factor. War is *still* used as a justification for denying rights to experimental subjects. Late in 1990, the US Food and Drug Administration and Department of Defense approved the use of investigational drugs and vaccines on American troops in the Gulf War against Iraq, without their consent. Yet there were no special circumstances relating to the Gulf War that could justify abrogation of subjects' right to consent (Annas and Grodin, 1991). The Australian mustard gas tests on armed forces personnel displayed an even more extreme abrogation of the rights of subjects. War conditions could not possibly have justified the Australian command in testing an offensive weapon on their own troops. I believe this ethical blindness is attributable in part to an attitude of superior ranking officers, officials and scientists towards lower

9. In a letter from Markey to Herrington (Markey, 1986).

ranking soldiers and airmen that regarded them as 'expendable'. The accusation that a patrolman had put the welfare of 'a handful of natives' ahead of the British nuclear testing program in Australia is an illustration of this attitude.

Superiority is one element but it is not enough to explain how doctors and scientists could be so indifferent to the risk of harm, or the deliberate infliction of harm, on others. Another explanation for unethical treatment of human subjects is Sir Macfarlane Burnet's simple observation (quoted earlier) that 'any group of men directly concerned in the success of an enterprise will be inclined to minimise danger and to resent any safety precautions which will impede the enterprise'. In a research context, the outcome of the project is regarded as more important than the risks of harm to the lives and well-being of the subjects.

The obvious question that this raises is 'What can be done about it?' In Burnet's view the solution was political. It required 'an uninvolved body to be available to satisfy itself that precautions for the public safety are adequate and to report this to Government and people'. The action of the University of Washington research ethics committee, which resulted in the termination of one of the nuclear radiation studies, supports this view. Committee review is one of the main protective measures considered in this book.

Indifference and at times outright cruelty have blighted the record of experimentation on human subjects. It is apparent that some means is needed to curb the excesses of those engaged in science in order for society to protect subjects from the infliction of harm. In my view, the lesson to be learnt from this historical account is that there should be *no* privilege extended to scientists to conduct experiments on human subjects without adequate protective measures.

In the following chapter, codes of ethics are considered as one of the protective measures, and the factors leading to the adoption of committees of review are outlined in Chapter 3.

CHAPTER 2

Development of Codes of Ethics

It was stated in Chapter 1 that the interests of scientists were seldom restrained by a concern for the interests of the subject. Some of the exceptions to this generalisation can be found in codes of ethics for research on human subjects. What these codes represent is an early attempt to protect subjects of experiments. The earliest codes on experimentation were personal codes. This century has seen the development of national and international codes of ethics for experimentation on human subjects.

National and international codes were sometimes imposed on experimenters as an external constraint from outside the profession, as in the early German codes and the Nuremberg Code, or they were adopted by various branches of the medical profession, as with the Helsinki Declaration. By and large, these codes attempted to balance the need for scientific experimentation against the need for protection of its subjects.

EARLY PERSONAL CODES

One of the earliest statements bearing some relation to the ethics of experimentation was a paragraph from Thomas Percival's *Medical Ethics* published in 1803. He stated that there should be no trials of new remedies and treatment 'without a previous consultation of the Physicians or Surgeons, according to the nature of the case' (reprinted in Leake, 1975: 76). This recommendation for peer review was finally incorporated in codes of research ethics in the 1960s – one hundred and fifty years after Percival's book was published. Some commentators (for example, Nicholson, 1986: 53-4 and Howard-Jones, 1982: 1430-1) have argued that Percival's code is not relevant to research review because it referred to innovative treatment rather than systematic research. This observation, although true, is a trivial objection in that systematic research was a development of a later era. It illustrates the tendency of many commentators to restrict the discussion of experimentation on human subjects to research in the strict and modern sense of the term. As I argued in the Introduction, many of the issues relevant to research are also relevant to non-systematic experimentation and to innovative therapy. Experimental subjects need some assurance that their well-being will be given greater importance than the conduct of an experiment whether or not the experiment is part of a well-conducted research program or a consequence of a non-systematic innovation in therapy. From this perspective, the fact that Percival's suggestion of peer review related to innovative therapy does not diminish its importance as a statement in the history of the development of codes governing human experimentation.

Percival was also criticised for not discussing the 'obligations of physicians' to inform patients about their treatment (Katz, 1972: 321). It may be wisdom in hindsight to require this of Percival and it could be argued that this was not a common practice in his day. However, a criticism that would completely undermine the value of Percival's code, if it were true, is the suggestion by Howard-Jones (1982: 1430) that Percival's code was part of 'an elaborate hoax'. The implication was that the code was not a genuine guide to practice but the product of moral posturing designed to fool the public into believing in the propriety of medical practice. In my view this is overstating the case. A more reasonable supposition is that Percival's code represented good intentions at the very least.

The oldest known American credo of ethics for research was William Beaumont's code of 1833. He recognised the importance of experimentation on humans but considered that voluntary consent of the subject was necessary. His code required abandoning the experiment if it caused the subject distress or if the 'subject becomes dissatisfied' (Beecher, 1970: 219). Faden and Beauchamp (1986: 188) have suggested that Beaumont's treatment of patients did not always live up to his own standards.

Claude Bernard's statement in 1865 was the first in the context of research in the modern sense. Bernard gave a clear expression of the primacy of the welfare of the subject over the scientific enterprise by stating that doctors should never perform 'on man an experiment which might be harmful to him to any extent, even though the result might be highly advantageous to science, i.e., to the health of others'. He added that, of all possible experiments, 'those that can only do harm are forbidden, those that are innocent are permissible, and those that may do good are obligatory' (Bernard [translated from the French], 1957: 101–2). This statement has also been criticised because it is not possible to know in advance whether an experiment will do good or harm and that not all harmless experiments should be permissible – only those that 'are properly organized and give promise of value' (Beecher, 1970: 226). Essentially, Bernard's statement begs the question because if it were known in advance that an 'experiment' would do good it would not be an experiment. Howard-Jones (1982: 1431) has pointed out that 'medical history is strewn with examples of interventions thought to be beneficial that were in fact noxious or even lethal'. However, modern codes of research ethics also require anticipating in advance whether experiments will do good or harm. Some modern codes, such as the Nuremberg Code and the Helsinki Declaration, require a balancing of anticipated benefits against potential risks to subjects. These codes make it clear that the assessment is to be based on the information available. However, the actual risks and benefits cannot be known until after the experiments have been conducted – and the anticipated risks and benefits may be misleading. So, while Bernard may have been overemphatic, there is some support for his general position that risky experiments should be avoided and experiments that appear to be beneficial should be encouraged. Furthermore, he should be applauded for his early recognition that the rights of the subjects of experiments should have priority over the interests of science.

Nevertheless, we should be on guard against reading too much into the statements of individuals such as Percival, Beaumont and Bernard. Their positions on ethics were probably not at all typical of the generally held views of their time. There is no evidence that their views were influential. As Rothman (1987: 1196) has put it, 'such statements reflect the moral acuity of individual commentators more than a shared sense of crisis'. Furthermore, these codes may have borne little relation to experimentation in practice. What they represent is an early awareness by some researchers of the need to protect subjects of experimentation from harm.

EARLY NATIONAL CODES: THE GERMAN CODES

Alongside the development of systematic research, the twentieth century saw the development of national and international codes of ethics applying to experimentation on human beings. Germany provided both the nursery for the early development of research and its commercial application. It was the first country to formulate a national code of ethics. Paradoxically, German atrocities during the Second World War, in contravention of its own codes, led to the first international statement on the ethics of research: the Nuremberg Code.

Directive of 1900

In the late nineteenth and early twentieth centuries, German medical science was the most successful in the world and led Germany to develop a modern pharmaceutical industry. This industry owed much to the work of Paul Ehrlich (Ackerknecht, 1982). Ehrlich was aware of the potential for abuse of subjects in experiments to test drugs and was cognisant of the need to adequately inform volunteers in drug trials of the risks that they ran (Howard-Jones, 1982: 1435). There could be no guarantee that early drug trials were free from risk. Given his standing and his sensitivity to these issues, he may have been influential in the development of a code of ethics to protect subjects.

Germany was the first country to proclaim ethical criteria for experimentation. A directive from the Prussian Minister of Religious, Educational and Medical Affairs was issued to the directors of clinics in 1900. It limited medical experiments (which were included in the description of 'medical interventions' other than those for diagnosis and treatment) to competent adults who had consented after a 'proper explanation of the adverse consequences that may result'. Experiments had to be conducted or authorised by the director and a record of compliance with the directive had to be noted (World Health Organization, 1987: Annex 1).

Richtlinien of 1931

Despite the directive of 1900 there were difficulties with drug trials in Germany in the 1920s. These difficulties highlighted the dynamic tension between science, society and the subject. The German medical profession was accused in the press of flagrant abuses of subjects of experiments (including children) in the name of science. The German pharmaceutical industry was developing rapidly and hospitals were also accused of working for this industry. In 1929 and 1930, the Berlin Medical Board discussed a recommendation for an official regulatory body to consider proposals for experiments on human subjects. This suggestion was supported by the press but publicly repudiated by a representative of the German National Health Council. Although the proposition was rejected, it is worth noting that this was the earliest record of a public call for the establishment of prospective review of research (Howard-Jones, 1982).

Following this public debate, the German Ministry of the Interior published *Richtlinien* (regulations or guidelines) on new therapy and human experimentation in February 1931. The initial statements reiterated arguments of the National Health Council: namely that, if medical progress was not to cease, new therapeutic agents had to be tested and that human experimentation could not be dispensed with (Howard-Jones, 1982). However, any experimentation had to be conducted according to a number of principles including previous tests on animals, consent after appropriate information, and the impermissibility of experiments on children that endanger them 'in the slightest degree'. These regulations were legally binding and 'remained binding law in Germany even during the period of the Third Reich' (Sass, 1983).[1]

Fischer and Breuer (1979) have declared that the regulations were better and more far-reaching than all the subsequent codes including the Nuremberg Code and the Helsinki Declaration. It is ironic that, within fifteen years of the promulgation of the clearest and most definitive guidelines for the ethical conduct of experiments on human beings, German doctors would actively participate in some of the worst atrocities of medical experimentation recorded in history (Capron, 1986). A German commentator, in something of an understatement, commented that this blunt disregard by German doctors of their own code in the concentration camps demonstrated how closely the regulation of ethical issues was 'intertwined with shifts in political fashions, preferences, and powers' (Sass, 1983).

1. Howard-Jones (1982: 1436) has stated that these guidelines 'were recommendations not having legal force'. However, I believe that Sass gives the correct account. Capron (1986: 231) has also stated that these 'regulations were in force at the time the experiments in the concentration camps were carried out'.

INTERNATIONAL CODES

The Nuremberg Code

The Nuremberg Code (as it became known) was part of the judgment of the Nuremberg Court in the case of *United States v. Karl Brandt* discussed earlier. The Court drew up the Code as a statement of a universal standard of ethics in research against which to measure the behaviour of the accused (Appelbaum, Lidz and Meisel, 1987: 212). The Court asked two of its expert witnesses, American doctors Andrew Ivy and Leo Alexander, to advise it on universal standards of ethics in experimentation on human subjects (Capron, 1986: 231).

Alexander referred to the earlier German codes of research ethics in advising the Nuremberg Court. Although it was apparent that these codes were little known and ineffectual, Ivy, with the endorsement of the American Medical Association, presented three basic principles of human experimentation: (1) voluntary consent; (2) previous animal experiments to investigate the risks of each experiment;[2] and (3) responsible, medically qualified management. It was these three points that the Court had taken and expanded into the ten principles of the Nuremberg Code. However, as Appelbaum, Lidz and Meisel (1987) pointed out, the testimonies of Ivy and Alexander were misleading in that they had based their recommendations on ethical principles which were more indicative of good intention than of actual practice at the time.

One of the strongest criticisms that can be made of the Nuremberg trial was that it was an exercise of moral indignation by the victor over the actions of the vanquished without regard to the fact that breaches of moral codes were condoned by both sides in the name of war. This was one of the contentions made in defence of Brandt and his co-accused (Katz, 1972). Howard-Jones (1982: 1436, 1442) argued that the circumstances of experimentation in concentration camps during the war bore little relation to normal medical practice and research in peacetime and that 'entirely atypical wartime medical experiments that were neither ethical nor intended as such' have led to a Code that was inappropriate and restrictive and has

2. Although the Nuremberg Court supported the use of animals to make sure that the risks for humans are reasonable, the assumption does not go unchallenged. See, for example, Singer (1977), Regan and Singer (1976), Gruen and Singer (1987).

threatened medical progress. I disagree and support the view that in the historical context of the Code, 'its importance cannot be over-stated' (Annas and Glantz, 1987: 3; Annas, Glantz and Katz, 1977: 21).

The contention surrounding the Nuremberg Code arose because of the emphasis given to the principle of consent. Consent was the first and major principle. However, Annas and Glantz (1987: 2–3) have argued that before consent becomes an issue, the scientific validity of a proposed study, the acceptability of potential risks to subjects and the competence of the investigator to conduct the study, need to be established. Fletcher (1983: 210–11) has suggested that the Nuremberg tribunal's concern with consent was a symbolic display of 'moral disgust' and that the pre-eminence given to consent as the *'first principle* and the only *absolute* principle of research ethics' (emphasis added) is inappropriate. He argues that the Court at Nuremberg side-tracked the debate into the issue of consent rather than the more important issue of adequate protection of subjects from harm. As a consequence, experienced investigators simply discounted the concern over consent and ignored the Code. Although the Code did require that the risks involved in experiments should be in proportion to the expected benefits, no suggestions were offered about who should make this assessment and how it should be made. In my view, Fletcher's argument is an overstatement of the shortcomings of the Code and does not give sufficient credit to the Nuremberg Code for prompting further positive developments such as the World Medical Associa-tion's Declaration of Helsinki.

Although the Nuremberg trial of German doctors and the Nuremberg Code are well known, it may be that this notoriety is relatively recent. It has been claimed that the Nuremberg trial itself received very little press coverage and that, before the 1970s, there were very few discussions of the Nuremberg Code or citations in medical journals (Rothman, 1987). The Nuremberg Code has also had little judicial application (Annas, 1991). Within medicine there was a tendency to dismiss the atrocities revealed in the Nuremberg trials as the work of morally bankrupt or deranged 'Nazi doctors' (Rothman, 1987: 1198; Jones, 1981: 188). This was a political and defensive reaction that blinded the medical profession and medical bureaucracy to the ethical and humanitarian concerns inherent in medical research. It took revelations of unethical medical research within the United States itself to shake this complacency.

The World Medical Association and the Helsinki Declaration

The Helsinki Declaration has been more influential in the medical profession than the Nuremberg Code largely because it is perceived to be a guide to researchers rather than a legal document and because it is less restrictive of research. The Declaration is a code of ethics for research on human subjects, adopted by the World Medical Association in 1964. The Association itself was formed in 1947 by doctors who had met during the Second World War at the British Medical Association House in London. It included doctors from countries invaded by the Germans in Europe and doctors from Australia, Canada, New Zealand, South Africa, Britain and the United States (Pridham, 1951).

The Association had spent many years considering principles for experimentation on human subjects. The Helsinki Declaration was not the first pronouncement. The Eighth General Assembly of the World Medical Association, held in Rome in 1954, adopted 'Principles for those in Research and Experimentation'. The first of these principles referred to the scientific and ethical requirements of experimentation (in very general terms) and the second to the need for prudence in the publication of the results of experimentation. The third principle required that healthy subjects be fully informed. It stated, however, that the primary factor was the responsibility of the researcher and not the willingness of the subject. The fourth principle allowed that 'operations or treatment of a rather daring nature' could be conducted on sick subjects in rare and 'desperate cases' if the decision could be made by the doctor in good conscience. The fifth principle required that subjects 'be informed of the nature of, the reason for and the risk of the proposed experiment' and that consent be obtained in writing. In the case of an 'irresponsible' patient (one without legal capacity) consent could be obtained from a legally responsible representative.[3] Commentators such as Annas and Glantz (1987: 7) have drawn attention to the early differentiation between experimentation on healthy and sick subjects contained in these principles (a distinction that appeared subsequently in the Helsinki Declaration) and to the general approval of proxy consent which had not been allowed for in the Nuremberg Code.

3. Editorial, 'Organisational News', *World Medical Journal*, 1955: 14–15.

The World Medical Association's 1954 principles were considered by a Dutch government body in preparing a report for the Minister of Social Affairs and Health in 1955. This report recommended that the 'investigator should consult other experts on the research project in order to intensify the sense of responsibility'.[4] This was an early move towards peer group approval for research proposals. The Netherlands Report was forwarded to the World Medical Association for information so that its recommendations could be considered in any further revision of the guidelines on research ethics.

In the early 1960s, the World Medical Association began to draft another code of ethics for research on human subjects. The first draft was produced in 1961 but the code was not adopted until 1964 at the Eighteenth World Medical Assembly in Helsinki. This delay was said to have been caused by the 'desire to produce a truly useful and practical document' (Winton, 1978). However, reading between the lines, it is not difficult to detect disagreement within the Association on the need for a code. Indeed, resistance to the adoption of guidelines for researchers within an organisation that had previously placed its confidence in the responsibility of the investigator was hardly surprising. Some support for this reading of events is to be found in a later editorial note in the *World Medical Journal* (1976) that referred to the 'hard work, mutual consultation, *argument* and discussion' involved in preparing declarations (emphasis added).

Annas and Glantz, two American commentators on the Nuremberg Code and the Helsinki Declaration, have suggested that the thalidomide tragedy and the Food and Drug Administration's proposal to tighten regulations on drug experimentation in the United States may have given the necessary push to the World Medical Association to adopt the Declaration (Annas and Glantz, 1987: 8). They also considered that the large increase in drug trials internationally made a new code necessary since neither the Nuremberg Code, devised as a yardstick to measure the abuses of 'Nazi' doctors, nor the Hippocratic model were sufficient to cope with this new situation.

Annas suggested that the World Medical Association had a more cynical motive in putting forward the Helsinki Declaration. He saw it as 'Recommendations to physicians by physicians' which watered down the restrictions that were imposed by the Nuremberg Code

4. Editorial, 'Human experimentation', *World Medical Journal*, 1957.

and preserved the rights of doctors to conduct research even when consent was not possible (Annas, 1991: 26). The medical profession had objected to the Nuremberg Code because the requirement for consent in the Code appeared to be absolute and would have excluded research on the very young, on the unconscious, and with those who lacked legal capacity, such as the mentally ill. The Declaration of Helsinki allowed for proxy consent by others for research on such subjects. It went further and allowed that, in clinical research on sick persons, the doctor could dispense with the need for consent if it was not 'consistent with patient psychology' (World Medical Association, Declaration of Helsinki, 1964). This extended the 'therapeutic exception' to research which was combined with treatment. The therapeutic exception allows a doctor to dispense with the requirement for consent in medical treatment if it is in the patient's interest. Some saw this loophole as a serious flaw (Swazey, 1978: 133). The exception has remained however, although a subsequent amendment to the Declaration required the doctor to state the reasons for not obtaining informed consent in the research protocol.[5]

Another feature of the Helsinki Declaration was the distinction between 'clinical research combined with professional care' and 'non-therapeutic clinical research'. This was the same distinction that appeared in the World Medical Association's 1954 principles. A change of wording in a subsequent revision of the Helsinki Declaration altered these terms to 'clinical research' and 'non-clinical biomedical research'. Generally, this has been referred to as a distinction between therapeutic and non-therapeutic research. The basic safeguard for therapeutic research was that research had to be justified by its potential benefit for the patient. Doctors were not constrained from using new diagnostic or therapeutic measures if they considered them to offer a health advantage to the patient. However, this distinction between therapeutic and non-therapeutic research, and the consequent lack of control over innovative therapy, has been criticised (see, for example, Levine, 1986: 4).

The medical profession clearly preferred the Helsinki Declaration. For example, Beecher, a prestigious Harvard professor, considered the Nuremberg Code to present a danger in that it was a 'rigid set of legalistic demands' whereas the Declaration of Helsinki was a

---

5. World Medical Association, Declaration of Helsinki, 1975, Principle II.5 (Tokyo).

'series of guides' (Beecher, 1970: 279). Underneath this rhetoric was a resistance to the intrusion of law and to restrictions on the practice of medicine and research. Beecher's preference was for guidelines which would leave the discretion for ethical conduct with doctors rather than impose it from the outside (Beecher 1966b). An editorial of the *Medical Journal of Australia* in 1976 noting that the Helsinki Declaration had gradually superseded the Nuremberg Code, suggested that this could be explained by the fact that the Declaration was issued by 'an international body representing the practising medical profession' and related to 'generally accepted medical traditions rather than to the specific matter of Nazi crimes'.

The Helsinki Declaration became widely accepted in the United States and other countries.[6] In Australia, the National Health and Medical Research Council's Statement on Human Experimentation (see Appendix 2) was developed originally from the Helsinki Declaration, and various medical and para-medical associations have also adopted the Declaration (Berglund and McNeill, 1989).

Up to this time all the codes had relied on the conscience of the individual investigator and the consent of the experimental subject. In 1975, however, an amendment to the Helsinki Declaration (Principle I.2) introduced the recommendation that research projects be considered by a 'specially appointed independent committee'. The development of committee review in the United States, which created the precedent for this amendment, is outlined in the next chapter.

Another interesting change in the revised Helsinki Declaration was a change in the rationale for experimentation on human subjects. The earlier Declaration claimed that 'it is essential that the results of laboratory experiments be applied to human beings to further scientific knowledge and to help suffering humanity'. The revised Declaration simply claimed that the purpose of medical research on human subjects was to 'improve diagnostic, therapeutic and prophylactic procedures and the understanding of the aetiology and pathogenesis of disease'. This rationale, in the revised Declaration, had dropped implicit assumptions about the value of research to society and replaced them with a more accurate statement of the motivation for research.

6. Many of the US bodies endorsing the Declaration of Helsinki are listed in Editorial (Special Article), *Annals of Internal Medicine* (1966). See also Beecher (1970: 279).

WHO/CIOMS guidelines

Other international guidelines have followed the Helsinki Declaration. The World Health Organization (WHO) and the Council for International Organizations of Medical Sciences (CIOMS) published *Proposed International Guidelines for Biomedical Research Involving Human Subjects* in 1982.

The issuing of those guidelines was prompted by concern that research might be conducted in 'developing countries' to avoid restrictions and to minimise expense. Such investigations could serve 'external rather than local interests' and have insufficient insight into local mores and customs. There was also concern that, on completion of the research, there would be no long-term commitment to the subjects and no compensation for any injury that might have occurred. It was considered that some of these difficulties could be overcome through collaboration with local institutions and a tangible commitment to service and training in these countries. It was also recognised that research relevant to local problems was needed and that there would often be insufficient resources or expertise to support a regulatory system (WHO/CIOMS, 1982: 3–6).

The principles behind these guidelines were that there should be an adequate assessment of the risks; that research design and practices needed to be justifiable and capable of leading to valid results; and that subjects who were otherwise beyond the reach of organised medicine would continue to have access to treatments that had been shown to be of value. The guidelines also dealt with issues of informed consent and research involving children, pregnant and nursing women, the mentally ill, and prisoners.

It was recognised that individual consent would not always be possible. The guidelines therefore adopted the principle that any decisions on behalf of others had to be made by an independent representative body with responsibility for protecting community interests. The guidelines also gave a strong endorsement to 'independent impartial prospective review of all protocols' by a committee of the 'the investigators' peers' that might also include 'other health professionals, particularly nurses, as well as a layman qualified to represent community, cultural and moral values'. Investigators with a direct interest in a proposal were precluded from participation in its assessment. It was suggested that review committees could be created either by national or local health administrations or by national medical research councils or other nationally representative medical bodies. The proposed guidelines have now been adopted by CIOMS.[7]

In 1987, the Canadian Medical Research Council was host to the International Summit Conference on Bioethics in Ottawa. There was little that was new in the recommendations of the Summit Conference. However, a principle from the WHO/CIOMS guidelines, reinforced by the Conference and subsequently adopted by the Economic Summit Nations, was that a 'nation should not allow or support in other countries research which does not conform to ethics review standards at least equivalent to those in force within the nation' (Miller, 1988).

Given the difficulty of regulating experimentation on human subjects in the Third World, the WHO/CIOMS guidelines are an important international recognition of minimum standards of research in those countries. Statements of support, such as those of the Economic Summit Nations are useful in reinforcing these ideals. As is discussed in Chapter 4 and Appendix 1, there is little evidence of review outside of the 'developed' nations. It means that, notwithstanding the WHO/CIOMS guidelines and other statements, Third World countries are vulnerable to exploitation by researchers seeking to conduct research with the minimum of restrictions.

International Covenant on Civil and Human Rights

The International Covenant on Civil and Human Rights seeks to protect human subjects of experimentation as part of its rejection of torture, cruelty and inhuman or degrading treatment or punishment. Article 7 states that 'no-one shall be subjected without his free consent to medical or scientific experimentation' (Bossuyt, 1987: 147). The Covenant took effect in March 1976. Australia, together with New Zealand, the United Kingdom, Canada and many other countries (87 countries in all) were parties to the Covenant. However, its implementation is difficult in that national guidelines for medical research in a number of countries allow experimentation on persons incapable of consent even when there is no therapeutic benefit to those persons. Many countries, including Australia, have therefore

7. Personal communication, Zbigniew Bankowski, Secretary-General of CIOMS, 20 October 1989.

become parties to an international covenant which prohibits experimentation which is expressly permitted by guidelines within those countries. This situation is unresolved but it is likely that the precise terms of Article 7 of the International Covenant will simply be ignored by medical researchers.

CONCLUSION

This chapter has examined the historical development of codes for experimentation on human subjects. The first international code of ethics, the Nuremberg Code, was itself part of the judgment of a court in the case brought by Allied forces against German doctors and scientists. The Code was largely ignored. Subsequently, the World Medical Association formulated a set of guidelines known as the Helsinki Declaration. This Declaration appears to have been more influential and has prompted the development of national guidelines and guidelines of professional bodies within countries. Of the other codes discussed, the WHO/CIOMS guidelines may have some value in the Third World but without adequate surveillance and review it can only be a starting point and offers little protection. Even in countries with established review processes, there are questions about the degree to which codes actually influence researchers' practices.

Codes on their own are not sufficient to safeguard research subjects and ensure ethical experimentation. The obvious illustration is the comprehensive rules of research ethics enshrined in the German Richtlinien of 1931 and the utter disregard of those provisions by the German doctors and scientists in Nazi concentration camps during the Second World War. Codes of conduct can be at best a statement of principle which will be adhered to and at worst, a public relations document which serves to hide unethical conduct which continues unchecked. The important issue is whether or not there are provisions for ensuring that agreed principles are put into practice. In my view there needs to be some mechanism for ensuring that the rules stated in codes of ethics are adhered to.

Subsequent chapters trace the evolution of research regulation and the development of review by committee which was instituted to ensure that accepted principles of research ethics are put into practice.

PART TWO

Research Ethics Committees: History and Practice

The Development of Committee Review in the United States, Britain, Australia, New Zealand, and Canada

While national and international codes have been important in setting the parameters of acceptable research, it is committees of review that have been relied on to ensure that research practices conform to the standards set out in these codes. Committees were first developed in the 1960s in the United States and rapidly became the standard means throughout the world for resolving the conflict between the scientific need to conduct research on human subjects and the humanitarian need to protect those subjects. This chapter traces the history of the regulation of research and the development of committees of review in the United States, and then traces the extension of committee review into Canada, Britain, Australia and New Zealand.

THE UNITED STATES

Developments in the United States were prompted by political pressure, particularly in the Senate, following publicity given to cases in which the welfare of patients and subjects of experiments had been disregarded. These cases are now considered in detail.

Regulation of pharmaceutical testing

Calls for the regulation of human experimentation in the United States resulted from the testing of drugs (as in Germany in the 1920s). In the United States it began with the release of a dangerous drug onto the market.

Elixir of Sulfanilamide
A drug known as 'Elixir of Sulfanilamide' was marketed by a pharmaceutical company in the United States in 1937. Prior to its

release, the solution had only been tested for 'flavour, appearance, and fragrance' (Howard-Jones, 1982: 1434). There were alarming reports in the press about the lethal effects of this solution which led to a public outcry. The American Medical Association initiated investigations which showed that diethylene glycol was included in the 'Elixir' and was a poison. It concluded that this substance (or the substance in a mixture with sulfanilamide) was responsible for more than a hundred deaths.[1] Yet the company had not been required to test the safety of the substance before releasing it onto the market.

In response to resolutions of the Senate and the House of Representatives, the Secretary of Agriculture proposed that all new drugs should be licensed only after experimental and clinical tests. Any drugs dangerous to health would be prohibited. Previously, the only restriction on the distribution of drugs had been that they should be clearly labelled, no false therapeutic claims made about them and that they not be adulterated. Because of strong opposition from business interests, the Secretary of Agriculture's proposal was incorporated in the Federal Food, Drug and Cosmetic Act of 1938 in an attenuated form (Howard-Jones, 1982). The Act gave control over any new drug or device for diagnosis, treatment or prevention of diseases in man or animals to the Food and Drug Administration (FDA), unless it had been shown to be safe. The legislation exempted the use of drugs for investigation by qualified scientists. The inadequacy of these requirements was brought home by the thalidomide tragedy.

Thalidomide

This drug had been used since 1958 and was initially considered to be effective for bringing about sedation without toxicity. In 1960 some suspicion began to arise that the drug caused peripheral neuritis and partial paralysis; and in 1961 doctors noticed an association between thalidomide and deformities in children (Teff and Munro, 1976). At this time thalidomide was still an investigational drug with the FDA in the United States. Dr Kelsey, the FDA Medical Officer assigned to review the application for a permit to sell the drug, had not been satisfied that the drug was safe. She was concerned about the reports of peripheral neuritis and the possibility that the drug might cross the placental barrier. She wrote to the company

---

1. See the Editorials in the *Journal of the American Medical Association*, (1937a–g; 1938).

to ask for evidence that it was safe for pregnant women and was not satisfied by the answer provided. The permit to sell the drug was not issued but, because of the lack of regulation of investigational drugs, the company was relatively unrestricted in its program of 'testing' thalidomide. The pharmaceutical company apparently used drug testing as a marketing exercise rather than as a genuine attempt to investigate the drug (Katz, 1972).

Concern about the adequacy of drug evaluation and the thalidomide tragedy gave the necessary impetus for the successful implementation of amendments to federal drug legislation in 1962. As a result, US federal regulations now require more extensive tests including testing for any teratogenetic effects of new drugs on several species of animals (Curran, 1969; Katz, 1972; Howard-Jones, 1982).

Although the FDA's action in restricting thalidomide meant that there were far fewer deformed babies born in the United States than in Europe and elsewhere, the issue for the United States was the inadequacy of the controls over testing of new drugs. Senator Estes Kefauver, as Chairman of the Subcommittee on Antitrust and Monopoly, and Senator Hubert Humphrey, chairman of another congressional subcommittee, joined forces and argued successfully for the Drug Amendments of 1962. These required the Secretary of the Department of Health, Education and Welfare (and, in effect, the FDA), to issue regulations for the control of investigational drugs. At the last minute, an amendment was accepted that introduced a consent requirement into the legislation (Faden and Beauchamp, 1986: 203).

The resulting FDA regulations of 1963 required information on pre-clinical testing and information on the proposed phases of testing on humans. The final phase of such testing required a detailed protocol setting out the names of the investigators, the number of subjects, the duration of the trials and provision for independent assessment and recording of the effects of the drug. These regulations dealt with abuses of subjects in the testing of drugs, not by banning human experimentation, but by making experimentation obligatory. In essence, testing was regarded as a good thing as long as it was carried out on a sound scientific basis (Curran, 1969; Howard-Jones, 1982).

During the 1960s, at the time that the FDA came under pressure to regulate experimentation, the National Institutes of Health (NIH) was also considering the regulation of all its funded research. This led to similar principles being applied by the National Institutes of Health to all its funded research.

NIH and the development of control over experimentation

At the end of the Second World War, the Public Health Service (PHS) gained the power to make grants to outside bodies including universities and private institutions, and inherited the extramural research grant program of the very successful wartime Committee on Medical Research. The PHS administered these programs through the National Institutes of Health (NIH). This was the beginning of a rapidly expanding program of NIH external research grants and fellowships within the United States and in many parts of the world. For example, foreign research grants increased from $130,000 in 1947 to $15 million in 1963; and between 1948 and 1968, the total NIH medical research budget rose from $17 million to $873 million (Swain, 1962: 1235-6; Curran, 1969: 571; Harden, 1986).

NIH peer review [2]

Intramural research at the Clinical Center of the NIH had been subject to peer review since the opening of the Center at Bethesda in 1953. No study raising ethical questions could be initiated without approval of a medical review committee composed of representatives of the research institutes within NIH and Clinical Center staff. There were clear precedents for using committees – the medical profession had turned to committees as long ago as the early 1920s to deal with difficult ethical issues.

Although there had been discussions about requiring extramural research programs to adopt NIH policies on committee review and consent they were not applied to other institutions funded by the NIH until the mid-1960s. This was in part because of a reluctance to interfere with the scientific freedom and judgment of researchers and their institutions. Professional standards and law were relied on by the NIH to maintain ethical conduct of research. It had been hoped that external institutions would follow the lead and adopt guides similar to the NIH policy for intramural research. However,

2. This section draws extensively from Faden and Beauchamp (1986), Curran (1969) and Katz (1972, 1987).

a study by the Boston University Law–Medicine Research Institute in 1962 (cited in Faden and Beauchamp, 1986) showed that few institutions funded by the PHS had any guidelines for research. All that was needed to bring the issue of lack of clinical guidance to a head was an ethical crisis in a PHS-funded research program. Such a crisis was created by the Jewish Chronic Disease Hospital Case.

Jewish Chronic Disease Hospital case
In 1963, at the Jewish Chronic Disease Hospital in Brooklyn, New York, three doctors conducted experiments in which 22 chronically ill and feeble patients were injected with live cancer cells in a study that was funded in part by the PHS. The doctors were interested in the rate of rejection in patients already afflicted with diseases such as cancer, Parkinson's and congestive heart failure. A number of other doctors took exception to these experiments on ethical grounds (some likening the experiments to the 'Nazi' atrocities) and prompted a court case for an order to inspect the records relating to the experiments.[3] The evidence revealed that patients were not informed that cancer cells were to be injected nor were they told that they were the subjects of an experiment. The investigators claimed that there was no need to inform the patients as previous studies had indicated that live cancer cells were rejected by healthy patients. They were led to believe that the injections were a part of their treatment. One of the doctors explained that 'there was no need to tell the patients that the injected material contained cancer cells because it was of no consequence to the patients' (Katz, 1972). This attitude was clearly arrogant and the testing of their hypothesis on these patients without their informed consent was both unethical and a breach of their duty of care.

Discussions within the National Institutes of Health
The Director of NIH, Dr James Shannon, was disturbed by both the Jewish Chronic Disease Hospital case and the unsuccessful transplantation of the kidney of a chimpanzee into a human being in a program at a university hospital that was receiving some support from the NIH. The surgeon in the transplantation case, Dr Rheetsma, had not formally consulted others and, although he reported that the patient had consented, there was no evidence of any likelihood of success of the operation or promise of new

3. *Hyman v. Jewish Chronic Disease Hospital*, 1964.

scientific information. Shannon was further unsettled by the report of the Boston University Law–Medicine Research Institute which warned of possible untoward events that could 'rudely shake' the NIH in the absence of any applicable code for the conduct of research. These events unsettled staff of the PHS – and the FDA – and created the conditions for change. All these events coincided with the Declaration of Helsinki being proclaimed in 1964 by the World Medical Association and its adoption by various national medical bodies. The climate of opinion within the United States and the world research community was shifting in favour of some restriction on the free hand of researchers with their subjects.

Peer review

Dr Shannon took his concerns to a meeting of the National Advisory Health Council in September 1965 where he argued for 'subjecting research protocols to impartial, prior peer review of the risks of the research and of the adequacy of protections of the rights of subjects'. He did not consider that researchers were sufficiently impartial for a proper scrutiny of their own research proposals. Nor did he consider that the NIH could continue to rely simply on subjects' ability to protect themselves through requirements for their consent.

The Council, while bemoaning the intrusion of law into research, was worried that it would be vulnerable to political criticism and litigation if it did not take action. It put its faith in 'institutional review committees' and passed a resolution in support of Dr Shannon's proposals at the September meeting. There was criticism at that meeting that the Council was relying on committees without telling them what to do. Katz (1987: 3) has criticised the Council for having 'ducked all the important issues' and placing its faith in a procedural solution (peer review) without establishing substantive guidelines. The Council's concern was that to go any further and suggest guidelines on the ethics of experimentation would have the effect of discouraging clinical research. However, its meeting in December 1965 recommended the briefest of guidelines suggesting that reviewers determine the 'appropriateness of the methods used to secure informed consent' and assess the 'risks and potential medical benefits of the investigation'.

This recommendation was adopted by the Surgeon-General in February 1966 with the additional requirement that applicants for

Public Health Service grants provide a description of the method of review and the associates who are to be included in the review committee. This was a concise statement that would eventually require interpretation, elaboration and revision but it was the first official, binding policy that established the rights and welfare of research subjects and the requirement of informed consent (Katz, 1987: 3). It was also the first official document that established the use of research ethics committees as the central means of protection for subjects of research. Initially, this ruling applied to research and research training grants; in July 1966 it was extended to all PHS grants (Curran, 1969: 577).

Factors leading to peer review requirement

Commentators have identified a number of factors which prompted the adoption of committee review for all research. One factor was the increasing volume of research that was conducted in the United States after the Second World War (Curran, 1969). Another factor was the increasing role of the NIH. An attitude of deference to the scientific freedom and judgement of researchers on the part of NIH officials was understandable when the federal government (through the NIH) funded very little research. With the growth of its power as the primary biomedical research funding body in the United States, there was an increasing sense of responsibility within the NIH for the proper ethical conduct of research. It was then seen as appropriate that the NIH should apply a similar requirement for review of its extramural research to that which already applied to its intramural research (Faden and Beauchamp, 1986: 210).

Political response to revelations of unethical research

The reliance on procedural review by committee came into question over a series of public disclosures of unethical research in the United States. Perhaps the most significant of these disclosures were contained in a paper by Henry Beecher, a respected Harvard professor of anaesthetics.

Beecher article
Beecher's article, published in 1966 in the *New England Journal of Medicine*, stated that hundreds of patients were experimented on

without knowing they were the subjects of research and, of those that were 'informed', many had not had the risks satisfactorily explained to them (Beecher, 1966a).

The paper listed 22 cases of unethical research. Some of these studies involved the withholding of known effective treatment from patients in need of treatment. In one study this withholding of treatment had led to deaths from typhoid and in other studies had led to the contracting of rheumatic fever in a number of patients. The thyroid gland was removed from children undergoing cardio-vascular surgery in one of the reported studies, to see what effect it would have on skin grafts. Neither the thyroid gland removal nor the skin grafts were necessary or relevant to the treatment. They were procedures done purely for research. In another study, melanoma was transplanted from a girl who was dying from the disease to her mother 'in the hope of gaining a little better understanding of cancer immunity'. The daughter died the same day and the mother died 15 months later from melanoma that had metastasised from the transplanted material. The mother was said to have 'volunteered' and to have been informed. On the record it is apparent that the doctors held out unjustified hope to a distressed parent for the sake of a frivolous study. In another study, babies less than 48 hours old were subjected to extensive X-ray exposure to observe the filling and voiding of their bladders without their parents' knowledge or consent.

Beecher had submitted 50 cases to the journal but the number had been reduced to 22 by the journal editors 'for reasons of space'. He had simply identified studies, published in reputable medical journals, that appeared, on the face of the article, to be in breach of ethics of human experimentation. Although Beecher did not identify the articles in his paper, they were identified for the journal editor. In a review of Beecher's paper some 20 years later, Rothman (1987) confirmed that the studies had been conducted by 'mainstream' researchers and that almost all of the 22 studies involved subjects who were either institutionalised or in a situation that compromised their ability to give informed consent.

Beecher's paper had an immediate impact. As Faden and Beauchamp (1986) noted, it came at a time when the NIH was considering the adequacy of its provisions for regulation of research and review by committee and added weight to the push for federal regulation.

Willowbrook

Included as one of Beecher's 22 cases was the Willowbrook State School Case. The case only gained public attention after Beecher again referred to it in his book *Research and the Individual* (1970), and after further criticism by theologian Paul Ramsey and correspondence in *The Lancet*. This was a major controversy involving mentally defective children who were deliberately infected with hepatitis. Although the parents were said to have 'consented', the consent form read as though the procedure was a vaccination. Furthermore, in the latter stages of the research, because of over-crowding in the school, only those children whose parents enrolled them in the study were admitted to the school. This was clearly coercive (Faden and Beauchamp, 1986).

The Tuskegee syphilis study

The Tuskegee syphilis case is probably the most infamous of the exposés of this period. Four hundred poor black men from rural areas in the South were diagnosed with syphilis. They were not informed of their condition and they were not treated. They were merely told they had 'bad blood'. Yet they were brought back for observation and testing on a regular basis to observe and to chart the course of the disease. The study proceeded from 1932 through to the mid-1960s and even after penicillin became available, which was an effective treatment for syphilis, the men were given no treatment. There were numerous doctors and officials involved and yet none of them objected to this study. One doctor wrote in 1966 to one of the authors of a paper reporting the study to suggest that the 'physicians associated with [the study] need to reevaluate their moral judgments'. He received no reply. Jones' examination of the case (1981) reveals that it was not until 1970 that any of the doctors involved at Tuskegee indicated that it may have been unethical. When details of the study were finally made public, the medical profession simply ignored it except for the *Southern Medical Journal* which exonerated the study and chastised the 'irresponsible press' for bringing it to public attention (Katz, 1987: 4).

During this period, from the mid to late 1960s, revelations of this sort led to public outrage at the abuse of subjects of experiments at the hands of callous researchers. This outrage was most clearly expressed in the American Senate.

United States Senate

By the early 1970s, various United States senators had been involved in committee discussions on matters relevant to the ethics of experimentation on human beings. There was concern about the Willowbrook School case and the impending Tuskegee Syphilis Report. Senators Jacob Javits and Edward Kennedy were active in seeking adequate review and regulation of research (Curran, 1968; Faden and Beauchamp, 1986). In a speech to the Senate in August 1972, Kennedy referred to the Tuskegee study and listed a number of other cases of concern. He gave information on a study in which Mexican-American women, believing they had been prescribed birth control pills, were in fact subjects in an experiment to test the effectiveness of a new contraceptive. No consent was sought and some of the women were not given contraceptive pills but a placebo. The argument of the officials in defence of the study was that 'the potential benefits in this kind of study outweigh the potential risks to the individual subjects'. Kennedy's response to that argument was that the 'essence of democracy is that we do not delegate to any officials the right to make such decisions for others' (Sobel, 1977: 61–3). He linked free choice and democracy with principles of research ethics and the right to decide for ourselves whether or not to volunteer for an experiment. Implicit in his speech was a civil libertarian argument dating back to John Stuart Mill.

Kennedy was expressing for the public generally the indignation engendered by a series of revelations of the cavalier use of human subjects by a profession that appeared to put science above the welfare of its human subjects. American society, through its politicians, reacted strongly in favour of the subjects and in opposition to unrestrained science. From February to July 1973, Kennedy convened subcommittee hearings on human experimentation. The hearings examined a number of cases including Willowbrook and Tuskegee, and ethical issues in psychosurgery, and research on human fetuses and prisoners (Faden and Beauchamp, 1986).

Several senators, including Kennedy, Javits and Walter Mondale, had been pushing for a *permanent* regulatory commission, independent of the NIH, to protect human subjects. Kennedy and Javits agreed to compromise on an *advisory* commission on the assurance that regulations covering human experimentation would be published. Consequently, in 1974, the Department of Health, Education and Welfare converted policy guidelines which had applied to intramural research at the NIH Clinical Center into federal regulations applying to all PHS funded research. In the same year, Congress passed the National Research Act which created the National Commission for the Protection of Subjects of Biomedical and Behavioral Research. The Commission was to recommend ethical guidelines for the conduct of research involving human subjects (Faden and Beauchamp, 1986: 214).

National Commission

The National Commission met between 1974 and 1978 and published a total of 17 reports and appendices. The Commission was particularly concerned with the issue of consent to research and the ethical issues posed by research with groups of vulnerable persons such as children, mentally incompetent persons and prisoners. The reports considered research on the fetus, prisoners, children, and the mentally infirm. It also published reports on research under freedom of information legislation, on psychosurgery, and on the delivery of health care by the Department of Health, Education and Welfare.

The important reports, in terms of the principles of research ethics (and methods for applying those ethics) were the Institutional Review Boards Report (including the recommendations and appendices) and the Belmont Report.[4] The Institutional Review Board Report included a research survey on the membership and functioning of committees known in the United States as institutional review boards (IRBs). Some of the findings of this study are reported in Chapter 4. The National Commission's last report, the Belmont Report, identified three 'basic ethical principles' for the conduct of research involving human subjects: 'respect for persons', 'beneficence' and 'justice'. These principles are discussed in detail in Chapter 6. The Belmont Report implicitly put confidence in the committee review system as a means of balancing the conflicting interests in human experimentation.

Ethical Advisory Board and the President's Commission
When the National Commission was wound up in 1978, it was superseded by an Ethical Advisory Board that remained in existence until 1980 (Yesley, 1980). The Ethical Advisory Board was followed in turn by the President's Commission for the Study of Ethical

4. National Commission for the Protection of Human Subjects of Biomedical and Behavioral Research (1978b, 1978c and 1978d).

Problems in Medicine and Biomedical and Behavioral Research which functioned from 1980 to 1983. The President's Commission study is described in more detail in Chapter 4.

Government regulations

During the period from the first promulgation of the regulations in 1974 until 1981, the Department of Health, Education and Welfare (and subsequently the Department of Health and Human Services) took note of the various suggestions for change to the regulations. The Department had its own committees working on these regulations and, in 1981, the Department promulgated amended regulations concerning the requirements for informed consent and the constitution and functions of IRBs.[5]

By the late 1980s there were 16 government departments and agencies with rules covering human experimentation. After protracted negotiations they all agreed on a 'common rule' which gave them identical regulations (with one minor exception) applying to all experimentation conducted within their jurisdiction. Essentially the 'common rule' is a standard for regulations which are applicable to research conducted by various federal departments. The standard applies to all federally funded research on human subjects or research conducted within federal government departments. It requires that research be considered by an IRB and sets out guidelines for the composition and functioning of IRBs and criteria that they should adopt for approval of research. There are no sanctions which apply directly to researchers included in the regulations. The understanding is that the head of the governmental agency or department would not support research which was not approved or would withdraw support for research which was found not to comply with the regulations (US Federal Policy for the Protection of Human Subjects, 1991; Porter, 1991).

Reasons for regulation in the United States

One of the obvious distinctions between the United States and other countries is this degree of governmental control over the regulatory

5. Department of Health and Human Services Rules and Regulations 45; Code of Federal Regulations (CFR) 46. These regulations paralleled the FDA Rules and Regulations 21 CFR 50 and 56, and are reprinted in part in Levine (1986: Appendices 1 and 2).

process of ethics review. Aside from the historical, cultural and political factors discussed later, there was an administrative factor that made it easier for the United States federal government to regulate research: namely, federal monies are distributed directly by a government department. This has allowed the government to maintain greater control than has been the case in any other country.

There are possible cultural reasons for this degree of control. As R. J. Levine (1988) argues, the notion of individuality and individual rights is an obvious feature of American culture. But the reasons are also partly historical. During the 1960s and early 1970s, questioning of the role of the establishment and all authority including medical authority became widespread. So, as details of the Jewish Chronic Disease Hospital, the Willowbrook State School, and the Tuskegee syphilis cases became known, there was a strong reaction from the public and from politicians. This reaction was much stronger than the reaction to cases of abuse of research ethics in other countries. The extent of public concern about unethical research in the United States, made federal regulation a politically acceptable option.

Committee review of research, having begun in the United States, now appears to be firmly entrenched there. Although it had been introduced by government as a departmental regulation, it was accepted by researchers and endorsed by both the National Commission and the President's Commission. It is supported by a voluntary organisation in the United States known as PRIM&R (Public Responsibility in Medicine and Research) and another organisation for the administrators of IRBs known by the acronym ARENA (Applied Research Ethics National Association). There is also an academic journal (the *IRB: A Review of Human Subjects Research*) which is devoted to issues of relevance to IRBs.

While the United States has relied principally on committee review to protect subjects of research, it has also gone further than any other country in debating the ethical issues underlying experimentation on human subjects in academic, governmental and professional forums. The Belmont Report, for example, represents a significant outcome of an attempt to deal with the difficult ethical issues presented by the need to protect subjects of experiments from harm while at the same allowing for medical and behavioural research in the interests of society.

As I have noted elsewhere (McNeill, 1989b), the United States is one of the most interesting of all countries in the field of human experimentation. There has been much more written, there are more regulations, and there is more detail in those regulations than in any other country. Even the publicity given to unethical research is a reflection of the degree of concern in that country.

As we shall see below, committee review has become the standard means for regulating research on human subjects worldwide. It started as a requirement in the United States in 1966 and was adopted by Canada in the same year. The Royal College of Physicians in Britain introduced committee review in their guidelines the following year. New Zealand introduced committee review in 1972 and Australia in 1973.

BRITAIN AND IRELAND

Guidelines for research on human subjects have been issued by various bodies in Britain including the Medical Research Council, the Royal College of Physicians, the British Voluntary Licensing Authority, and the Department of Health. The earliest was a statement on 'Responsibility in investigations on human subjects' issued in 1963 by the Medical Research Council (MRC).

Royal College of Physicians Guidelines

In 1967, the Royal College of Physicians (RCP) considered the MRC statement, the Declaration of Helsinki and the Australian NHMRC Statement on Human Experimentation (none of which made any mention of committee review of research) and recommended that all experimentation on humans should be subject to peer review (Bassiouni, Baffes and Evrard, 1981: 1651). In the same year, M. H. Pappworth published *Human Guinea Pigs*, a book containing allegations of unethical research by British researchers. It had been published the year after Beecher's article. Unlike the response in the United States to Beecher's article, however, Pappworth's book drew very little response from the public or the medical profession in Britain (R. J. Levine, 1988).

A subsequent report of the Royal College of Physicians in 1973 was superseded in 1984 by a document entitled *Guidelines on the Practice of Ethics Committees in Medical Research*. A further edition was issued in January 1990. Until recently the RCP guidelines have been the effective standard for ethics committees in Britain.

The guidelines state that research ethics committees are to 'maintain ethical standards of practice in research, to protect subjects of research from harm, to preserve the subjects' rights and to provide reassurance to the public that this is being done'. The guidelines also state that committees are to 'facilitate good research' and to 'take care not to hinder it without good cause'. A study of research ethics committees in the United Kingdom has found that committee members are confused by a perceived conflict between the requirement to facilitate research and their need to be critical of research (Neuberger, 1992: 44). Elsewhere, I have been critical of the emphasis that was given to facilitating medical research in the RCP guidelines (McNeill, 1989a). Although the 1990 edition re-ordered the objectives of ethics committees to put protection of subjects in first place, it again emphasised the 'need' for committees to avoid 'impeding' research and the need 'to facilitate' research. The guidelines also emphasised protecting researchers and the research enterprise by shielding them from criticism and reassuring the public. The need for surveillance of research, after committee approval, is played down. It is simply accepted that 'it is impracticable, even if it were desirable, for an Ethics Committee to *monitor* in detail the conduct of ongoing investigations' (Royal College of Physicians 1990a: 12 [emphasis in original]). My conclusion is that the Royal College of Physicians guidelines are conspicuously less demanding of review committees and tend to emphasise, to a greater extent, the role of committees in supporting researchers' interests than guidelines in the other countries dealt with in this chapter.

The Royal College of Physicians guidelines are supported by a document (Royal College of Physicians, 1990b) which sets out principles for the ethical conduct of research on patients. They are also supported by a document from the Voluntary Licensing Authority of Britain which reiterates many of the RCP guidelines and adds recommendations relevant to *in vitro* fertilisation (Voluntary Licensing Authority, 1989).

Department of Health guidelines

Whereas the Royal College of Physicians guidelines emphasise research interests, the United Kingdom Department of Health guidelines for 'Local Research Ethics Committees' (LRECs) are more balanced between the interests of science and subjects and are preferable for this reason. These guidelines were issued in April 1991 and apply to all research projects that take place within the National Health Service (NHS). The Department of Health guidelines also recommend that lay members be appointed by consultation with the relevant Community Health Council. This is a movement towards greater independence of lay members which I firmly support. I return to this point in Chapters 8 and 9. There is some doubt whether all NHS institutions will adopt the guidelines, however, as there is no sanction for non-compliance (Editorial, *Bulletin of Medical Ethics*, 1991).

National committee and training

There have been suggestions for the establishment of a national committee in Britain to provide more uniform standards of ethics committees and ensure that members of committees have some training in ethics.[6] Chairpersons of district research ethics committees have met to explore ways of improving the overall performance of committees including the provision of training for committee members.

Ireland

The Republic of Ireland made review by research ethics committee mandatory for clinical drug trials and set out some limits for clinical trials in the *Clinical Trials Act 1987*. The committees were required to include 'medical representatives, business and legal experts, and a competent member of the lay public' (Dooley, 1991). Prior to 1987, there was no legislation governing clinical trials. The need for such legislation was accepted by the government following the death of a student volunteer who died after being injected with an experimental heart drug. The fatality was caused by an interaction between the experimental drug and another drug the student was taking (unbeknown to the clinician researcher). The Clinical Trials Act was amended in 1990 to make it clear that committee members

6. These issues have been raised in Neuberger (1992), in Editorials of the *IME Bulletin* (1989g) and the *Bulletin of Medical Ethics* (1990a), and in Warnock (1988).

were no longer required to guarantee funds for compensation (as discussed in Chapter 9).

AUSTRALIA

In Australia recognition of the need for national guidelines on the ethics of experimentation on human subjects was prompted by overseas events. Unlike the United States, this recognition was not the result of concern and public alarm about unethical experimentation or dangerous drugs. There were almost no public suggestions of unethical experimentation, other than that raised by Senator G. Georges (and reported in the *Sydney Morning Herald*, 4 November 1972: 24) concerning dying patients being kept alive 'for experiments with drugs or new hospital techniques'. This issue, however, did not lead to any controls on research. There was nothing equivalent to Beecher's (1966) allegations in the United States or Pappworth's (1967) allegations in Britain. Nor were there any public scandals such as the Tuskegee study in the United States. The cases that were relevant to the ethics of experimentation in Australia (namely the mustard gas experiments and atomic testing discussed in Chapter 1) were not generally known and were not instrumental in prompting concerns about experimentation on human subjects and medical research. Thalidomide had been an issue in the 1960s with Australian children being born with deformities (Costa, 1989). However, this had not led to any concerns about experimentation as such but was dealt with as a matter for the proper investigation of the safety of imported drugs.

In the 1960s and 1970s, politicians were reluctant to become involved in the issue. Although the medical profession came in for increasing critical comment in the press during the 1970s (Sackville, 1980), there was almost no public concern with the issues of experimentation on human subjects other than the issue raised by Senator Georges (above). In the 1980s, the concerns of politicians and academics were expressed in relation to particular issues, such as *in vitro* fertilisation and the ethics of experimentation on embryos, but not about experimentation on human subjects in general. The impetus for change in Australia was largely prompted by concerns expressed within the National Health and Medical Research Council and within the medical profession.

The National Health and Medical Research Council's role

The National Health and Medical Research Council (NHMRC) took the initiative, at the national level, and developed broad ethical guidelines for researchers on experimentation with human subjects and a system of review of research. The NHMRC is a body responsible for funding of medical research and was established by an Order of the Governor-General in 1936. Members of the NHMRC wished to avoid the consequences of unguided research. These consequences included the possibility that unethical research could harm individuals and reflect on medical research in general. They wanted to ensure that 'what was revealed at Nuremberg must never happen again' and they were concerned to forestall the possibility that 'the epidemic of litigation in medical practice in the United States of America might spread' (NHMRC, 1986a). They had also been prompted into action by the Declaration of Helsinki and considered that the NHMRC 'should provide guidance on this important matter, as it relates to Australian conditions'.[7]

The first NHMRC Statement on Human Experimentation

In May 1966, the Council formally endorsed a 'Statement on Human Experimentation'. Although inspired by the Declaration of Helsinki, the NHMRC Statement was different in several respects. First, the NHMRC Statement appeared to put the emphasis on the goals of science; second, there was no distinction between therapeutic and non-therapeutic research as there was in the Declaration; and third, the Statement was simpler than the Declaration of Helsinki and less restrictive of experimentation especially in the clinical context. Provision for formal peer review was not mentioned in either document, although the NHMRC Statement referred to 'appropriate consultation' which presumably meant consultation between the doctor/researcher and his or her peers. Subsequent amendments to both the NHMRC statement in 1973 and to the Declaration of Helsinki in 1975 made provision for peer review by committee.

NHMRC revision – 1973

Changes in the NHMRC statement on research were the indirect result of concerns about testing for the effects of marijuana on

7. Minutes of the NHMRC Medical Research Advisory Committee, May 1965.

healthy volunteers. In a meeting in November 1972, the NHMRC established a subcommittee to consider whether proposed experiments with marijuana were ethical. Having formed the Ethics in Clinical Research Subcommittee, the Council asked it to 'examine the need to revise the Council's Statement on Human Experimentation having in mind that it was now over six years old'.[8] The subcommittee found that testing of marijuana was ethical if properly conducted by competent researchers and resolved the issue by endorsing a proposal for testing the effects of cannabis on human volunteers.

Peer group review

In examining the Statement on Human Experimentation, the subcommittee considered that 'there was a need for peer group assessment of experiments involving human subjects'. It therefore recommended 'that each medical research institute should have a medical ethics review committee on which at least one of the members is a person not connected with the institute'.[9] The minutes do not disclose what prompted this policy. It preceded the amendment to the Declaration of Helsinki which introduced peer review. However, it is likely that both the United States and British requirements for peer group assessment were influential. To be eligible for research grants from the United States Department of Health, Education and Welfare, Australian researchers needed to satisfy NIH requirements. There were several research ethics committees in Australian hospitals (such as the committee at the Royal Prince Alfred Hospital, Sydney) which had been instigated as a result of NIH requirements for peer review. Members of the subcommittee are likely to have been aware of the United States requirement for peer group assessment and may have been persuaded that this was an appropriate mechanism of review. The Royal College of Physicians of London adopted peer review for clinical investigations in 1967. Given the close nexus between Australian medical specialists and British medical specialist colleges it is also likely that members of the subcommittee were aware of the British guidelines requiring peer review.

8. NHMRC Ethics in Clinical Research Subcommittee Minutes, 27 March 1973.
9. ibid.

Subsequent developments in the mid-1970s

The NHMRC was prompted by amendments to the Helsinki Declaration in 1975 to make further changes to its own Statement on Human Experimentation in 1976. One change was that the policy of requiring ethics committee approval was to be made explicit in the Statement. This policy had been adopted in 1973 but not included in the Statement at the time. What was curious about the 1976 Statement was the obvious tension between medical and behavioural research. The United States National Commission had laboured over writing a set of guidelines that would be appropriate for medical and other research. The NHMRC appeared to have simply added the words 'investigations on human behaviour' to a Statement that was obviously designed for medical research. The other amendments adopted at the same meeting were clearly addressed to medical research. These included the requirement that researchers have 'appropriate clinical competence' (which would not fit for most academic psychologists who might be conducting research on human subjects) and the description of the required committee as a 'medical ethics review committee' in an institution 'undertaking medical research'.

Developments from 1976 to 1981

After the adoption of the 1976 guidelines, pressure for further development of the guidelines came from various sources. One of these included the Commonwealth Department of Health which gave research ethics committees a greater role in the evaluation of drugs (discussed further in Chapter 9). In addition, the College of Paediatrics (and others) expressed concerns about issues of consent in subjects with limited comprehension and capacity (Editorial, *Australian Paediatric Journal*, 1981). Medical developments in fertilisation and embryo research also raised ethical questions, and experience with the system of committee review suggested the need for further development. The Secretary of the NHMRC was also concerned about the risk of 'over-exposure' of groups such as prisoners and students to 'zealous researchers' (De Souza, 1981: 166).

There was criticism of the system from outside the NHMRC. It was suggested that the value of medical research had been assumed and that committees, having been set up by the principal funding body for medical research, might see their role as facilitating research rather than protecting the subjects of research (Osborne, 1983b). It was also alleged that some research ethics committees were more concerned with protecting their institution from legal liability than protecting subjects (Campbell and McEwin, 1981). The NHMRC's response was to convene a Working Party on Ethics in Medical Research in January 1982. The Chairman was Professor Lovell who (prior to his retirement) had been a physician and professor at the University of Melbourne.[10]

NHMRC Working Party
The most significant addition made by the Working Party to the NHMRC Statement on Human Experimentation as a policy document was the statement that the rights of research subjects took priority over the advancement of knowledge. This requirement (in its present form) is for research ethics committees to ensure that:

> while accepting that doctors have a duty to advance knowledge by research . . . the rights of individual patients, or subjects of research take precedence over the expected benefits to human knowledge.[11]

Prior to 1982, the NHMRC had endorsed the need for research without stating this priority. It was asserted that no application to the NHMRC for funding would be considered until a research ethics committee had certified that it complied with the Statement. The Working Party recommended a number of additions to the NHMRC Statement in the form of 'Supplementary Notes'. These dealt with the composition and function of research ethics committees and a number of substantive issues including research on children, the mentally ill and those in dependent relationships, therapeutic trials, and *in vitro* fertilisation and embryo transfer (NHMRC, 1983a).

Institutional ethics committees
Prior to 1982, the only guide for the functioning of ethics committees was that a medical ethics review committee should have at least one member who was not connected with the institution. The Working

---

10. Professor Lovell went on to serve as the Chairman of the Medical Research Ethics Committee for a further ten years.
11. Supplementary note 1.6 (ii) of the NHMRC 'Statement', Appendix 2. The original wording is given in NHMRC Working Party Report (1983a).

Party produced a set of more detailed guidelines on the membership and function of ethics committees. It changed the name of the committees from 'medical ethics research committees' to 'institutional ethics committees' (IECs). This was presumably to accommodate the fact that the Statement had been amended to cover behavioural research in addition to medical research. The name for these committees is a source of confusion, however, because in the United States the term 'institutional ethics committee' refers to clinical ethics committees (or hospital ethics committees) and not to research ethics committees as it does in Australia.

The function of Australian IECs is to determine whether research proposals are 'acceptable on ethical grounds', monitor research projects until completion, keep a record of all projects, and communicate with the NHMRC. In carrying out this function, committees are to ensure that researchers consider 'local cultural and social attitudes' and that consent from subjects will be obtained. The committees were to include a minister of religion, a lawyer, a medical graduate with research experience, a 'lay woman' and a 'lay man'. This degree of specificity for required membership categories was unique to Australia (at that stage) and underscored the Working Party's commitment to the involvement of people from different backgrounds. Of course it was open to committees to include many more than one medical graduate and most have done so. The Working Party also suggested including members of different ages and both sexes.

An issue of concern to the Working Party was that the NHMRC had no power to ensure that institutions undertaking medical research on human subjects had an ethics review committee (NHMRC, 1983a). The support of Ministers of Health for the states and territories was sought and they were requested to make it 'mandatory for every institution in which medical research is undertaken to maintain an institutional ethics committee'. However, none of the states or territories has acted on this recommendation.

There were criticisms of the Working Party Report. For example, Osborne (1983a), Rutnam (1988) and Caton (1990b) considered that the Working Party had not determined the philosophical values underlying its medical research ethics and had instead devoted its attention to mechanisms for review. Similar criticisms had been made in the United States by Veatch (1979: 27) and Katz (1987: 3) about the lack of underlying principles for research ethics review.

The Medical Research Ethics Committee

The Working Party also considered that there was the need for a national committee and made recommendations on the role and functions of the 'Medical Research Ethics Committee' (MREC) as a standing committee of the NHMRC to continue to review the work of IECs. The MREC began its work in 1982.

1985 Amendments

In 1985, the MREC made amendments to Supplementary Note 2 on the composition and functions of IECs. A major change was the requirement that *all* research on human subjects be subject to review by an IEC. It was suggested that institutions not complying with this requirement could lose NHMRC funding. This threat has been sufficient for almost all committees to comply with the NHMRC's guidelines on committee composition.

The MREC continued to put its confidence in review by committee and made changes to strengthen the impartiality of committees by requiring that lay members were 'not associated with the institution' and 'not closely involved in medical, scientific or legal work'. It took the step of reducing an obvious bias by requiring that no member of a research ethics committee 'adjudicates on proposals in which they may be personally involved'. The MREC continued to add guidelines in specific research areas by way of Supplementary Notes to the NHMRC Statement including guide-lines on research involving the human fetus and fetal tissue, epidemiological research, somatic cell gene therapy, and guidelines for experimentation on unconscious patients. (The NHMRC Statement together with Supplementary Notes is reproduced in Appendix 2.)

Australian Health Ethics Committee

In 1988, the Australian Commonwealth Government established the National Bioethics Consultative Committee (NBCC) to advise both the federal and state (and territory) governments on bioethical implications of new developments in medicine. However, in 1991 the NBCC and the MREC were combined by the federal government into a single committee known as the Australian Health Ethics Committee (AHEC). The AHEC has many of the functions of both former committees including responsibility for formulating guidelines on research ethics and monitoring the functions of IECs. It has been established as one of the principal committees of the NHMRC in place of the MREC (Bates and Dewdney, 1990: 57, 420).

The formation of research ethics committees in New Zealand was prompted by circular letters from the Department of Health, the first of which was sent in 1972. By 1975 the Medical Research Council required applicants for grants from the Council to state that they had 'consent' of a local committee. Until 1978 there were ten research ethics committees identified in New Zealand. Two of those conducted their business by mail without meeting in person (Burrell, 1978; 1980a). The number of members on each committee varied between three and six. There were no lay members from outside the hospital system serving on ethics committees with the exception of the Auckland Hospital ethics committee (Richmond, 1977). Nor were there theologians, lawyers or nursing staff serving on any New Zealand committees. The committees included medical superintendents and senior consultants and (in the medical schools) some academic medical staff. The lack of members other than medical graduates was not surprising given that the only guide on committee membership was in the 1972 Department of Health memorandum recommending that committees should include 'experienced members of the professional staff' (Burrell, 1978; 1980a).

The New Zealand system for review of experimentation on human subjects was to be dramatically altered as an outcome of an 'unfortunate experiment' – so-called by C. G. Skegg in a letter to the editor of the *New Zealand Medical Journal* (Skegg, 1986).

Committee review and the cervical cancer inquiry

The term 'unfortunate experiment' refers to a cervical cancer study at the National Women's Hospital in Auckland which proceeded from 1966 to the mid-1970s. Women diagnosed with carcinoma *in situ* had been left untreated to observe the natural history of their disease. Many of them had developed invasive carcinoma unnecessarily and some had died. When some of these events were given publicity an inquiry was instigated.

The Inquiry conducted by Judge Cartwright found that the cervical cancer study had been unethical on a number of grounds: the risk of progression to invasive carcinoma was known; many of the women had not consented; the study was poorly designed and conducted; and there had been inadequate scientific and ethical review. Many of the women had thought they were receiving treatment and had not known they were the subjects of research. The Inquiry was especially critical of the lack of proper review and the failure of responsible doctors and administrators to intervene in the interests of the women (Cartwright, 1988; McNeill, 1989b; and Paul, 1988).

Judge Cartwright also found that the National Women's Hospital Ethical Committee was inadequate in several respects. It had 'limited understanding of ethical principles and their application to research projects', it lacked impartiality, and was 'heavily weighted with medically trained personnel'. Furthermore, the Committee had failed to ensure that patients had given their full consent prior to their inclusion in a research trial. There was little if any surveillance of research projects once approved. Judge Cartwright found that the Committee had failed to ensure adequate scientific assessment of projects. The Inquiry's view of the ethics committee was substantiated by the New Zealand Medical Council which found the chairman of that Committee (Professor Bonham) guilty of 'disgraceful conduct in a professional respect' for his failure to carry out an adequate review of the cervical cancer study (Editorial, *New Zealand Medical Journal*, 1990).

The Inquiry made a number of recommendations including many suggestions for improving the review, conduct and surveillance of research, and recommendations for the review of new medical treatment proposals. On submission of its report, the New Zealand Minister of Health adopted all its recommendations (Barber, 1988).

Department of Health guidelines

The recommendations of the Inquiry were implemented by the New Zealand Department of Health in its 'Standard for hospital and health board ethics committees' of October 1988. One of the outcomes was that a government department (the Department of Health) took over the role of guiding ethics in research from the New Zealand Medical Research Council. Another significant change was that the new standard extended the role of the ethics committees beyond research review to ethical aspects of clinical care and gave them a broad range of responsibility.

Under the guidelines for ethics committees as amended in 1991, all health research proposals involving human participants and all 'untried and unorthodox treatments or procedures' are to be approved by an ethics committee before they can be instigated. In addition, New Zealand ethics committees are authorised to 'consider any matter of ethics relevant to health care delivery' (New Zealand Department of Health, 1991). There are no sanctions specified for non-compliance although reference is made to professional licensing bodies requiring that practitioners submit research proposals for ethical review. The Health Department followed the recommendation of the Inquiry in stipulating that the lay membership should constitute approximately half the total membership of each committee. It took the recommendation even further by stipulating that the committee should be chaired by a lay member. In appointing members to ethics committees, the relevant authorities are to 'take account of the need' for 'medical/scientific expertise' and to provide a balance of knowledge, experience, and perspectives including 'ethics, law, nursing, women's health, patient advocacy and Tikanga Maori . . . cultural diversity' and 'gender'. The guidelines state that members are 'representative of the community at large rather than of any single profession or group'. This is a point I discuss further in Chapters 8 and 9 in arguing that there is no need to exclude representation of particular groups.

The crucial issue for me, however, is whether the subjects of experiments are adequately represented. The New Zealand recommendation for including 'patient advocacy' may go some way toward satisfying this concern, particularly in Auckland and Otago. In these areas the relevant health authorities have adopted a novel approach for the appointment of patient advocates. They have funded a non-profit company (in the Auckland area) and a trust (in the Otago area) to appoint and pay patient advocates who act within hospitals but are independent of hospital management. The advocates are also members of the ethics committee. These structures allow patient representatives to act more independently than advocates elsewhere, such as those in the United States, who are employed by the hospital where they work.

The Department of Health 'Standard' has received some criticism within New Zealand. There was concern that it may be difficult to find members with 'ethical expertise' which is appropriate to medical decisions and that, in some parts of the country, representation of Maori people may be less relevant than a 'Pacific Island or Asian perspective' (Gillett, 1989). There was also concern that the needs of research and academic medicine might not receive proper consideration by the new committees and that the new provisions 'could have a stultifying effect on clinical research' (Paul, 1989; Neutze, 1990). I agree that there is still a need for adequate and knowledgeable consideration by scientific experts. Nevertheless, the power of these experts needs to be balanced by members who have no particular commitment to research. The New Zealand solution of including an equal number of non-medical and non-scientific members on ethics committees is necessary for this reason and comes close to the model for committee review which I discuss in Chapter 9.

The New Zealand cervical cancer case illustrates what can happen when ethics review is not conducted impartially. There was no 'outside voice' on research ethics committees in New Zealand and the National Women's Hospital Ethical Committee was apparently incapable of impartial review. The ensuing tragedy for some women with carcinoma *in situ* led to radical changes in the review system over the whole country. Lay members were given considerably more power and control within committees and the role of the committees was extended to include a consideration of the ethics of clinical treatment.

Health Research Council

In August 1990, a new Health Research Council was formed by an Act of the New Zealand Parliament.[12] The Council includes an ethics committee that advises and is responsible for ensuring that all grant applications to the Council are reviewed by an ethics committee. The national ethics committee can review research itself (where the research is of national importance or is of great complexity) and can be requested (by an applicant) to review an ethics assessment made by one of the local ethics committees. The national ethics committee is also to advise local committees on their composition and on standards and procedures. The responsibility for issuing guidelines

12. *Health Research Council Act, 1990, No. 68.*

for ethics committees is not clear. By this legislation the government appears to have returned the role of formulating and amending research ethics guidelines to the new Council. However, since this Act was passed, the Department of Health has issued amended guidelines. Whether the government will continue to exercise control over human experimentation through the Department of Health or relinquish it to the Health Research Council is yet to be established.

Continuance of ethics committees

As I write, the major issue in human experimentation in New Zealand is the continuance of ethics committees and (if they are to continue) the structure under which they will operate. They were constituted in 1988 as part of the Area Health Boards within the New Zealand Area Health Boards Act 1983. However, in July 1991 all 14 Area Health Boards were abolished and are now due to be replaced by four regional health authorities. Unlike the health boards, the new health authorities are to be independent of the hospitals and other health institutions within their regions and will contract for the provision of health services with privately and publicly owned hospitals. According to the Editorial of the *British Medical Journal* (1991), the regional authorities will be operating by July 1993. In the meantime, the administration of the (previous) Area Health Boards is being conducted by Commissioners.

Ethics committees had been disbanded at the same time as the Area Health Boards, but the first act by the Commissioners (apparently on instruction from the Minister of Health) was to reinstate them. The longer term difficulty, however, is that ethics committees do not fit easily into the proposed new structure of regional health authorities set up on a commercial basis and contracting with many health enterprises. In response to these changes, chairpersons of Area Health Boards met in April 1992 and recommended that the various health enterprises be required by legislation to make contractual arrangements with Health Care Ethics Committees for ethical review of their functioning. If these recommendations are accepted, the Committees would be 'stand alone bodies' funded by health enterprises within such contracts.[13] This is an endeavour to maintain

13. Report of discussions (30 April–1 May 1992) between chairpersons of Area Health Boards in New Zealand, sent to author by the 'Policy Group', Department of Health, Wellington, New Zealand.

ethics review within a health care and research system established on a commercial basis. Given that unethical research was allowed to continue for many years in the absence of adequate review, it is readily apparent that the New Zealand government needs to take seriously plans such as these for maintaining effective review and monitoring of research on human subjects.

CANADA

In Canada there are a number of national bodies with an interest in the ethics of research on human subjects. These include the Medical Research Council, the Royal College of Physicians and Surgeons of Canada and the Social Sciences and Humanities Research Council of Canada. The Royal College, in cooperation with the Medical Research Council, has spawned a further body, the National Council on Bioethics in Human Research, which was set up to publish guidelines, advise on ethical issues and sponsor conferences. A study paper by Baudouin, Ouellette and Molinari (1990) of the Law Reform Commission of Canada has recommended the formation of a further national body: the Canadian Advisory Council of Biomedical Ethics. It is suggested that the Advisory Council act as a national 'think-tank', promote interest in current issues, publish opinions, advise government, and provide information on research both internationally and within Canada.

There are two systems for local committee review of experimentation throughout Canada. One of these was established by the Medical Research Council and the other was established by the Canada Council and is now administered by the Social Sciences and Humanities Research Council.

Medical research review

Since 1966 the Medical Research Council (MRC) has required that biomedical research using human subjects be reviewed by a local ethics review committee. The current guidelines for review committees were published by the MRC (1987a) and are presented in a small booklet which is easy to read, educational and informative. The purpose of the guidelines was described as 'sensitizing' and 'guiding' decision-makers. There are no sanctions provided for non-compliance.

The guidelines on review are preceded by an outline of the history and an explanation of the need for research ethics. This includes a simple statement describing ethics and an outline of fundamental ethical principles; a concise history of human experimentation and the development of ethical codes; and a few paragraphs on the nature of research and the need to blend rigorous science and ethical principles. Other issues canvassed are the preference for guidelines over legislation in the control of research, the combination of research with treatment, and the relationship of law and ethics. This booklet provides an ideal model for other countries in presenting guidelines in a form that is readily accessible to committee members.

The 1987 MRC guidelines adopted the name Research Ethics Boards (REBs) for Canadian committees. Membership of these Boards was described in general terms, with a stated need for 'members who can reflect community values', scientists with a 'broad understanding of research design and of research in the areas usually considered by the REB' as well as 'at least one specialist in the relevant discipline of the research', and a 'clinical psychologist or other mental-health expert' who could 'aid in assessing the subject's capacity to understand the protocol and exercise a free choice'. It was also recommended that members from other disciplines be included, such as a bioethicist, philosopher or theologian; and a lawyer who would provide legal expertise but 'not sit to represent the institution'. The guidelines acknowledge that membership of an REB is demanding but recommend that members sit for two or three years and attend regularly in order to develop the necessary expertise.

The previous version of the guidelines (MRC, 1978) had presented strong arguments for the inclusion of lay members and suggested they 'might even form a majority'. The guidelines, as amended in 1987, omitted this suggestion but stressed the importance of community representation, preferably by members who were unaffiliated with the institution.

Humanities and social sciences review

Research in the humanities and social sciences involving human subjects is covered by guidelines originally published by the Canada Council and now administered by the Social Sciences and Humanities Research Council of Canada (SSHRC). These are contained in a booklet entitled: 'Ethics: Report of the Consultative Group on Ethics' (Canada Council, 1977). This booklet presented guidelines on informed consent; deception in research; the need to assess the risk in relation to the benefit; privacy and confidentiality. These guidelines were given further elaboration in relation to research in special fields such as anthropology and with groups of subjects for whom there are special considerations such as children and captive populations.

The SSHRC guidelines recommended an institutional review committee as a standing committee within all universities to which appropriate persons could be added on an *ad hoc* basis depending on the nature of the applications. It was suggested that the review committee be 'broadly based and include representatives both from inside and outside the department and discipline in question'. Lay members in this sense were not community representatives, as in REBs, but were 'lay' in the sense that they were academics from another discipline.

There was no recommendation to include a lawyer although committees were advised to seek legal advice where necessary. One of the issues for these committees, stated in the guidelines, was the conflict of interest that arises when a committee member is competing for academic advancement with one of the applicants to the committee. This was the reason given for the guidelines suggesting that committees 'should protect the "rights" of both subject and researcher'.

This separation of the review of medical and social science research in two systems has some advantages. Catherine Berglund and I have suggested that there is a significant difference in the emphasis between medical research and social science research (Berglund and McNeill, 1989). Risks in medical research are often to do with the invasion of 'physical integrity' whereas the risks for non-medical research are more likely to concern the invasion of 'psychological integrity'. Another reason for separate review systems is that researchers in one discipline are not always able to appreciate research methods of another. This point is developed further in Chapter 9.

DISCUSSION

There are clear links between the development of review in these five countries. The United States requirement for review in 1966 was

quickly followed by a requirement for review by committee in
Canada. The following year, Britain recommended committee
review, with New Zealand doing likewise in 1972 and Australia in
1973. None of these countries has introduced explicit sanctions for
researchers who do not comply with these guidelines. However, in
many cases both funding and publication of results are dependent
on committee approval. Each country expanded the membership
from what were initially peer review panels to include lay members,
lawyers and others. Whereas the United States has required the
presence of representatives of law and the community since 1974,
New Zealand was the last to broaden the membership of committees
and only did so in 1988.

There are differences in the extent of government involvement in
committee review. Significantly, the two countries in which the
governments are most directly involved are those in which there has
been a public outcry about unethical research. These countries are
the United States and New Zealand. From the mid-1960s to the early
1970s, the 'scandals' in medical research in the United States
prompted government reaction including the issuing of regulations
as well as the establishment of national and presidential commissions. In New Zealand, the cervical cancer study prompted
an inquiry and the publication by government of a wide-ranging
standard for committee review. Although there were revelations of
unethical research in Britain, they did not appear to excite any
response from the public or politicians. The Canadian system was
developed by a medical funding body, the Medical Research Council.
Interestingly though, the Royal College of Physicians and Surgeons
of Canada is now active in this area having promoted the National
Council on Bioethics in Human Research. The Australian ethics
review system was largely the creation of a medical funding body
(the NHMRC) and there has been little governmental involvement
in its development.

All comparisons between countries are necessarily suspect given
the differences in many of their dimensions. Nevertheless, one of the
obvious differences, namely the extent of government regulation and
control, would appear to be directly related to the response of the
public and politicians to reports of unethical experimentation.

CHAPTER 4

The Practice of Review by Research Ethics Committees: An International Study

This chapter presents descriptive and empirical information on research ethics committees from different countries around the world. The accounts of review in the various countries cover mainly Anglo-American and European countries, with some historical material presented for the latter. Descriptions of research ethics committees from the Anglo-American group are drawn from reports of studies in the United States, Australia, Canada and Britain. European countries presented include France, The Netherlands and the Scandinavian countries. I have added a separate section on Germany and Japan in order to draw from the experiences of the atrocities committed in the name of medical science by German and Japanese doctors during the Second World War. Given that history, it is a conspicuous anomaly that there is apparently little review of the ethics of experimentation in either country.

Some reports from a number of other countries show very little evidence of review activity, others indicate that little information is available, while others use information that is out of date. Given the length of this chapter I have presented my findings on those countries in Appendix 1.

THE UNITED STATES

As was stated in Chapter 3, institutional review boards (IRBs) are the committees responsible for review and monitoring of experimentation on human subjects in the United States. There are 'non-institutional review boards' but very few of them (Herman, 1984; 1989). In the years from 1966 to 1976, IRBs were the subject of many studies.[1] A study of IRBs was commissioned by the National

---

1. See, for example, Barber et al. (1979), Gray (1975), Cowan (1975) and Melmon, Grossman and Morris (1970). There was also an earlier study (in 1962) by the Boston University Law–Medicine Research Institute which is discussed in Faden and Beauchamp (1986) and referred to in Chapter 3 of this book.

Commission for the Protection of Subjects of Biomedical and Behavioral Research and was conducted by the University of Michigan's Survey Research Center based on data for the period mid-1974 to mid-1975. Their report was presented in 1978. There have been some studies of individual IRBs and many reports on aspects of their functioning since that time but no comprehensive study of IRBs across the country.[2] After the National Commission study, a study of twelve IRBs was undertaken by the President's Commission which is discussed later.

The National Commission study, 1978

Although the National Commission study is now dated, many of the findings are still relevant and some have been affirmed by similar findings in Australia and elsewhere. The National Commission review of IRBs was the most thorough study in any country on record, having been based on questionnaires and interviews of committee members, researchers and subjects from a sample of 61 institutions out of a population of more than 420 institutions. Almost 4,000 people were interviewed. These included researchers, subjects of experiments and IRB committee members (National Commission for the Protection of Human Subjects, 1978b; 1978c).

The study found that the average number of research proposals considered by IRBs was 43. Most of the activity related to review of the information contained on consent forms although there was no evidence that IRBs helped to improve the readability of consent forms. Both researchers and members of IRBs considered that IRB review protected subjects and improved the scientific quality of research. Even though the researchers found the process interfered with their research to some extent, they were generally supportive of IRBs and accepted the legitimacy of their function. Social and behavioural researchers, however, were less convinced of the need for review of their research and less supportive of the system than medical researchers.

Of the research proposals reviewed by IRBs, 60 per cent were biomedical (usually involving the administration of a drug or the study of samples of tissues or body fluids) and 30 per cent were

2. Charles R. McCarthy, Director of the Office for Protection from Research Risks (OPRR) has stated that the OPRR intends to conduct further research at some stage (interview with author 30 November 1987).

behavioural. Of the remaining research proposals, approximately 6 per cent involved secondary analysis of data or the study of body tissues or fluids obtained for another purpose. Broadly speaking this represents a ratio of medical to non-medical studies of 2 : 1. This ratio was found to be 4 : 1 in Australia in a similar study (McNeill, Berglund and Webster, 1990).

The average number of members on IRBs was fourteen and the committees met on average ten times per year. Ninety per cent of IRBs had a 'community representative' and approximately 75 per cent had a lawyer as a member of the committee. Of the members of IRBs, 50 per cent were medical scientists, 21 per cent were behavioural scientists, and the remainder included administrators, lawyers, nurses, and members of the clergy. The National Commission found that lay members were not as active as their scientist counterparts. This finding was based on the difference between scientists and non-scientists in requests for additional information from researchers or initiations of requests to modify studies. We also found a similar difference in the influence of professional and lay members on committees in Australia (discussed later). This is an important point and one I return to in Chapters 8 and 9 as it relates to whether or not these committees adequately represent interests other than those of researchers.

Most IRBs required a written report from the investigators of approved studies after periods ranging from three months to three years, but usually after one year. More than one-third of these committees had at some time delegated a member or associate to observe the manner in which projects were conducted: of those, half reported that this was done routinely and the other half reported that this was done only under certain circumstances such as when there was a particular risk, when children were involved, or when there had been problems in the past. Porter (1987: 5) found that none of the 198 'unaffiliated/nonscientist' members of IRBs in her study group had participated in the observation of consent processes or, by implication, monitoring of research.

President's Commission study

The President's Commission for the Study of Ethical Problems in Medicine and Biomedical and Behavioral Research functioned from 1980 to 1983. The Commission made site visits to 12 IRBs from

October 1981 to June 1982. The performance of the IRBs was rated on a number of measures such as whether there appeared to be a genuine process of ethical review and whether proper weight was given to protecting subjects' rights and welfare (President's Commission, 1983). Inadequacies were identified in some of those IRBs. For example, one committee was considered to be a 'creature of the regulations, not of conviction'. The Commission considered that the relation of that IRB to the parent organisation was one of subservience. Its composition was criticised for not being sufficiently diverse and the Commission found that non-institutional members were 'either co-opted or frozen out' (President's Commission, 1983: 111). The impression given was of a committee that existed to satisfy the letter but not the spirit of the regulations and which thereby allowed the organisation to continue unimpeded with its research.

Another problem identified was that some IRBs appeared to delegate the consideration of research proposals to a primary reviewer (or to a subcommittee of primary reviewers) and simply rubber-stamp the primary reviewer's recommendations without giving any opportunity for all committee members to see the full protocol and discuss it. The President's Commission made a number of recommendations including the suggestion that research proposals should be examined and discussed by the full range of members. The Commission also questioned the appropriateness of the composition of membership of some IRBs in relation to the type of research being considered and it suggested that there should be a broad educational program for IRB members and monitoring of the committees themselves.

AUSTRALIA

Descriptive study of research ethics committees

At the time of writing, the most recently published report on research review in Australia is a study in which my colleagues and I identified 101 institutional ethics committees (IECs) responsible for reviewing research on human subjects (McNeill, Berglund and Webster, 1990). Of these committees, 86 responded to our request for detailed answers to a survey questionnaire during 1988 and 1989. An average committee was made up of eleven people: four medical graduates, two lay persons, one lawyer, one minister of religion, and representatives of two or three other professions, including nurses, psychologists, non-medical graduate researchers and statisticians. Although medical graduates form the largest group of members on Australian ethics committees, the proportion of non-medical graduate members was greater on Australian committees than was found on equivalent committees in other countries including the United States, Britain and The Netherlands, with the exception of Denmark and New Zealand.

We found that research projects considered by Australian IECs were overwhelmingly from the medical sciences, including health services and epidemiology research (80 per cent of projects), with the remainder being from the behavioural and social sciences (20 per cent of projects). The existence of a committee within the institution which considered the scientific validity of research apart from the research ethics committee was reported by 36 per cent of the respondents. The average number of research protocols considered by committees in the year from mid-1987 to mid-1988 was 41. This more than doubled the average number of proposals given in a 1983 study by the Medical Research Ethics Committee of the NHMRC which found that committees reviewed on average 19 new proposals for research per year (National Health and Medical Research Council, 1985d). Our report included the speculation that the increase in the average number of studies considered by committees between 1983 and 1987/88 was the direct result of the NHMRC requirement in 1985 that all research on humans be reviewed.

We found that 63 per cent of studies were approved on first consideration by the committee, 14.7 per cent were approved after clarification and further consideration, 17.3 per cent were approved after modification by the researcher, 2.7 per cent were rejected and 1.6 per cent lapsed. The earlier study by the Medical Research Ethics Committee had found that 73 per cent were approved at once; 23.5 per cent were approved after further consideration (sometimes after modification) and 3.5 per cent were rejected. In sum, both studies found that 95 per cent or more of new research proposals were approved by Australian IECs either on first consideration by the committee or after further clarification and sometimes modification by the researcher. Very few were rejected outright. These findings are also consistent with the results of a study of ethics committees in Australia conducted in 1978 (Burrell, 1980a). The reported rates of rejection of new research protocols in that study were between 0 and 3 per cent for nine of the eleven committees studied.

We found that fewer than half of the committees monitored research in progress as a general practice. Most monitoring was based on a written report from the researcher. Only 23 per cent of committees had ever sent a representative to observe research as it was being conducted. In a subsequent study, based on questionnaires and interviews with researchers (McNeill, Berglund and Webster, 1992a), we found that only 4.9 per cent of researchers reported either having been visited during the progress of their research by members of their ethics committee or having their research documents audited. Although monitoring of research in progress was included in the guidelines for IECs, 10 per cent of committee representatives responding to our questionnaire in 1988–89 disagreed that monitoring was the role of the committee. There was, however, some evidence of committees taking action on reports of unsatisfactory conduct of research: 20 per cent of committees were reported to have required a researcher to provide evidence of satisfactory conduct of research; 15 per cent were reported to have received formal or informal reports of unethical research practices; and 14 per cent had formally or informally warned or disciplined a researcher about questionable conduct of research.

We had a number of concerns about the committee process. One of these was the finding that some committee members took part in the review of projects with which they were involved. In 74 per cent of committees, one (or more) members had presented a research project to the committee for approval. In more than half of these cases (53 per cent) the member had remained in the meeting during the discussion of the ethical acceptability of that proposal and in some of those cases was present while the decision was made. We considered that this practice called into question the impartiality of the committee.

We were also concerned about the process of selection by institutions of lay and non-institutional members for committees. Appointments were made, in the main, from recommendations given by other committee members or by staff within the institution. This appeared to undermine the intention of the NHMRC that these members be independent of the institution.

We had concerns about the ways in which the lay members and other non-medical members of the committees could be marginalised. They were found to be used less often as primary reviewers of research protocols and their non-attendance at meetings was regarded as less critical than the non-attendance of the medical graduate members. Another concern was that 25 per cent of committees met only twice a year or less. We considered that several meetings were necessary each year for a committee to develop a philosophy and to create an atmosphere in which full and open discussion was possible.

The influence of various committee members

In a later study (McNeill, Berglund and Webster, 1992b), we interviewed 118 members of IECs drawn from every state in Australia and asked them to rate their own activity in contributing to committee discussion. We also asked our interviewees to rate the importance of their own contributions to the committee decisions. Having rated themselves, they then rated the activity of each of the other members of the committee on the same scales both on activity in committee meetings and on the importance of the contribution of each of the members. These ratings were made on scales of 1 to 5: 'inactive' to 'active', and 'unimportant' to 'important', respectively. The data were analysed according to the membership categories of the NHMRC Statement: lay members, ministers of religion, lawyers and medical graduates. We added another category, 'administrators', to this and looked for significant differences between the ratings for each category and the average of other members (see Table 4.1).

Lay members were rated as being significantly less active and significantly less important in their contribution to committee meetings. Both administrators and medical graduate members were rated as significantly more active and more important than remaining members. Lawyers were rated as significantly more important but not significantly more active. The ratings of importance and activity of lay members were supported by comments in interviews.

Although the differences between the mean ratings are not large, the findings suggest that lay members, and to some extent ministers of religion, have less influence on committees than medical graduates and administrators. The implications of the study are, I believe, that the addition of lay and non-scientific members to review committees may not make an appreciable difference. Lawyers (who are not

Table 4.1 *Mean assessment of activity and importance by NHMRC committee membership group*

Committee Membership Group		Mean	SD	N	p
All members	Activity	3.55	0.55	454	
	Importance	3.69	0.65		
Lay member	Activity	2.92	0.99	112	0.00**
	Importance	3.10	1.02		0.00**
Minister	Activity	3.30	1.19	83	0.03*
of religion	Importance	3.58	1.17		0.44
Lawyer	Activity	3.71	1.09	91	0.17
	Importance	3.97	0.96		0.02*
Administrator	Activity	3.85	1.03	79	0.00**
	Importance	3.92	1.05		0.00**
Medical	Activity	4.03	0.73	89	0.00**
graduate	Importance	4.14	0.69		0.00**

SD = standard deviation; N = number of members.
** p < .01, * p < .05, where p = probability of significance.

Source: P. McNeill, C. Berglund and I. Webster, 'The relative influence of various members of research ethics committees', unpublished manuscript, 1992.

defined as 'lay members' in Australia) appear not to fit this generalisation. They were rated highly on both scales. Interviews with committee members confirmed that finding. Typical comments of interviewees which illustrate their view of each role are presented in Table 4.2. Lawyers were valued, both for their contribution from their knowledge of the law, and as intelligent lay people. Most of the lawyer members we interviewed, however, did not see their role as giving legal advice but as representing a lay perspective. I believe that lawyers have the advantage and status of being respected as 'fellow professionals' along with the medical graduates and other professional members. Lay members were much less confident and were seen by other members as not being assertive and as contributing on minor issues. Ministers of religion were similarly tentative about their role. Nurses saw themselves, and were seen by other members of committees, as caught in a traditional role of being subservient to doctors. Although we had not included nurses in the statistical analysis of the data, the mean rating by committee members for the activity of nurses was 3.1 and their importance in reaching a decision was 3.4. This was lower than the rating for ministers of religion.

Table 4.2 *Typical quotes from interviews with committee members about their perception of their performance*

Lay person
Initially I found it very hard in the meetings. Being a lay person, you sit there and think all these other people know so much more than me about the protocols: the lawyers, and the ministers, and the doctors are from high up in medical things. But then you realise that you have to put your two cents worth in when it's there because they often forget how the little people feel. . . . The main problem in the meetings is thinking how to say what I want to say and make it sound important. Really, the best way is to say what you feel, but it often appears unimportant compared to the other issues.

Minister of religion
My role in the committee meetings is from the back seat. I would only speak if I had problems after the science and drug aspects were explained. The discussion is largely up to the medical people. . . . There have been protocols where I seriously questioned the infringement on patients, but I've never opposed them on these grounds. I've always been convinced by the medical argument that the research had to be done.

Lawyer
There's six medical type people as against myself, a minister of religion, a lay man and a lay woman. And then you find the lay man and the lay woman more often than not are intimidated by the doctors, so they won't disagree with them because there's not the knowledge, there's not the confidence in having a view . . . to stand up to them. And without the confidence I suppose that you have from being a fellow professional . . . it's a bit terrifying for them. I have the confidence to express my views, but the other people just sit there and say nothing.

Medical graduate
The routine protocol that has no problems about it, is presented, usually by a medical man, and the others understand it, and we all come to a very quick decision and there's no problem. When there's a problem, where ethical issues as opposed to scientific issues are at stake, then the other people come into it.

Administrator
The number one thing that concerns me is that they [research proposals] are properly presented, because many of our committee now don't have medical training and they don't necessarily have scientific training. . . . My prime concern is to get a protocol to the committee in a form in which it can be understood by almost everyone present. The second thing is to get it through and to see that there are no obvious gaps.

Nurse
The nurse is a subservient role, she's still calling all the doctors 'Doctor'. So even though she might be quite active it's never going to be an active that actually challenges what is going on.

A lawyer's comment about the nurse
The nurse is very much subservient to the specialist doctors in the hospital. And it's difficult to change that. Always I feel that it was a conditioned response on

continued

Table 4.2 (*cont.*)

the nurse's part that one didn't challenge, or shouldn't challenge, the specialist's view, which for medical things is fair enough but these were not necessarily just medical things. So, the area in which she was conditioned to do what she was told tended to spill over into the non-medical and ethical issues.

These ratings were supported by comments in interviews (see Table 4.2) which indicate that nurses also have relatively little influence.

In summary, the impression from both the ratings and from comments offered in interviews is that lawyers are regarded as influential members of committees whereas lay members, nurses and ministers of religion, have relatively little influence.

Researchers' opinions on review and monitoring

In 1989 and 1990, my colleagues and I sought the opinions of researchers on committee review. Our findings were based on questionnaires completed by 449 researchers and subsequent telephone interviews with 92 of those respondents (McNeill, Berglund and Webster, 1992a). Although researchers found the review process to be time-consuming and saw it as impeding research, they nevertheless supported the review system. Eighty per cent considered their effort in applying to a research ethics committee to be justified by the protection offered to subjects and 83 per cent saw the review system as protecting subjects. This was similar to a finding of the National Commission in the United States (National Commission for the Protection of Human Subjects, 1978b: 74; 1978c: 1–80). This is not surprising given that very little research is rejected by committees in either country. Yet we also found that researchers who had had their research rejected by an ethics committee, or who had had their research actively monitored by committee members, were more likely to agree that review and monitoring protected subjects and ensured the ethical conduct of research. We concluded that this result should 'encourage those REC [research ethics committee] members who are fearful of intruding on researchers and inhibiting their research' (McNeill, Berglund and Webster, 1992a). There were a number of concerns raised by this study about researchers not following ethical guidelines. These findings give weight to the argument that review committees, or their institutions, should be more active in the monitoring and surveillance of research practices and not be solely concerned with plans for research.

CANADA

As shown in the previous chapter, there is a dual system for review of research in Canada. There is some information on committees of review of medical experimentation (research ethics boards) but apparently none on committees of review of social science and humanities research.

It has been claimed (for example, by Baudouin, Ouellette and Molinari, 1990: 5) that it is impossible to establish the number of committees in Canada, how they work and what influence they have. However, some information on Canadian committees is already available, and the most recent information on Canadian research ethics boards (REBs) was gained from a questionnaire conducted during a workshop on ethics review held in 1989 by the National Council on Bioethics in Human Research (Miller, 1989). Of the REBs represented at the workshop, 53 were included in the survey. The survey results (published in 1989) indicate that there were community members on 75 per cent of committees represented in the survey although many of those members had another affiliation with the institution and (by implication) were not independent. Lawyers were present on only 28 per cent of those committees; philosophers, bioethicists or theologians on 36 per cent; and 'mental health experts' on 55 per cent. Although nurses were not mentioned in the guidelines, 60 per cent of committees included a nurse. All 53 committees had medical or scientific specialists.

The consensus of views from the workshop was that there should be at least one community member on each committee who was unaffiliated with the institution; members should serve staggered terms of three years to allow time to develop expertise and facilitate education of new members; committees should meet at least monthly; and each committee should define how an investigator could appeal from a decision of the committee.

From the figures given in the report of the workshop, it is estimated that, in the preceding year, REBs considered an average of 104 research proposals (with a range between 4 and 594). These figures are not representative of REBs throughout Canada in that the 53 REBs represented at the workshop and responding to the questionnaire are likely to have included a disproportionate number of more active committees. There was no information in the workshop report to suggest the total number of REBs.

The Medical Research Council's 1987 guidelines had introduced the provision for independent monitoring of research. It had been anticipated that in some circumstances researchers would be obliged to pay for monitoring from their research funds. Many researchers in Canada were opposed to those provisions (McNeill, 1989a). The 1989 questionnaire, however, established that very few committees did any monitoring at all. Although some REBs seemed 'prepared to act on complaints they may receive', the main form of monitoring was the requirement for annual reports from researchers. There was no report of active 'on-site' surveillance of research in progress by outsiders.

The Medical Research Council guidelines of 1987 contained the strongest provisions of any guidelines internationally for active monitoring and surveillance of research. Yet it was apparent at the workshop that committees had not adopted active monitoring. It is understandable that committees whose influential members are from within the institution will be less inclined to actively monitor research out of concern for intruding upon colleagues. In this respect, research ethics committees are typical of most forms of 'self-regulation' in not dealing adequately with non-compliance. This is an issue that I explore further in Chapter 8. However, the failure of committees worldwide to conduct monitoring, even when they have the explicit power and encouragement to do so (as in Canada), raises wider concerns about the adequacy of a system of research review which relies on committees (as presently constituted) to detect and respond to cases of non-compliance.

BRITAIN

Studies in Britain have shown considerable variability in the standards of review by British committees.[3] An editorial in the *British Medical Journal* concluded that 'evidence suggests that the ethical control of medical research remains inconsistent and ineffective'

3. See, for example, Denham, Foster and Tyrrell (1979); Thompson, French, Melia, et al. (1981); Ethical Committee, University College Hospital (1981); Allen, Waters and McGreen (1982); Nicholson (1986: 153–94); and Gilbert, Fulford and Parker (1989).

(Lock, 1990). A group from Edinburgh who studied Scottish committees (Thompson, French, Melia, et al., 1987) pointed to a considerable and confusing lack of uniformity across committees with some serving as little more than debating forums. They were of the opinion that committees in Scotland provided only limited protection and considered that more effective and standardised procedures were needed. Their study was based on responses to a questionnaire from 34 committees. Many of the committees met infrequently if at all. They were concerned that few proposals (1.2 per cent) were rejected outright and that there was no correlation between the number of proposals considered by committees and the number of meetings held. The authors took this to mean that the degree of rigour with which committees scrutinised proposals varied considerably. There was a difference in the size of committees between one and 73 members, most of whom were medical. They considered that there was inadequate lay representation and inadequate use of expert assessors and they suggested greater public accountability.

A survey questionnaire conducted in 1983 by the Institute of Medical Ethics was completed by 174 (69 per cent) of the committees in England and Wales (Nicholson, 1986: 153–4). The size of these committees varied from 3 to 41 members with an average of 8.4 members. Of these, 6.2 were doctors and 2.2 were 'others' including representatives of Community Health Councils, health authorities or administrators, lawyers and lay people. Five per cent of committees were composed entirely of doctors. It was reported that 11 per cent of committees did not meet in person but conducted their business by mail or telephone. (The UK Department of Health (1991) has since recommended against conducting business in this way.) Few research proposals (1 per cent) were found to have been rejected outright. Twelve per cent of chairpersons responding to the questionnaire reported that they were aware of research projects conducted during 1981 and 1982 that had not been approved by an ethics committee. Reports on research ethics committees in Britain continue to give the impression of poor quality in the work of some committees (Editorial (News), *IME Bulletin*, 1988a and 1989b). The most recent report was based on a survey of 25 research ethics committees and interviews of 96 of the members from those committees. The study was conducted by the King's Fund Institute – an independent centre for health policy analysis. Considerable variation was found in standards of review between committees. Some committees did not abide by accepted guidelines and did not accept that they should. Many of the committees functioned as advisory committees having no powers to require that their recommendations be adopted (Neuberger, 1992).

The Institute of Medical Ethics study found that at least 20 per cent of committees surveyed in England and Wales were responsible to a district health authority or management team (Nicholson, 1986: 162). This proportion is likely to have increased following the support for regional committees in the guidelines of the Royal College of Physicians (1990b) and in the Department of Health guidelines (1991). In interviews with members of research ethics committees in Edinburgh in 1987, I found support for the regional basis of their committees. Members believed they were more impartial than institutional committees (McNeill, 1989a).

FRANCE

The body responsible for public funding of research in France, the National Institute of Health and Medical Research, set up a national ethics committee for examining the ethics of experimentation on human subjects in 1974 (Isambert, 1988). This was replaced by the National Consultative Ethics Committee for Life Sciences and Health (a politically illustrious body inaugurated by President François Mitterrand and made up of prominent members) in 1983 (Fagot-Largeault, 1987; Isambert, 1988). The purpose of the committee is to 'provide guidance on the moral problems raised by research in medicine, biology, and health' (Ambroselli, 1984). It functions by debating issues publicly and issuing recommendations. One of its recommendations was that research proposals be considered by ethics committees. Isambert (1988, 1989) has reported that the central committee has very little influence on the local research ethics committees.

Most researchers apply for approval only when they need it for some purpose such as to be eligible for a grant from another country (usually the United States) or for publication in an international journal.[4] There are hospital and regional committees in

4. Isambert (1989) and Professor Pierre Jouannet, Président, Groupe de Réflexion sur l'Ethique Biomédicale of the Kremlin-Bicêtre region (interview with author, 1 June 1987).

various parts of the country but few research proposals were put to the committees for consideration. For example, the research ethics committee for the Kremlin-Bicêtre region considered only 19 research proposals in 1986. This was a small number for a region that includes several hospitals (including a teaching hospital), several laboratories and a university (McNeill, 1989a). In 1989 it was reported that the average number of studies reviewed by ethics committees each year had increased to 23.5 (Isambert, 1989).

In December 1988 a law was passed establishing a 'network of regional multi-disciplinary committees' to protect research subjects.[5] The committees were given the power to inform the Minister of Health if they disapproved of a project. Projects reported to the Minister could not commence for two months, and the Minister could stop the project altogether if it was considered to be dangerous or contrary to law. Breach of the law was a criminal offence. There were provisions for consent, payments to subjects and the establishment of a national register of research subjects. In March 1989, a Bill entitled *Sciences de la vie et droits de l'homme* was introduced in the French Parliament. It requires investigators, who are members of committees, to refrain from taking part in discussions on review committees which relate to projects in which they have an interest.[6] In 1989, however, there was still no law or regulation requiring that research proposals be reviewed although it was expected that such a law would, at some time, be passed in France (Isambert, 1989).

A study in 1984 of 17 committees had found that medical doctors were in a clear majority on all committees although no committee was composed solely of doctors. Most committees included a lawyer and other hospital staff. Only a minority of committees had social scientist members and only one committee had theologian members. Only in rare instances were members of the community or patients included (Isambert, 1988; 1989: 449). By December 1986, the number of committees had increased to 34. The numbers of members on these committees ranged between 6 and 30 with most committees having between 12 and 15 members (Bergkamp, 1988a: 14).[7] In 1987, a group

---

5. For reports on these developments, see Editorial (News), *IME Bulletin* (1989a, 1989e).
6. An earlier draft Bill prepared by a previous government, which would have made it mandatory for researchers to gain ethics committee approval, was never introduced in the Parliament (interview with François-André Isambert, Directeur d'Etudes, Ecole des Hautes Etudes en Sciences Sociales, Paris, 3 June 1987.
7. Isambert (1989: 449) reports committee size as between 8 and 30 with most being between 10 and 15.

was established to discuss the organisation, composition and modes of working of research ethics committees with the intention of exploring the issue of uniformity between committees. In 1989, Isambert reported that 93 per cent of research proposals reviewed by committees were approved (49 per cent approved outright and 44 per cent after slight modification). The remaining 7 per cent were substantially modified or rejected. There is no monitoring of the execution of any research after approval. Research ethics committees in France are said to work in an almost 'feudal' environment of medical patronage in a profession that has 'extreme reserve' about the role of ethics (Isambert, 1989: 445).

THE NETHERLANDS

The first research ethics committee in the The Netherlands was formed in 1970 at the Free University of Amsterdam (Bergkamp, 1988b). By 1981, every university teaching hospital had an ethics committee.

A ministerial decree in 1984 on hospital accreditation in the Netherlands led to 'an explosion of ethics committees' (de Wachter, 1988). In 1983, the year before the decree, there were 14 committees; by October 1986, there were 63 established committees with 40 others in the making. The number of members on these committees ranged between 3 and 13 with a majority of medical specialist members. On one committee, all of the members were medical graduates. Other committees included research workers and pharmacologists. About half of the committees included an ethics specialist or a clergyman. Some committees included members from outside the organisation although few committees included a lay represen-tative of patients' organisations or consumer groups.[8] By 1988, few committees had complied with the membership guidelines in the explanatory note accompanying the 1984 ministerial decree (Bergkamp, 1988c: 67).

Research ethics committees reviewed an average of 17 proposals in 1985. These numbers are low compared with the numbers of research proposals considered by IRBs in the United States and elsewhere. Committee members had reported that they were aware

8. The information on committees in 1983 is drawn from de Beaufort's (1985) study and that on committees in 1986 is drawn from Bergkamp (1988c).

of studies that had been conducted without having received committee approval. Bergkamp (1988c) concluded that there was a need for legal sanctions against researchers who failed to put forward research proposals for review.

BELGIUM

In 1976 the Scientific Medical Research Fund in Belgium established a commission which prompted all eight university medical faculties to appoint a 'faculty medical ethics commission'. Their role was to assess the ethics of research projects before such projects could be considered for support from the fund. In 1984 this requirement was incorporated into the *Code de deontologie medicale* which made approval by an ethics committee mandatory for all research involving human subjects. Committees were required by the code to have at least five members including a lay member and a professional member who was independent of the institution (Bergkamp, 1988c).

A survey in 1987 found 37 research ethics committees operating in Belgium with a further seven being planned (Barthelemy, 1988). Two-thirds of the committees included a lawyer as the lay member. Committees in Catholic hospitals also included a priest or a philosopher. The procedure for review was for researchers to complete a questionnaire which was then circulated to all committee members. Members then sought clarification from the researcher, or asked for outside expert opinion if they had queries. It was reported that most research proposals were accepted, although changes were proposed for some, and few proposals were rejected. Although it is not clear from the report, it appears that most committees did not meet in person but conducted their review by mail (Barthelemy, 1988).

SWITZERLAND

The Swiss Academy of Medical Sciences (SAMS) published its 'Guidelines for experimental research on man' in 1984. Many of the provisions of these guidelines are drawn from the Helsinki Declaration, and some of the cantons in Switzerland have declared that the SAMS guidelines are mandatory within their area.[9] The

9. Bergkamp (1988a: 16) stated that Swiss regulation of health care is largely within the power of the cantons (political divisions in Switzerland equivalent to Australian states), ibid, p.16.

guidelines recommend that institutions establish advisory bodies to consider the medical and ethical aspects of experimentation on human subjects. The membership of these medical ethical committees is determined by the institution (Bergkamp, 1988a: 17).

SAMS has also established a Central Committee for Medical Ethics which deals with questions of medical ethics in general as well as issues of the ethics of medical experimentation. One of the Committee's roles was to co-ordinate the medical ethical committees in hospitals and universities. It was also available to act as the medical ethical committee for an institution that did not have its own committee.[10] In 1979, there were 21 such committees, and all five university hospitals had a committee which also served other institutions within its region. Bergkamp (1988a) gave no details on the functioning of these committees presumably because of a lack of published information.

SCANDINAVIA

Denmark[11]

In Denmark there are seven regional ethics committees. Each committee has three lay members and three medical/scientific members. The Danish Medical Research Council appointed the 'medical/scientific' members from nominations of various medical and scientific bodies in the region. The regional county councils appointed the lay members from nominations of individual citizens, or societies. Professor Riis, the main architect of the Danish system of review, concluded that the 'lay representation was both necessary and very valuable' (1988). More recently he has reported that lay members and scientific members work cooperatively together and, in spite of the parity between scientific and lay members and the representational nature of their membership, decisions are 'never the result of voting within blocs' (1991).

In 1985, a total of 1,301 new projects were proposed. By 1990, the total number of projects had increased to 2,234. For each committee this represented an average of 319 projects, with a range of 135 to 711 (Central Scientific–Ethical Committee, 1991). Overall, Danish

10. Editorial (News), *IME Bulletin*, No. 39 (1988c); Bergkamp (1988a: 17).
11. This section draws extensively on the works of Professor Povl Riis (1979, 1983, 1988 and 1991).

committees are responsible for a far greater number of proposals than is reported for ethics committees anywhere else in the world. Their average figure contrasts markedly with average numbers considered by committees in France and The Netherlands. However, not all research proposals are considered by committees. It is required that all research be *registered* with an ethics committee but *approval* by the committee is only necessary when the investigator wishes to dispense with informed consent, or when there is doubt about the ethical acceptability of the project (Riis, 1983: 127).

Although Danish committees undertake no direct monitoring of research, staff are advised of a contact person within their region to whom they can take any concerns about research. These contacts act as 'informal monitors' of research within institutions.[12] In the United States it has been stated that 'informal surveillance' is 'probably the most effective means' by which IRBs can become aware of research which may be putting subjects at risk because 'almost every activity in a university hospital is subject to observation, discussion, and review by physicians, nurses, students of various sorts, and others' (Levine, 1978; 1986: 349).

In Denmark there is a national body with two representatives (one lay and one medical/scientific member) from each regional committee. The main function of this Central Scientific–Ethical Committee is the formulation of guidelines. The national committee can also review multi-centre trials. In addition, any researcher who had been unable to gain approval from a local committee is entitled to appeal to the national committee. In practice, very few proposals are submitted to the Central Committee.[13]

The Danish system of review offers an interesting model for other countries. I examine the issue of parity between lay and scientific members and the size of committees in Chapter 9 when making general recommendations for changes to committee composition.

Norway

In 1988, a White Paper published by the Norwegian Ministry of Cultural and Scientific Affairs recommended that ethics committees

---

12. Interview with Professor Riis, 7 June 1987.
13. The range was between 2 and 15 proposals in any one year, representing an average of 0.6% of the total proposals considered by the seven regional committees (Denmark, Ministry of Health, 1989: 30).

be set up in three research areas: (1) medicine, including health and life services; (2) social sciences and the humanities, including law and theology; and (3) natural science/technology, including research in biotechnology and genetic engineering that was not dealt with by the committee in medicine. In June 1989, the Storting (Norwegian Parliament) passed legislation which accepted these recommendations and established the three national committees. The Storting also provided 16 million kroner (approximately US\$ 2.5 million or A\$ 3.3 million) to establish a Centre for Biomedical Ethics in Oslo which would support an information service, scholarships for training in research ethics and research in biomedical ethics. This was a significant and rare commitment to the importance of education (Editorial (News) *IME Bulletin*, 1989d).

All three national committees have been established with similar terms of reference. The mandate for the National Committee for Medical Research Ethics was issued in May 1990. The role of the medical committee is to keep abreast of current issues in research ethics and to advise and co-ordinate regional medical research ethics committees. At last report, the national medical committee comprised nine members, including those with medical, ethical and legal expertise, and a minimum of two lay members (Editorial (News), *Bulletin of Medical Ethics*, 1990b).

Sweden

In the 1960s, the Swedish Medical Research Council ruled that no experiment on human subjects would be funded unless an ethical committee had 'scrutinised' the protocol, the competence of the investigators and 'all other circumstances of an ethical nature' (Werko, 1982). There were committees in the university hospitals and in the pre-clinical departments of medical schools. Initially, these committees were composed of members who were all medical graduates, but one or two non-medical members were added subsequently as a result of a recommendation of the Parliament. Research ethics committees were subsequently found to have ten members on average, with six doctors or researchers, a pharmacologist, a nurse, a lay person and, on some committees, a 'paramedical person' (Bergkamp, 1988a: 25–6).

Ethics committees in Sweden were originally set up in the six medical schools and served the teaching hospitals. Subsequently they came to serve other hospitals and institutions in the region and thus acquired a regional base. As a consequence of their increased workload, some committees delegated a portion of their work to sub-committees. Part of this increased workload came as a result of legislation enacted in 1983 by the Swedish Parliament which stipulated that an ethics committee must have 'given its advice' before a drug trial could commence. Subsequent to this law, ethics committees within some pharmaceutical companies were dissolved and their work taken over by hospital committees (Bergkamp, 1988a: 27).

In a detailed study of committee minutes, Giertz (1982) found that some committees approved studies in which information on the use of placebos was withheld from subjects. He found that other studies were approved which gave deceptive and incomplete information. It is also apparent that not all medical research projects are submitted to Swedish ethics committees for approval and there has been a great deal of pharmaceutical experimentation and testing conducted by non-university hospitals and out-patient facilities which has received no ethics committee scrutiny (Bergkamp, 1988a; Werko, 1982).

Finland and Iceland

A report published in 1983 indicated that the Finnish system was similar to that in Sweden, with local ethics committees in hospitals and in university medical faculties. There were no lay members on those committees. At that stage the need for ethics committees had been acknowledged in Iceland but had not been implemented (Riis, 1983: 129).

GERMANY AND JAPAN

As stated at the beginning of this chapter, information on review of research in Germany and Japan is included because of the involvement of both countries in the abuse of the rights of human subjects of experimentation during the Second World War (outlined in Chapter 1). It is interesting to consider this history and the possible reasons for the subsequent lack of action in introducing safeguards for the protection of subjects of experiments in both countries.

Germany

The political situation in Germany has altered dramatically as a result of the unification of East and West Germany. However, the only published information relates to East and West Germany as independent countries. I therefore present the information on East and West Germany separately.

East Germany
The only report of ethics committees in East Germany that I have been able to find is that of Rappoport (1979). It gives a brief outline of the system for review of research projects in the German Democratic Republic. Researchers presented their research projects before either local or central boards of scientists (depending on the importance of the project). The members of these boards were appointed by the government. Rappoport stated that one of the concerns of the boards was the extent of risk to human subjects.

West Germany
In West Germany, the central Research Foundation (Deutsche Forschungsgemeinschaft) established local ethical review committees on a trial basis in selected 'special research areas' in 1973. The members were researchers from different disciplines within particular universities (Fischer and Breuer, 1979: 68–9). It was reported in 1987 that the Foundation required review and approval by an ethics committee before it would support a research project (Medical Research Council of Canada, 1989b: 42). In 1979, the West German Federal Medical Association issued guidelines on the structure and function of research ethics committees. It recommended that the regional Medical Associations should set up independent committees with a multi-disciplinary membership including two clinical and one theoretical researcher, a representative from the Medical Association and a lawyer. The recommendation had been prompted by the introduction of peer review in the 1975 amendment to the Declaration of Helsinki (Bergkamp, 1988a: 21–2). In 1981 a combined meeting of West German medical faculties accepted the importance of ethical review and the need for uniformity between committees; and in 1989 it was reported that all medical schools and the state and federal branches of the Medical Association have research ethics committees which are known as *Ethikkommissionen* (Sass, 1989).

A study in 1984 and 1985 had identified 24 *Ethikkommissionen*.

The number of members varied between three and nine with most committees having between five and seven members. The majority of members were medical graduates although two-thirds of the committees included a lawyer. A few of the committees had other members including a statistician, nurse or medical student. One-quarter of the committees functioned by mail and did not meet in person (study cited in Bergkamp, 1988a: 22).

All *Ethikkommissionen* appear to function as peer review committees (Sass, 1989: 407). More than half the committees were clinical case review committees that gave little attention to ethical issues. Most committees considered between 5 and 15 research proposals each year and acknowledged that only a small part of research on human subjects which was conducted within their institution was submitted for review (Bergkamp, 1988a: 22–3). In 1986, the *Ethikkommissionen* formed an association which formulated by-laws for the operation of the committees. *Ethikkommissionen* were to comprise a minimum of five members including four doctors and one lawyer. It has been argued, on behalf of that association, that lay members are neither necessary nor warranted (Sass, 1989: 470). Furthermore, Illhardt (1988) has reported that none of the decisions of ethics committees were binding on researchers.

The impression created by various reports of *Ethikkommissionen* is that they do not act effectively as research ethics committees.[14] They function in a 'traditional paternalistic' medical culture which is focussed on 'protecting first of all its own turf' and does not encourage the exercise of patients' rights, such as the right of consent (Sass, 1989: 465). This is not an environment conducive to ethical research and it appears that *Ethikkommissionen* cannot be relied on to ensure that experimentation conducted on human beings is conducted ethically. This conclusion sits uncomfortably with a recognition of the proven atrocities of German doctors in experimentation on human subjects during the Second World War.

Japan

It has been observed that there is a strong research orientation among medical practitioners in Japan who 'treat patients as interesting

14. See, for example, Bergkamp (1988a) and Illhardt (1988). Maurice de Wachter (Director, Instituut voor Gezondheidsethiek) expressed a similar view in an interview with the author (10 June 1987).

medical cases rather than as persons deserving of respect'. There appears to be little genuine review by ethics committees to counter this attitude (Kimura, 1989: 458).

By July 1987, there were said to be 64 ethics committees in 81 per cent of 'medical' universities. A survey conducted in May 1986 found that each committee was made up, on average, of 10 members. Of these, 1.7 were from outside the institution but none of these was a 'lay' community member (Kimura, 1989). Earlier reports indicate very little review of research.[15]

The committees have been said to exist 'merely as a public relations mechanism for the medical "insider" to show the "outsider" that ethical problems are being considered seriously'. They serve a perfunctory role in giving approval to studies to allow publication in international journals. 'Japanese-style ethics committees' are described as 'only a camouflage to distract the public's gaze' (Kimura, 1989: 461).

The rules for reviewing drug research are not any more encouraging. The Japanese Ministry of Health and Welfare requires that medical institutions conducting clinical trials of drugs on human subjects establish an Institution Review Board. The Boards are to contain at least five members including medical, dental and pharmaceutical experts and another member who is not from these disciplines. The committee's role is to 'review the validity of conducting the clinical trial' and to 'verify that consent has been obtained'. Other than this mention of consent, there is no indication that the Boards are *ethics* committees as they might be understood elsewhere. As I argue in Chapter 6, reviewing the validity of studies is a scientific and technical question that precedes ethics review.

The only ethical obligations are on the researchers themselves. The requirements for drug trials place an obligation, presumably on the researcher, to review the selection of subjects in terms of their health condition, ability to give consent, and their involvement in other trials. There are also some rules on the information that should be given to subjects. However, researchers have a divided loyalty between their research and the welfare of subjects. History has shown that it is not sufficient to rely on researchers to act ethically.

15. See, for example, Bassiouni, Baffes and Evrard (1981: 1647), World Health Organization (1987: 253–4) and Medical Research Council of Canada (1987b: 41). Interesting material is also found in the 'Discussion' by H. Tanaka in Bankowski and Howard-Jones (1982: 254–5) and 'Special report: Japan' in the *World Medical Journal*, 7, 1960: 85.

In the Japanese context, the provisions of rules for testing drugs are small comfort indeed. The indications are that there is little ethical review of experimentation on human subjects in Japan and that Japanese experimenters lack genuine concern for their subjects. In view of the role of Japanese doctors and scientists before and during the Second World War (Williams and Wallace, 1989) this, as with Germany, is a disturbing finding.

CONCLUSION

Given the reliance on committee review, research ethics committees clearly deserve greater attention. The United States study was a thorough review but is now dated. With the exception of the United Kingdom, Australia, France, The Netherlands, and Denmark, many countries have not undertaken studies of the workings of their procedures for committees of review while others appear to have little or no review.

Generalisations across a number of countries are necessarily tentative, given the many differences in culture between nations. However, there are some trends that can be identified across review systems in the various countries described in this chapter.

The first generalisation is that national guidelines which include a 'requirement' that research proposals for experimentation on human subjects be reviewed have been effective in leading to an increase in the number of research proposals offered to review committees. This is the case even though national guidelines carry no strong sanctions for failure to comply (as is discussed in Chapter 3). The main incentive for researchers to seek committee approval is the threat of withdrawal of support. This can occur directly through refusal of funding bodies to fund unapproved research or through withdrawal of support by the researcher's department. For example, the United States 'common rule' and the Royal College of Physicians of London guidelines both suggest that the research ethics committee can ask the sponsoring department to withdraw support from research which does not comply with the guidelines. I would suggest therefore that a national requirement for review is effective to the extent that it is supported by research institutions, funding agencies and academic journals.

The United States, Australia, and Denmark have long-standing requirements that all research on human subjects be reviewed by a research ethics committee. Those requirements appear to have been taken seriously by researchers because failure to comply could have implications for funding and publication. The number of new proposals considered on average by Australian committees was found to have increased from 19 in 1983 to 41 for the year from mid-1987 to mid-1988 after a stipulation that *all* research on human subjects be reviewed by a committee. The National Commission study in the United States had found that committees considered 43 new proposals on average in that year. The American regulations apply to almost all research by virtue of the system of 'assurances' which are offered by institutions to the relevant government agency. The Danish requirement that research be registered with a local committee has resulted in a large number of proposals being put before the seven regional committees. From these findings I conclude that a national requirement, that *all* research involving human subjects be reviewed by a committee, which is accepted by other agencies, does prompt more researchers to put their proposals before committees for ethical approval.

This conclusion is supported by the finding that in most continental European countries, with the exception of Denmark and Belgium, there is no compulsion for researchers to present their proposals for review and few of them do so. In The Netherlands, for example, there was little incentive for researchers to offer their proposals for review. Committees had few proposals to consider because the only researchers obliged to put their proposals to a research ethics committee were those seeking overseas grants (usually from the United States) or publication in international journals. In France and The Netherlands the number of projects volunteered for review was relatively small.

The second generalisation about ethics review internationally is that there is very little monitoring of experimentation after its initial approval. Most countries rely on prospective review of research proposals by committees. There are no countries in which monitoring of research in progress is consistently employed. Only 23 per cent of Australian committees had ever sent a representative to visit a study in progress, and only 5 per cent of researchers reported having had their research actively monitored or their documents audited. The National Commission study in the United States found that one-third of committees had delegated a person to monitor studies in progress although only half of those committees claimed to have done so routinely. The British Royal College of Physicians guidelines disclaim the need for committees to monitor ongoing investigations. Canada confronted this reluctance to monitor research and introduced specific provisions and powers for committees to require monitoring of experimentation. As was discussed above, the evidence is that those provisions have been ineffective. Denmark appears to have been more successful in providing for informal reporting by subjects and 'spot-check' audits of researchers. Suggestions for a more active role for committees in monitoring of research have been made in England (Neuberger, 1992).

My colleagues and I have suggested that to rely on prospective review of research proposals in the absence of comprehensive monitoring of the projects is to place undue confidence in researchers' intentions rather than their research practices (McNeill, Berglund and Webster, 1990). The results of our study in Australia should give support for a more active role of institutions in monitoring and surveillance of research projects.

The third generalisation is based on the simple observation that almost all countries have a decentralised system of review and rely on committees within institutions or within regions to ensure that proposals for research on human subjects are ethical. In many countries (including the United States) research ethics committees are based within a particular institution. Where ethics committees are within institutions, those institutions are also responsible for research. In other words, research ethics committees are often to be found within an institution with a research commitment. There appears to be a trend toward regional committees particularly in New Zealand, and to some extent in Britain and Australia (through district health areas or area health boards). Denmark is the clearest case of committee review based on a regional system.

Few countries can demonstrate effective co-ordination between committees and a national appeal body to allow for consideration of multi-centred trials and for appeals. Denmark again is the only country with an obvious centralised system. Although the Danish Central Committee has the power to consider proposals, and although it may serve as an appeal body, in practice it considers very few research proposals. It would seem therefore, that the function of a central committee (where there is one) is predominantly the issuing of guidelines on research ethics review. In some countries, such as Australia and Canada, central committees also play a role in establishing workshops for research ethics committee members.

The fourth generalisation is that most Anglo-American and European countries include lay members within the recommended composition of review committees. In almost all countries, the lay members are considered to be representative of the community. New Zealand is the only country requiring patient representation, although there has been a proposal for patient representation in Denmark and there may already be some patient representation in The Netherlands. However, in general, most countries require community representation rather than representation of patients or subjects of experiments. This is a point I return to in Chapters 8 and 9.

The fifth generalisation is the simple observation that medical graduates and researchers make up the major part of committees in most countries, with the exception of Denmark and New Zealand. Lay members are typically part of a small minority. Denmark and New Zealand are exceptions in that they now require the same number of scientific and lay members. Recent unpublished research discussed earlier in this chapter (McNeill, Berglund and Webster, 1992) suggests that when they are in the minority, the non-professional members contribute relatively little and their participation is given little importance. It is my concern that, in these circumstances, ethics committees lack balance between the interests of science and subjects.

The sixth generalisation is that publicity of unethical research, together with resulting public concern, is effective in prompting government action. This is most apparent in the United States where the system of review grew out of public concern over unethical research. The federal government played an active role in the extension of the system of review throughout all the states by issuing regulations. Public concern about unethical research in New Zealand similarly led to decisive action. At the direction of the government, one of its departments issued standards that extended the committee review process to treatment as well as research and gave greater representation to lay members. In Denmark, public concern about reports of unethical research, together with controversy over the ethics of experimentation on embryos, prompted a government commission which proposed legislation that would contain substantive rules for the review of research (Denmark Ministry of Health, 1989: 9).

The development of review systems in Canada and Australia was not the consequence of revelations of unethical experimentation in those countries. In both countries the major funding body for medical research was active in developing a review system. Perceptions of public concern were a factor, however. In Australia and Canada it was anticipated that the public would not tolerate abuses of research subjects. This was one of the factors prompting the respective medical research councils to take action to ensure that research was conducted ethically.

I regard publicity about unethical experimentation as one of the major factors in implementing a system of review of experimentation on human subjects. Publicity of abuses of subjects in the United States and in New Zealand was one factor. Another was the strength of public reaction and a third factor was the willingness of the political authorities in both countries to take relevant action.

Publicity is a factor that warrants special consideration in relation to Germany and Japan. In spite of findings that medical graduates and researchers in both of those countries carried out major atrocities against human subjects in the name of science during the Second World War, neither country has developed a system of review that is independent of investigators proposing research and that requires all experimentation on human subjects to be reviewed. In 1988 the editors of the journal *Laboratory and Clinical Medicine* reported that they had received four manuscripts reporting unethical studies from countries that have 'less than ideal historical records or respect for the rights of individuals' (Daniel, Cherniack, Douglas et al., 1988). The editors did not specify the countries but, given the countries that fit their description, there is some justification for concern about the lack of review.

In the case of Germany, there has been a great deal of publicity given to medical atrocities whereas in Japan, until recently, there has been very little. I suggest that the critical factor for the failure to deal adequately with the issue of research regulation in Germany is that there is extreme sensitivity about any issues that are reminiscent of atrocities committed in the name of medical science in 'Nazi' Germany. There is a reluctance to discuss the issues in public but this moral sensitivity does not necessarily extend to a concern about medical research practices. Postwar Germans appear to be more inclined to bury the past than endeavour to draw lessons from it. One example of this can be seen in the demonstrations in 1987 against the views of Australian philosopher Peter Singer – demonstrations which forced the cancellation of meetings in Germany at which he would have discussed euthanasia for severely disabled newborn infants (Singer, 1990). The protesters opposed any public discussion of the issues but did not challenge the accepted medical practice in Germany of allowing babies with a poor prognosis to die (Singer, 1990; Schöne-Seifert and Rippe, 1991). Human experimentation is in a comparable position as a result of the atrocities committed under National Socialism. There is a reluctance to discuss the issues publicly. Paternalist attitudes of doctors and researchers are not effectively challenged and medical researchers are free to conduct research within their own professional guidelines. The horror of Nazi Germany seems too much for postwar Germans to come to terms with. So, while these issues are politically very sensitive, it seems that rational discussion is difficult – and, in that climate, any discussion of effective controls by the wider public is thwarted.

Japan, however, is in a different situation. Japanese researchers are still protected from scrutiny by an extremely paternalist medical environment (Kimura, 1989). Furthermore, the medical atrocities prior to and during the Second World War led to few sanctions other than for those experimenters tried by the Russians (discussed in Chapter 1). Indeed, with the connivance of the American armed forces, some of the people responsible for the atrocities were permitted to continue their research on human subjects and to become prominent and respected members of Japanese society (as discussed earlier). Effectively, there were no sanctions for the most degrading and extreme forms of unethical experimentation imaginable. Japanese people, unlike the Germans, were deprived of any information about the extent of the horrors committed by their own medical fraternity in the name of science. They appear to have been more intent on building a new Japan than on dwelling on the past.

In neither Germany nor Japan has there been any public outcry or political pressure on the medical fraternity (or other experimenters) to review scientific research adequately to ensure that human subjects are not put at undue risk. It is only recently that the Japanese press has begun to publish material on the atrocities committed in China and Japan by Japanese doctors. As the material on unethical experimentation in the United States and New Zealand indicates, effective action resulted only when the press persisted with revelations of abuse and when politicians were willing to pursue the issue and demand effective action.

I conclude from the comparison of review systems in this and the previous chapter that an effective review system for experimentation on human subjects depends on a combination of publicity, expressed public concern for the welfare of the research subjects and a willingness on the part of professional and political authorities to discuss the issues. Publicity itself depends on public concern. The press is unlikely to persist with issues for which there is no public sympathy – but there must be publicity. When the authorities withhold the facts, as with Japanese experimentation, there is little likelihood of a public reaction. In New Zealand, it was only when the facts of the cervical cancer study were made public by two persistent journalists that there was a public reaction and an immediate response from government. A willingness on the part of the political authorities (either government or responsible medical/scientific authorities) to respond to expressed concerns is clearly vital if any change is to occur.

PART THREE

Law and Ethics
in Human Experimentation

CHAPTER 5

Law and Human Experimentation

Law is a means of balancing competing claims within society. Courts have exercised an important role in balancing the interests of researchers against the protection of the interests of subjects of human experimentation. In early cases, the balance was almost entirely weighted in favour of the protection of subjects. Since the 1930s, however, courts have shown a greater appreciation of the need for medical experimentation and have been more careful to weigh the issues on either side.

This chapter explores some of the relevant cases and examines the development of legal principles that parallel more closely the accepted ethical principles and practices in human experimentation.

ATTITUDES OF THE COURTS

Prior to the Second World War, courts were protective of patients when it was deemed that doctors had been experimenting on them. The courts at this time could be seen as acting as an external restraint on science in the interests of the welfare of the subjects of experiments. In the few cases which reached courts of appeal before the 1930s, the word 'experimentation' was defined broadly and the courts held doctors to be strictly liable for damage resulting from an experiment. In all of these cases, the word 'experiment' was used to mean 'any departure from standard medical practice'. The courts were disparaging and regarded experimentation as 'something improper'.[1]

---

1. *Slater v. Baker and Stapleton* (1767); *Carpenter v. Blake* (1871); *Jackson v. Burnham* (1895); *Sawdey v. Spokane Falls* (1902); *Allen v. Voje* (1902); *Owens v. McCleary* (1926). Full citations of cases referred to in this book are listed under 'Legal Citations' before the list of References.

English and American cases in the years before 1930 leave no doubt about the attitude of courts to innovative practices. They were regarded as 'mere experiments' and the doctors seen as rash, reckless and ignorant (Annas, Glantz and Katz, 1977). In the cases of *Carpenter* and *Allen* which were decided 30 years apart on opposite sides of the Atlantic, the courts weighed up the argument that holding doctors to standard practice would inhibit progress in medicine and science. In both cases, the argument was rejected in favour of a conservative standard, weighted towards the safety of the patient and against experimentation.

Changing attitudes to science and experimentation

Since the 1930s there has been a change in the status of medicine and science in society and a change in the attitude of society to science and research. Subsequent judgments have given greater recognition to the value of experimentation in medicine and allowed for more experimentation.

The beginning of this change of attitude is apparent in *Fortner v. Koch* (1935). In this case the court upheld the award of damages against a doctor who had failed to do the appropriate diagnostic test for syphilis and had treated a patient for bone cancer. The court's judgment included the proposition that 'if the general practice of medicine and surgery is to progress, there must be a certain amount of experimentation carried on'. The court insisted, however, that 'such experiments must be done with the knowledge and consent of the patient' and that the experiments 'must not vary too radically from the accepted method or procedure'. Another favourable view of experimentation is found in the decision on *Stammer v. Board of Regents of the University of New York* (1941). A doctor had been successful in treating cancer on a patient's face with an experimental treatment. In spite of this success, he was suspended from practice by a disciplinary body for fraud and deceit. On appeal, the court held that it was legitimate to use a new method when 'so-called orthodox methods of treatment had failed'. The court believed that '[i]nitiative and originality should not be . . . stifled, especially when undertaken with the patient's full knowledge and consent, and as a last resort'. The attitude toward experimentation, in both *Fortner* and *Stammer*, is closer to the modern position. So too is the need for the patient's knowledge and consent.

Non-therapeutic experimentation

Most of the cases reported before 1945 concerned experimental treatment that was conducted for the benefit of the patient. One of the few cases to consider a non-therapeutic experiment was *Bonner v. Moran* (1941). The point at issue was whether consent from a child, who had donated tissue to his severely burned cousin in an experimental treatment, was adequate. It was held that there could be no exception to the requirement for consent from parents of a child in an experiment that had no benefit for the child. Whether or not this meant that parents could consent to a non-beneficial experiment on behalf of their child remained unclear (Annas, Glantz and Katz, 1977: 78). This is an issue that is discussed further in Chapter 6.

LEGAL PRINCIPLES IN POST-1945 CASES

Since the Second World War, courts have accepted experimentation on human subjects within certain limitations. There are, however, very few cases on human experimentation. Most of the reported judgments rely on legal principles established in cases concerning medical treatment. For this reason I will briefly outline the relevant law in relation to medical treatment.

Actions for damages: the emphasis on consent

The majority of medical cases are actions brought by an injured party to recover compensation for injuries sustained in the course of a medical treatment. Broadly speaking, the plaintiff has to convince the court that there has been some failure on the part of the doctor which rendered the doctor liable in law for the damage done. The injured party alleges that the doctor has committed a civil (as opposed to a criminal) wrong. This is known in law as an 'actionable tort'. The plaintiff needs to establish that either the doctor has acted without the consent of the patient and thereby committed a trespass (which includes the torts of assault and battery), or that the doctor was in breach of some duty owed to the patient and, by failing in that duty, became liable for the resulting damages. This is known as an action in negligence (Dix et al., 1988: 93).

One of the duties owed by doctors to their patients is the duty to disclose sufficient information for patients to be able to decide for themselves whether to go ahead with the recommended treatment or not. If a patient is not given adequate information and is injured in the course of that treatment then the patient may be able to show that the doctor is liable for the injuries sustained. This aspect of the law is particularly relevant to human experimentation. The doctor may also be liable for negligent treatment and diagnosis even though, in the majority of cases concerning human experimentation, the doctor/researcher is likely to have carried out the procedures competently. Cases on human experimentation are more likely to hinge on whether or not patients/subjects have been given sufficient information on which to base their consent.

There are exceptions to the obligation on doctors to disclose relevant information in medical treatment. In the case of an emergency, or with patients who are not competent to decide for themselves, or where an anxious patient may be dissuaded from embarking on necessary medical treatment by a full disclosure, then doctors may be under no obligation to inform the patient.

Cases on human experimentation

There have been very few court cases involving non-therapeutic human experimentation. Most cases have arisen from experimental treatment that promised at least the possibility of some benefit to the subject. In the few cases of 'non-therapeutic' medical experimentation, courts have consistently held that there can be no exceptions to the obligation to disclose all the relevant information.

Two significant cases of 'non-therapeutic' treatment are from Canada. One of these is *Halushka v. University of Saskatchewan* (1965) which was decided by the Saskatchewan Court of Appeal. Another more recent case is *Weiss v. Solomon* (1989) from the Quebec Superior Court.

In the first of those cases, Halushka, a second-year university student looking for vacation employment, had approached two doctors who were conducting research into comparative anaesthetics. He was offered $50 to be the subject in a trial of a new drug in a 'safe test that had been conducted many times before' (*Halushka*: 444). That statement was substantially untrue in that the doctors were testing a new anaesthetic agent 'Floromar' for the first time. Halushka was also told that a catheter would be inserted in his arm but he was not told that it would be 'advanced to and through his heart'. After administering the anaesthetic and observing its effect, the doctors increased the dosage to take the subject to a deeper level of anaesthesia. The level became too deep and, although the amount of anaesthetic was decreased, the subject (Halushka) went into complete cardiac arrest.

The doctors made a long incision in Halushka's chest, pulled two ribs apart and manually massaged his heart. It took a minute and a half before his heart began to beat again. Halushka remained unconscious for four days. Before discharging him ten days later, the doctors gave him $50 with a promise of more if he would sign a document releasing the doctors from liability. Halushka did not sign the document and claimed damages for both trespass and negligence (the two grounds of action discussed above). He gave evidence that he was unable to think or concentrate and became very tired. As a consequence, he had withdrawn from his university course. Expert evidence was not conclusive but consistent with there being damage to the higher intellectual functions of the brain resulting from cardiac arrest. The jury found that there had been no consent and that the doctors were liable in both trespass and negligence. In other words, they had committed a trespass and had been negligent. Halushka was awarded $22,500 and the case was upheld on appeal.

The main issue was the lack of consent. The appellate court took the view that in ordinary medical practice a doctor has a duty to inform the patient of the proposed treatment, the likely outcome and 'any special or unusual risks'. The court acknowledged that the rule was subject to some exceptions in treatment, but would allow no exceptions in the case of an experiment. It was a researcher's duty to give a 'full and frank disclosure of the facts, probabilities and opinions which a reasonable man might be expected to consider before giving his consent'.

The court stated that the doctors' relationship with the subject was based on trust – the subject was entitled to rely on their advice. The effect of finding that this was a relationship of trust (in legal parlance, a fiduciary relationship) meant that the doctors were liable for any 'error amounting to a misrepresentation' even when the advice was given in good faith.[2] This case has established a more demanding standard for experimentation than may apply to medical treatment in Commonwealth countries. Lord Scarman in *Sidaway v. Bethlem*

2. Here the court was quoting from *Nocton v. Lord Ashburton* (1914), p. 972.

Royal Hospital Governors (1985) rejected the argument that the doctor–patient relationship was of a fiduciary character (*Sidaway*: 650–65). While this may be taken to be so in Britain and other Commonwealth countries, Dworkin (1987: 204–5) considered it likely that other courts would follow *Halushka* and find that the researcher–subject relationship is fiduciary. Unlike the position in Commonwealth countries, the doctor–patient relationship *is* regarded by courts in the United States as fiduciary (Obade, 1991) and there is little doubt that the courts would also regard the researcher–subject relationship to be so (Delgado and Leskovac, 1986: 109–10).

An American decision which relied on the distinction between treatment and experimentation is *Hyman v. Jewish Chronic Disease Hospital* (1964). This case (mentioned in Chapter 3) concerned injections of live cancer cells into debilitated patients to see whether those patients would reject the cells or not. There is no doubt that it was purely an experiment as there could have been no therapeutic advantage for those patients. In disciplinary proceedings against the doctors, the Medical Grievance Committee made the point that there could be no exception to the requirement for full information. The Committee considered that the 'consents' from the patients were 'fraudulently obtained' because the doctors had withheld the 'key fact' that this was an experiment. Similarly, in *Weiss v. Solomon* (1989) – discussed in detail in the section 'Review by Committee' later in this chapter – the judge found that in this case, where there was no therapeutic benefit to Weiss, the highest standard of disclosure was expected (Freedman and Glass, 1990: 396).

The case of the German doctors and scientists charged with war crimes and crimes against humanity, *United States v. Karl Brandt*, is also relevant. As mentioned in Chapters 1 and 2, the *Brandt* case was determined by a court established by the Military Governor of the American Zone on behalf of the Allied Control Council of Germany. The judges, all American attorneys, were appointed by the Governor. Their opinions were issued as international criminal law (Annas, Glantz and Katz, 1977). One of the significant outcomes of this case, and the foremost principle of the Nuremberg Code, was the requirement that subjects must have given their voluntary consent to any experimentation conducted on them. Adequate consent was defined as requiring that subjects have legal capacity to consent; can freely choose to participate without force, fraud, deceit, duress, constraint or coercion; and have knowledge and understanding of what is proposed. Annas, Glantz and Katz (1977) considered that the Code contains one of the most thorough statements of the ingredients of an adequate disclosure for a valid consent to experimentation.

Very few subsequent cases have referred to and applied the findings of *United States v. Karl Brandt* (Annas, 1991). One exception is the judgment of the Michigan Circuit Court in Wayne County in the unreported case *Kaimowitz v. Department of Mental Health for the State of Michigan* (1973). Even though this was a decision of a relatively low status court in the American judiciary, the judgment was perhaps the most thorough of all judicial considerations given to human experimentation. It concerned two investigators who wished to perform psychosurgery on the brain of Louis Smith, a 'sexual psychopath,' as an experiment in the control of aggression. The plaintiff Kaimowitz brought an action for the release of Smith. The issue that the court had to decide was whether an involuntary detainee could give a valid consent to experimental psychosurgery and (if so) whether the State could carry it out. The court ruled that psychosurgery could *not* be conducted on involuntarily detained populations. In coming to the decision, the court upheld the common law right of inviolability of the person.[3]

As in the cases already discussed, the main issue was consent. The court paid particular attention to the requirements stated in the Nuremberg Code: the person must have the legal capacity to consent, not be subject to any form of coercion, and 'have sufficient knowledge and comprehension' to understand the decision. These elements of consent were considered under three headings: competence, knowledge, and voluntariness. The court made no finding on whether Smith was in fact legally competent. The element that assumed importance in the case was the inability of patients confined (against their will) to a mental hospital to give a voluntary consent, rather than the issue of competence.

The court found that Smith's consent could not have been voluntary because the nature of the mental hospital was 'inherently coercive'. Indeed, it was reported that on his release Smith withdrew all consent to taking part in the experiment, in spite of having

3. Bromberger (1977) pointed out that although this 'was a lower court decision in a single state' it nevertheless had a big impact. He cited the *New York Times* of 18 March 1973 which reported that 'practically all psychosurgical research had terminated' following the Kaimowitz decision.

made statements at the time that he had voluntarily consented. The finding that non-voluntary mental patients are unable to consent to an experiment could be particularly troublesome for psychiatric research. It could mean that experimentation is restricted to voluntary patients or to research that is justified by a therapeutic benefit for patients (Roth et al., 1987: 427–9).

On the question of knowledge, the court referred to the need for experimental subjects to be informed of the risks involved and found that the subject could not have had sufficient knowledge for his consent to be adequate. In its view, which was 'based on the state of knowledge at the time', there was not enough known about psychosurgery by *anyone* (including the experts) to make a 'knowledgeable consent' possible. The court did not endeavour to establish what the subject actually knew, as the relevant information was not available. This case has potential application beyond psychiatric research. It could mean that, where there is insufficient information to give a reasonable estimation of the risks involved, *no-one* can give a legally adequate consent. This proposition applies to *all* research where the risks are not known, not simply to research with involuntarily detained mental patients (Bromberger, 1977: 139).

The need for consent in behavioural science research has been upheld in an American case, *Merriken v. Cressman* (1973). The court decided that parents needed to be given adequate information on the content of a questionnaire that was given to eighth grade students as part of a drug addiction prevention program. Although there was no formal research proposal the court treated the program as experimental.

Treatment or experimentation?

Given that the courts have consistently found that there can be no exception to the requirement for consent in experimentation as opposed to treatment, it is necessary to make a clear distinction between treatment and experimentation. The common law essentially sees medical treatment as an established procedure with a known beneficial outcome, and experimentation as the use of an innovative procedure that has no established beneficial outcome for human beings (Capron, 1986). The courts have found that the main distinguishing features of experiments are the risks to the subjects and the lack of any therapeutic benefit to them.

In other contexts, it has been assumed that the only significant difference between experimentation and treatment is in the intent of the doctor. The British Royal College of Physicians guidelines (1990a: Section 3.1), for example, distinguish between medical research and medical practice on the ground of intent. Judge Cartwright (1988: 63, 69), in the New Zealand Inquiry into cervical cancer, similarly took the view that it was intention, or 'primacy of aim', that established whether an investigation was research or treatment.

The focus on intent is misleading, however. The difficulty arises in cases in which treatment and research programs run together. There may well be situations in which a doctor uses an experimental procedure with the intent of benefitting the patient. In this case, the intention is both to treat and to conduct research. Under these circumstances, the doctor's intention to treat may not dissuade a court from finding that the procedure is experimental. The court is likely to consider the nature of the procedure and circumstances of the case. In *Bonner v. Moran* (1941), the court, after considering the procedure itself rather than doctors' intentions, found that the operation (which involved partially removing tissue from Bonner and connecting it to his cousin) was of no benefit to Bonner and was an experiment. In the *Kaimowitz* case, it was the fact that the procedure was very risky and the likelihood of any benefit was slight which had prompted the court to find that the contemplated psychosurgery was experimental. That court went on to say that, in the case of risky experiments, it is more important that doctors are 'certain that a patient has consented adequately' (*Kaimowitz*: 148–50). In drawing a distinction between experimentation and treatment, the court found that the explicit intention of the parties and the existence of a research proposal was of no material import.

Distinguishing trespass (battery) and negligence

Whether or not subjects have consented to experimentation is critical in determining whether they can bring an action for trespass or negligence. The essential difference between actions for trespass (including the torts of assault and battery) and actions for negligence, hinges on consent. It is an important difference in that a plaintiff needs to establish fewer elements for a successful action in trespass. To establish trespass, or battery, it is only necessary to show that there was no consent to a physical invasion. Indeed, in the Australian case

Hart v. Herron (1980), the judge held that a patient has only to allege there was no consent to put the onus on the doctor/defendant to show that there was consent.

By contrast, for an action in negligence to succeed, it is necessary to establish a number of things: that there was a duty of care owed to the injured person by the defendant doctor (or researcher), that there was a failure on the part of the doctor to fulfil that duty, and that the injury sustained was a direct result of the doctor's failure. A result of this distinction between the two actions is that all damages are recoverable in battery. This includes an injury that was not the 'fault' of the doctor, such as a surgical incision that is slow to heal. By contrast, the only damages recoverable in negligence are those that result from the doctor's failure to fulfil a duty of care (Mason and McCall Smith, 1987: 149–50).[4]

However, an action in battery is limited to those cases in which there is clearly no consent. A consent, even when it was based on inadequate information, may preclude an action in battery. The generally accepted rule is that 'unless there has been a fraud to secure consent to the treatment, a failure to disclose the attendant risks, however serious, should go to negligence rather than battery'.[5] The question is whether this rule, established in cases concerning medical treatment, is applicable to experimentation given that courts have been more demanding in requiring a full disclosure of information and adequate consent in cases of experimentation.

The American case *Mink v. University of Chicago* (1978) drew a careful distinction between battery and negligence in medical research. The case concerned a study of 1,000 pregnant women who were included in a research program to test the effect of a drug in preventing miscarriages. The important point in the case was that there had been a 'total lack of consent by the patient'. The administering of a drug for experimental purposes without the consent of the women was therefore a battery. The court distinguished this situation from two previous cases where patients had 'consented' to the procedure although they had not been adequately informed of the inherent risks in procedures to which they had consented.[6]

---

4. Not only is it easier to establish an action in battery, but the plaintiff may be able to claim exemplary damages when there is evidence of 'contumelious' disregard for another's rights (*Hart v. Herron*: 67, 824).
5. Laskin CJC in the Canadian case *Reibl v. Hughes* at p. 10.
6. The two cases were *Rheingold v. E. R. Squibb & Sons, Inc.* and *Needham v. White Laboratories*.

The difference may depend on whether or not there is any potential benefit to the subject. The effect in practice is that where there is no benefit to the subject, as in the cases of *Halushka* and *Weiss*, all the relevant information must be given by the researcher on the nature of the intended procedure. Less than 'full disclosure'[7] would mean in effect that there had not been an adequate consent (Dworkin, 1987: 208). Someone injured under those circumstances would be entitled to compensation even if there had been no negligence on the part of the doctor in carrying out the procedure. However, where the research was combined with a treatment as in the *Mink* case, then a consent to a procedure, even if it was given on the basis of insufficient information, would mean that a doctor may only be liable to compensate the plaintiff if negligence could be established. However, it has been suggested that where research is combined with therapy there would be 'a higher obligation of disclosure on the researcher than in "normal therapy"' (Bromberger, 1990).

The requirement for consent in practice

There is a difficulty in reconciling the law's requirement for consent from subjects of experiments with the current practice of allowing experimentation on those incapable of consent. It is clear that a number of international and national codes of ethics allow parents to consent on behalf of their children to non-therapeutic research. As was stated in Chapter 2, the Declaration of Helsinki allows research on those not capable of consent. The Australian National Health and Medical Research Council (NHMRC) Statement on Human Experimentation allows parents or guardians to consent to research on a child where that child does not have 'sufficient maturity and intelligence to make this practicable'.[8]

The guidelines relating to unconscious and semi-conscious patients are even more difficult to reconcile with the well-established legal requirement for consent. The NHMRC Statement allows that these patients can be the subjects of non-beneficial experimentation even when there is *no-one* from whom consent can be obtained. There is a qualification that 'the experimental intervention will be

7. For a critique of 'full disclosure', see Freedman, 1982.
8. NHMRC Statement (1992, Supplementary note 2.4) [see Appendix 2].

one which will involve no material risks' (Supplementary note 2.2 (iii)). The qualification of 'material' risk should not deflect from the recognition that an experiment, by definition, has unknown effects. If there is any risk that an experiment with an unconscious patient involves the possibility that the subject's condition may be adversely affected, then it would be contrary to the requirement for consent in the law. In other words, professional practice allows experimentation on unconscious subjects where there can be no consent. The established legal principle is that there should be no exceptions to the requirement for consent. In my view, however, the courts are unlikely to insist on this requirement in the face of professional practice that allows research without consent of the subject. There is a need therefore to reconcile the differences between law and research practice in a way that does not undermine the general requirement for consent.

Reconciling consent in law and research practice

Gerald Dworkin, a legal scholar, has attempted to reconcile the apparent conflict between law and research practice on the need for consent (Dworkin, 1977). As he put it, the law had always been assumed to limit the right of parents and guardians to acting in the 'best interest' of their charges. That principle had been understood to mean that parents could consent to beneficial procedures on behalf of their children but could not consent to non-therapeutic experimentation in which there was a risk of harm and no corresponding benefit to the child. It had been stated by the American Supreme Court (although in a different context) that: 'Parents may be free to become martyrs themselves. But it does not follow [that] they are free . . . to make martyrs of their children' (*Prince v. Massachusetts*: 170). This could amount to a total ban on experimentation on children and would contradict national and international codes of ethics that appeared to validate non-therapeutic research on children and others (Dworkin, 1977: 198–200).

Dworkin's preferred option for reconciling research practice and legal theory was to shift the test from 'the best interests of the child' to a test in which parents acted in a manner that was 'not against the interests of the child'. By this criterion, although the welfare of the child was an important consideration, there were other considerations that could be balanced against the 'best interests of the child'. He reviewed cases in which courts have been prepared to find that other interests prevailed over the interests of the child. In one of these, a court found that freedom of publication was an interest that prevailed over concern for the welfare of a child who might have suffered harm if she was to read a publication describing the depraved behaviour of her father (*Re X (a Minor)*). Another case concerned the taking of blood from a child in order to establish paternity (*S. v. S.*). Dworkin argued that these cases illustrated a movement away from the 'best interests of the child' test toward a rule that simply restricted parents from doing or allowing anything that was 'clearly against the interests of the child'. Although the law is not clear, Dworkin's test is in accord with ethical codes that allow research on children. It is still open to the courts to follow this suggestion.

The South Australian Supreme Court has ruled that Australian courts have the power to question a professional practice. However, it was also stated that '[i]n most cases an approved professional practice as to disclosure will be decisive'.[9] On this test, the prevailing research practices appear to have wide acceptance among the profession and it is unlikely that any Australian court would rule that experimentation research (regarded as ethical by the profession) would be excluded. Legal scholars have argued similarly that professional guidelines on research have a practical effect and 'any test of reasonable behaviour on the part of the researcher will be measured against those guidelines' (Drahos, 1989; Bromberger, 1990).

The English position on whether or not courts of law have the power to question accepted medical practices is not entirely clear following the judgments in *Bolam v. Friern Hospital Management Committee* and *Sidaway v. Governors of the Bethlem Royal Hospital*. The Bolam test appeared to rely entirely on accepted medical practice. The court allowed that a professional standard was conclusive of what was reasonable. In *Sidaway*, however, a surgeon had withheld information on the risk of damage from surgery to a patient's spinal cord. The Court of Appeal did not find the surgeon liable for damages caused to the patient. However, two of the judges indicated that a court could find that a medical practice of withholding information was not reasonable in particular circumstances: such as where the accepted practice of withholding information was

9. *F. v. R.* at pp. 193–4; Cole J, in *Ellis v. Wallsend District Hospital*, cited *F. v. R.* with approval.

'manifestly wrong' or where the 'circumstances of the particular patient' might indicate that disclosure was warranted. In other words, there might be some limited circumstances in which the medical professional practice of withholding information could be challenged by a court. In the House of Lords, the Law Lords were divided on whether or not the court could challenge an accepted practice of withholding information (Iles, 1987).

The general position is that English courts have been more reluctant to question accepted medical practices than United States, Canadian or Australian courts. Even though the English cases (considered above) dealt with medical treatment not medical experimentation, it is unlikely that well accepted research practices would be found unreasonable by an English court.

Review by committee

As was stated in the Introduction, the main protection relied on for the protection of the interests of subjects of experimentation is review by a research ethics committee. The only case (of which I am aware) that considers the responsibility of research ethics committees is the Canadian case: *Weiss v. Solomon*. Weiss was a 62-year-old man who had been treated for cataracts. At his doctor's suggestion he volunteered for a study of a drug designed to reduce retinal oedema although he had been told that his participation would offer him no therapeutic benefit. He was given a fluorescein angiogram (which detects defects in blood vessels) to assess possible side-effects of the drug. Seconds after being injected with the dye fluorescein, Weiss experienced a sudden loss of blood pressure and died. His family brought a successful action, on the grounds of lack of consent and negligence, against the researcher and the hospital.

Judge De Blois held that both the researcher and the hospital, through its research ethics committee, were liable for failure to adequately protect Weiss and inform him of the risks of the fluorescein angiogram. This case was analysed by two Canadian commentators, Freedman and Glass, who observed that the judgment set a 'very high standard for committees to meet' (Freedman and Glass, 1990: 398). The judgment implied there were two requirements of a research ethics committee. The first was that, when a member of a research ethics committee has knowledge that a proposed procedure *might* have severe effects on some subjects (such as Weiss who had a heart condition), the committee was also deemed to know. Secondly, the committee was expected to take action on the basis of that 'knowledge'.

On the first of those points, the judge gave importance to the evidence of one of the medical members of the committee, that he had been aware of two previous cases of cardiac arrest following a fluorescein angiogram. The member himself had not considered those cases established a causal connection. At the time there was no literature relating angiograms and cardiac arrest, and there were very few doctors who suspected this relationship. The decision implies that there was an obligation on the committee member to share any concerns or suspicions with the committee. The question of whether the committee would still have been liable had there been no committee member with this knowledge was not dealt with by the court.

On the second point, the action expected of the committee was that it would minimise the risk – either by requiring the exclusion of subjects who might be adversely affected or by requiring that the information to all subjects include the advice that the angiogram could have fatal effects for some class of patients. This again is a demanding standard. It requires that a committee act on the suspicions of one member against the judgment of the researcher who might well be more knowledgeable in that field of medicine than the committee member.

The judgment of the court appeared to assume that the committee was an agent for the institution in setting and policing minimum standards for research. Freedman and Glass observed that this assumption is not compatible with the finding that the standard of care expected of the committee was as demanding as that expected of the researcher. In other words, if the committee is an agent of the institution, it could not be expected to have and act with the same knowledge and skill that might be expected of a researcher at the cutting edge of research in a particular field.

In my view this judgment has not realistically examined the role of a research ethics committee. The court is right to find that there is a reasonable standard of knowledge and skill that can be expected of a practising doctor and medical researcher. However, to expect the same standard of a research ethics committee (in terms of having, and acting on, up-to-date information) is to see the committee in a medical (technical) supervisory role. This is not an appropriate role for a research ethics committee. While there should be an obligation on researchers to put all material facts before the committee, it is for the committee to weigh up the interests of the various parties from an ethical perspective, on the basis of information before the committee. Although I advocate that committees should seek to be well informed, I maintain that it is not reasonable to expect that a committee should be expert in all the areas of research being considered.

The *Weiss* case also gives rise to the possibility that research ethics committee members may be personally liable if a plaintiff were to bring an action against them. This issue did not arise in *Weiss* because the committee was only considered as a part of the institution. The situation may have been different had the plaintiffs joined the committee members, jointly and severally, in the action.

The possibility of personal liability of committee members is considered to be remote (see UK Department of Health, 1991: 8; and discussion in Chapter 9). Even if a court were to find research ethics committee members individually negligent, staff members would not be in the position of having to pay compensation from their own resources. In most jurisdictions, they would be indemnified by the institution as employees acting for the institution. Community members, as unpaid volunteers, may be in a more vulnerable position, however. This possibility calls for an explicit indemnity to be offered by institutions for all members of research ethics committees. It would seem particularly unjust for those members, who were unpaid volunteers on the committee to be the only ones to suffer a personal loss.

Even though *Weiss* was a case decided in Quebec (which is in a 'civil code' as opposed to common law context), the recognition by a court of the role of a research ethics committee raises the question of whether common law courts might also recognise responsibility of research ethics committees for review and approval of the ethics of experiments on human subjects. Dworkin (1987: 206) was of the view that the 'value of research ethics committees in safeguarding the ethical and legal standards of research projects cannot be too highly emphasised'. The requirement of official bodies in most countries for committee review could be regarded as setting a professional standard against which to measure the actions of researchers and institutions in other jurisdictions. In this regard, it appears strange that the judgment in *Weiss* did not refer to the standard set by the Medical Research Council of Canada's guidelines, but referred instead to the Helsinki Declaration (Freedman and Glass, 1990: 401). It is open to courts to find that the system for review establishes the reasonable standard of care and skill for researchers both in the conduct of the research and in the extent of the disclosure to subjects.

Broader policy issues

Few courts have considered broader policy issues in human experimentation. The case of *Kaimowitz* (discussed above) was an exception. There it was stated that the 'Court does not in any way desire to impede medical progress' yet it recognised that medical progress must be restrained by public policy. One of the policy issues considered was the need to balance research in the interests of society against the protection of subjects of that research. However, that court put the obligation on the doctor, not on the hospital or its research ethics committee, to weigh the risks and benefits of experimentation. This case indicated that unreasonable risks of harm to subjects are not acceptable but that benefit to society may justify experimentation in which the risks are relatively low. This was an application of one of the principles of the Nuremberg Code. It is a further indication that other courts may be willing to consider principles beyond consent in deciding whether experimentation is reasonable.

In my view, the historical emphasis of courts on consent is plainly inadequate to deal with the complexities of experimentation on human subjects. I suggest that it is open to courts to endorse the elements of guidelines on research ethics (for example, the Helsinki Declaration, Principle I.2) that require the prior review of proposals for experimentation by an ethics committee. It is also open to courts to uphold other established standards, such as the requirement that precedence be given to the rights of subjects of research over the expected benefits to human knowledge or to the community (Helsinki Declaration, Principle III.4).

The situation is less ambiguous in the United States where government regulations incorporate many of the standards of ethical research. These regulations are likely to be regarded as setting a reasonable standard for research – especially for federally funded research (US Federal Policy, 1991; Porter, 1991).

LEGISLATION

There still remain many divergences between principles of law and ethics. The common law has not been well developed in this area because there have only been a few cases from which to draw. I agree with Dworkin (1987: 208-9) that there is a need for legislation. He saw the role of legislation as

- providing legal answers to the doubts about whether research was permissible on certain classes of incompetent subjects;
- indicating the circumstances in which proxy consent could be given;
- ensuring that all research projects were required to be submitted for review by an ethics committee; and
- providing for a general body to monitor and advise research ethics committees.

To this list I would add the need for protection for members of research ethics committees by granting an immunity from personal liability against claims for damages arising from research ethics committee deliberations. A precedent for this from the Republic of Ireland is discussed in Chapter 9. In New Zealand chairpersons of area health board ethics committees have recommended legislation to establish a national committee which would set standards for ethics review.[10] In England a report from the King's Fund Institute has recommended that there be 'legislation to strengthen RECs' role'. The report made similar points to those of Dworkin (above) on the advantages of legislation and added that legislation should require regular training of committee members (Neuberger, 1992).

Dworkin (1987: 206-7) also suggested that there might be some advantage in enacting a code of research subjects' rights as in California. He did not favour incorporating the detailed content of the rules of research ethics in legislation however. Many of these points are in line with the suggestions that have been made in Australia by the NHMRC (1983a). The NHMRC took the view that the substance of rules should continue to be in the form of guidelines but that the system itself needed legislative backing. In Australia, the State of New South Wales took a small step in this direction

---

10. Report of discussions (30 April-1 May 1992) between chairpersons of Area Health Board Ethics Committees in New Zealand, sent to author by the 'Policy Group', Department of Health, Wellington, New Zealand.

in issuing regulations under the *Children (Care and Protection) Act 1987*. Those provisions restrain anyone from carrying out research on a child under the age of 16 that does not conform to the NHMRC guidelines.[11] In the main, however, Australian states have ignored the request from the NHMRC for legislative backing.

Although I accept the need for legislation, I recognise a difficulty in that, in federal systems such as those of the United States, Canada and Australia, human experimentation (and animal research) is regarded as a state matter. This means that for effective control over the whole country, all state and territory governments would need to adopt adequate provisions for control. There are problems in having different legislative provisions for the control of research within each state. The ideal would be that each State would enact the same, or very similar, provisions for the control of experimentation on human subjects. Suggestions along these lines have already been made in Canada in a working paper published in 1989 by the Law Reform Commission of Canada. It suggested a number of criteria within which non-therapeutic biomedical experimentation should be considered legal and permissible within the criminal law. These were recommended to deal with any question about the legality of experimentation on human subjects in Canada (Law Reform Commission of Canada, 1989).

In Australia there are precedents for a number of different states acting together to develop legislation.[12] If Law Reform Commissions from several states could work together to develop legislation for the control of research on human subjects, this might hopefully become the model for legislation to be enacted in each of those states. Other states and territories could then be encouraged to adopt the same, or very similar, provisions.

CONCLUSION

The courts have relied principally on subjects protecting themselves by withholding their consent. The emphasis has therefore been on the adequacy of consent. However, consent is not always possible,

11. Clause (2), Regulation 1989: No. 502, issued under the NSW Children (Care and Protection) Act 1987.
12. See, for example, the joint report and recommendations for legislation published by the Law Reform Commission of Victoria, the Australian Law Reform Commission and the New South Wales Law Reform Commission (1989).

for example in research on children, the unconscious and the mentally impaired. Furthermore, consent is an insufficient protection for subjects of research. There needs to be further protection of the interests of subjects by the review and supervisory roles of a research ethics committee acting on established principles and rules. The next chapter considers the application of principles and rules to human experimentation.

Many countries now have guidelines for the protection of research subjects. These have the standing of a professional code of ethics. In most of these countries, the guidelines establish a review system by committee and require prior approval for all experimentation on human subjects. Even though the court in the *Weiss* case appeared to have ignored the relevant Canadian guidelines on research ethics, I suggest that such guidelines could well be regarded by courts of law as part of the standard of reasonable care of a researcher and research institutions. It is unlikely, however, that the courts will be in a position to develop a thorough and consistent set of principles to cover the areas of concern and it is suggested that legislation is needed to control and regulate experimentation on human subjects. Without further legislation, the law provides an inadequate basis for balancing the interests of science and the interests of subjects, and for protecting human subjects of experimentation from harm.

CHAPTER 6

Ethical Principles, Rules and Discretion

There are many relevant issues that have not been dealt with by courts or by legislation. While law provides for a minimum standard, ethical guidelines are more directly applicable to balancing the interests of science and the interests of subjects. This chapter explores the basis of those guidelines and the discretionary application of those principles and rules to research practices.

Ethics and law both share the problem of determining how to apply general rules to particular cases. In law, it is not always obvious how principles and rules will be applied by a court in the circumstances of a particular case. Similarly, it is not always obvious how ethical principles and ethical rules should be applied in a particular case. Furthermore, there are conflicts between different rules and between different principles, both in law and in ethics, that make the application of the rules and principles problematic.

Decisions still need to be taken, however, about the application of rules to a particular case. The rules themselves do not make this obvious. In law, courts necessarily have some discretion in applying the rules. In this chapter I argue that there is a similar need for a discretionary body in resolving ethical issues and deciding what ethical principles or rules should apply. In most countries this discretion is exercised by research ethics committees.

PRINCIPLES AND RULES OF RESEARCH ETHICS

The argument for principles of research on human subjects is that, on their own, rules may be inadequate for complex situations, they may conflict, and be difficult to interpret and apply. Principles can play a useful role in that, while not resolving disputes, they provide a framework for analysis and an *aid* in the resolution of ethical problems.

In this chapter, I follow the principles of research ethics which are set out in the Belmont Report (National Commission for the Protection of Human Subjects, 1978d). Although there are alternative statements of principles relevant to research ethics I have adopted the National Commission's statement for two reasons: first, it resulted from a consideration of ethics of experimentation on human subjects rather than of the broad area of bioethics; and secondly, the ethical principles identified by the Commission make it obvious that there are conflicts to be resolved in particular circumstances and that there are conflicts inherent within and between the principles themselves. The National Commission arrived at its principles of research ethics inductively. Toulmin, a consultant to the National Commission, stated that the Commission proceeded 'taxonomically, taking one difficult class of cases at a time and comparing it in detail with other clearer and easier classes of cases' (1981: 31). The resulting principles provide a shorthand reminder of important values and considerations.

Respect for persons

The first of the principles stated by the Commission was 'respect for persons'. It is derived from two different sources. One source includes the classical ideas associated with autonomy, while the other includes ethical notions about the need to protect those with diminished autonomy.

Autonomy

Autonomy is a philosophical concept or 'family of ideas' to which a number of philosophers have contributed. The two principal philosophers associated with the concept are Immanuel Kant and John Stuart Mill. For Kant, autonomy was understood as freedom of the will; for Mill, autonomy was freedom of action. Kant was concerned with moral autonomy – a person should not be the slave to outside coercion and should struggle to be free from the compulsion of inner desire or habit. Kant considered that we should treat others as autonomous ends and never as means to our own ends. Persons, for Kant, were of unconditional value in and of themselves. His was a deontological position. Deontology (from the root *deon* meaning duty) is the position that certain moral precepts are right in and of themselves and they impose a moral duty to act in certain ways regardless of the consequences.

A consequentialist position on the other hand is that the right or appropriate action is to be determined by the desirability or appropriateness of its consequences. For Mill, the issue was liberty of the individual in action and in thought. The only justification for limiting the liberty of an individual was to prevent harm to other individuals. Mill's position is also known as utilitarian. Mill argued that particular actions should be justified in terms of the outcome that would lead to the greatest utility (variously translated as satisfaction or happiness) (Mill, 1962: 33–77). It is justification in terms of outcome that places utilitarianism among the consequentialist theories. Deontological and consequentialist theories can lead to opposing positions (as is illustrated by the discussion of 'Fundamental principles or *prima facie* duties?' later in this chapter).

Autonomy includes the idea that an individual is free to choose and to act. Both rational capacity and freedom from constraint are necessary elements. 'Respect for persons' includes respecting the decisions of autonomous beings. It also means providing the information needed to be able to make rational decisions. In practice, respect for autonomy translates into the requirement for informed consent. Historically, the development of the notion of informed consent in law was paralleled by the increasing importance given to notions of autonomy in philosophy and ethics.

The notion of autonomy assumed particular importance in medical ethics in the United States during the 1960s and 1970s. It was a foil to the entrenched assumptions of paternalistic benevolence of the medical profession. As philosopher Robert Veatch put it, autonomy was used as a 'trump card' to counter the argument that doctors knew what was in the patient's best interest (Veatch, 1984). In a number of different areas of medicine there were demands for the patient's choice to be given priority over that of the doctor's. Veatch pointed to the rights of women to know the results of amniocentesis tests on their fetuses, the rights of psychiatric patients to refuse electro-convulsive shock treatment, the demands of teenagers for confidentiality of information on their contraceptive use *vis-à-vis* their parents, and the demands of terminally ill patients for the right to refuse treatment.

Since the 1960s and 1970s, there has been dissatisfaction expressed about the notion of autonomy as a fundamental principle. Cassell (1984), for example, considered that autonomy treated 'the individual as an entity distinct and independent from other individuals when, in fact, no such separate individual exists'. Another writer (Callahan, 1984) argued that autonomy was not an end in itself but a value among other values. He considered, from a community perspective, that justice was the principal ethic. Veatch himself argued that beneficence rather than autonomy was the fundamental principle. In his view, we should seek to benefit all of society while at the same time ensuring that individuals are respected and receive their fair share.

This was a challenge to the predominance of autonomy that could ultimately mean a very different emphasis in ethics. The beginning of this is seen in the willingness of the National Commission to qualify the notion of autonomy by combining it with provisions for those with diminished autonomy within a single principle of 'respect for persons'.

Protection for those with diminished autonomy
The second element of the National Commission's principle of 'respect for persons' was that 'persons with diminished autonomy are entitled to protection'. This was a recognition by the Commission that people are not capable of self-determination at all times and in all circumstances. Maturity and independence from the control of others is needed before a person can be described as autonomous. Children lacking this maturity and independence, and those in circumstances that are coercive or restraining, such as prisoners, are not regarded as autonomous. Similarly, an injury or illness might reduce one's capacity for autonomous action or choice. The Commission concluded that 'respect for the immature and the incapacitated may require protecting them as they mature or while they are incapacitated'. This protection meant, in practice, that some groups of persons would not be allowed to participate in research unless it was research particularly designed to further understanding of their conditions. Prisoners, for example, were no longer to be used for the testing of drugs as they were thought to be in a coercive situation and were susceptible to undue influence. These circumstances made it impossible for them to be true volunteers. This view parallels that of the court in the *Kaimowitz* case discussed in the previous chapter.

The Commission acknowledged that there could be a conflict of competing claims within the principle of 'respect for persons'. On one hand, the principle entailed respecting the choices of autonomous individuals while, on the other, it might entail disallowing the choices of people where the judgement was made that in their circumstances they were not fully autonomous. There is therefore an inherent conflict in this principle. The Commission had moved some distance from the notion of autonomy as a protection from paternalism. Respect for autonomy, in the Commission's view, occurred within a broader paternalist concern for determining whether a person was autonomous or not. The overriding issue was protection of the person.

Rules for applying the principle of respect for persons
It followed from the principle of 'respect for persons' that if research subjects are autonomous they should be given the opportunity to decide for themselves whether or not to contribute to a research project. The Commission acknowledged the controversy over whether informed consent was possible.[1] However, it skirted that issue by suggesting that, at the very least, subjects should be given the *opportunity* for informed consent. The Commission outlined three elements of the consent process that were necessary for that opportunity to exist: information, comprehension and voluntariness. This was a restatement of accepted views on the content of an informed consent and was consistent with legal definitions of consent discussed in the previous chapter. These applications of the principle of 'respect for persons' could be considered as ethical rules.[2]

Information. One of the elements was the need to inform potential subjects of 'the research procedure, their purposes, risks and anticipated benefits, [and] alternative procedures (where therapy is involved)'. Subjects must be informed that they are free to ask questions or to withdraw from the research at any time. The Commission took the view that the standard for how much information to give was that of a 'reasonable volunteer' who would want to know (as a minimum) that the procedure was not necessary for their care; that it may not be fully understood; and that he or she could decide whether or not to participate. Even in cases where subjects might benefit from the research, they should understand

1. In the debate on informed consent, the reader is referred to the following: Beecher (1966b), Ingelfinger (1982), Epstein and Lasagna (1969), Schultz, Pardee and Ensinck (1975), Fellner and Marshall (1970) and Appelbaum, Lidz and Meisel (1987: 138–46).
2. For an examination of the distinction between principles and rules, see Beauchamp and Childress (1989: 6–9).

the risk involved in the study and that their participation was entirely voluntary. The Commission was prepared to allow research involving incomplete disclosure in some circumstances according to the goals of the research, but never for the purpose of co-opting subjects in the first place.

Comprehension. The Commission was concerned that the manner in which information was conveyed should be as important as the substance of that information. The potential subjects had to be given enough time to come to a decision and an opportunity to ask questions. The obligation was on the researcher to make sure that the subject understood the information given, and the obligation was more onerous the greater the risk of harm.

In the case of subjects who were mentally incompetent by virtue of their age, mental capacity, or illness, the Commission considered that respect for those persons demanded both that they be informed to the extent possible and their objections be honoured; and that, in addition, permission be sought from other persons who were most likely to understand the subject's situation and act in their best interest and who were authorised to act for the subject. Persons representing the subject in this way should be given the opportunity to observe the research in process and withdraw the subject if the research did not appear to be in the subject's best interest.

Voluntariness. The third ingredient of informed consent was that consent be voluntary. This meant freedom from coercion or undue influence. Coercion in the form of some threat, or undue influence in the form of 'unwarranted, inappropriate or improper reward or other overture in order to obtain compliance' would mean that the consent was not voluntarily given. The Commission acknowledged that it was not possible to draw the line precisely between justifiable persuasion and undue influence. However, it stated that unjustifiable pressure could take the form of a person in the position of authority, or commanding influence, urging a particular course of action. It could also take the form of a threat of withdrawing health services or influencing a close relative.

Limitations of consent

One of the fundamental questions is the 'value of medical research as an end in itself' when subjects are at risk of harm (Osborne, 1983b). Consent is not sufficient to protect subjects. In the previous chapter the point was made that there are other important factors that need to be considered including the value of the research, the extent of risk of harm to subjects and the scientific validity. The philosopher Hans Jonas put forward a similar view in asserting that the research objective itself should be worthy: 'For less than adequate cause, not even the freest unsolicited offer should be accepted' (Jonas, 1969: 236). The importance of the principle of autonomy and the need for consent is acknowledged. However, on its own, consent is insufficient to protect subjects of research. As another commentator put it, reliance on informed consent put the 'onus of making a decision' on the person 'least qualified to decide: the subject' (Howard-Jones, 1982). There is clearly a need for others to consider the validity and value of a research proposal before consent even becomes an issue.

Beneficence

The principle of beneficence, as described by the National Commission, includes the idea of both non-maleficence and beneficence. In other words, it included the dual requirement to avoid harm and to endeavour to benefit where possible. The principle of non-maleficence is expressed by the maxim *primum non nocere* – 'above all do no harm'. The principle extends beyond physical harm to include protection from psychological, social and economic harm (as discussed in the Introduction). In the context of medical research on human subjects, the duty of non-maleficence imposed a duty to avoid actual harm and the duty to minimise the risk of harm (Beauchamp and Childress, 1989: 120–4). There is also a tradition within medicine that doctors have a positive duty to benefit others when they are in a position to do so. This is the major justification for medical research. The difficulty is that determining what will be of benefit and what may be harmful necessitates a program of research. Subjects of research are put at risk of harm so as to know what will be of benefit and what may be harmful to future patients.

The Commission considered therefore that investigators and members of their institutions were obliged to maximise possible benefits and minimise the risk of possible harm to experimental subjects. This duty carries with it the obligation to weigh carefully the evidence for possible benefits and potential harms. The Commission acknowledged that this may involve difficult choices between different claims within the principle of beneficence. This principle, as formulated by the Commission, is similar to the principle of 'respect for persons' discussed above in that it involves resolving a conflict inherent within the principle itself.

In the Belmont Report, the Commission declared that applying the principle of 'beneficence' included considering whether proposed research was properly designed, and whether the risks to subjects were justified (1978d: 15). Although the Commission did not say so, these are two separate issues: the issue of design deals with validity of research while the issue of risk and justification deals with the value of research. The Canadian philosopher Benjamin Freedman pointed out that validity and value of scientific research are often conflated. The first is a technical issue and concerns the 'formal relationship between the data and conclusions' of a study; the second concerns the social value of a study and is to do with the 'significance of the hypothesis itself' (Freedman, 1987).

Validity and value of research
The Commission considered that assessing the benefits of research meant assessing whether research is properly designed (National Commission, Belmont Report, 1978d: 14–15). Freedman stated that it is 'well established' that poorly designed research is unethical because it can not result in scientifically valid results. In his view, although validity was a separate issue, it affected the value of research and should therefore be a part of the business of an ethics committee (Freedman, 1987: 7; also Rutstein, 1969: 524). In interviews of members of research ethics committees, both in Australia and in other countries, this was a position that was often put to me by scientific and researcher members.

I question this view. The issue that concerns me is that an emphasis on validity has the effect of giving researchers a principal position in discussing the ethical merit of proposed studies. However, scientific validity is not primarily an ethical issue. It is technical. As I argued in the Introduction, the important ethical issue is not whether studies are scientifically well grounded but whether there is a risk of physical or psychological harm, or risk of economic loss to subjects. The difficult ethical issue is balancing the relative *value* of the research against the interests of subjects. Obviously, to be valuable a study needs to be valid. In other words it needs to be capable of establishing what it sets out to establish. But the issue of validity is a 'threshold condition' (Freedman, 1987) which precedes the question of relative value. Contrary to Freedman, I maintain that there *is* an advantage in separately considering questions of validity and value. Not all members of ethics review committees have the relevant expertise to resolve issues of validity. Expecting ethics committees to resolve such issues leaves those without the necessary expertise being (and feeling) superfluous. For these reasons I argue that validity of studies ought to be established prior to a research ethics committee consideration.

This has become an issue of some importance in Australia where, as a result of cost-cutting measures in the early 1980s, the Drug Evaluation Section of the Department of Health (as it then was) suggested that research ethics committees should take over the authorising and supervising of clinical trials for new drugs.[3] Changes introduced in the clinical trial notification (CTN) scheme in Australia, and to some extent in the clinical trial exemption (CTX) scheme, have put even greater reliance on research ethics committees for technical assessment. The NHMRC, the Consumers Health Forum and research ethics committees themselves, have expressed concern about the capacity of committees to make the necessary technical assessments (Baume, 1991: 115–16).[4] Because of similar concerns in Britain, the King's Fund Institute report has recommended a 'separate research methods committee which can vet the research design for scientific validity' (Neuberger, 1992).

This issue is more than a question of the *capacity* of research ethics committees to deal with the issue. It is a question of the *appropriateness* of relying on ethics committees to provide technical assessment. It is inappropriate to rely on *ethics* committees to resolve technical issues. Such matters ought to be resolved before a research ethics committee is asked to consider ethical issues arising from drug trials. Otherwise, the non-technical members on the committee are rendered superfluous and the quality of review overall is reduced. Thus, the point of this distinction is that research ethics committees are appropriate for considering questions of value but not for considering questions of validity, and the temptation

---

3. Copy of letter (undated, c. 1980) from R. E. Wilson, Acting First Assistant to the Director-General, Therapeutics Division (Secretariat for the Australian Drug Evaluation Committee) to Dr D. de Souza, First Assistant Director-General, on file with the NHMRC Division of the Department of Health. [A copy of the letter was contained in a file of historical material made available to me by the Chairman, Medical Research Ethics Committee.]
4. This area of review is changing very rapidly in Australia and modifications are expected.

to ask committees to take on further technical assessment should be resisted.

Balancing of risks and benefits

It has been said that risks to subjects should be outweighed by the anticipated benefit to the subject or to society. This is a deceptive formula, however. It suggests that a calculation can be made to determine an acceptable point of balance between risk to subjects and benefit to society (Douglas, 1985: 14). As benefits are not easily calibrated and are of a different order to harms, there is clearly no simple calculation but a balancing between competing interests. 'Risk' is a term often expressed as a probability. However, the term refers to both the probability of the occurrence of harm and to the severity of the injury that could result. The term 'benefit', on the other hand, does not indicate a probability. As the National Commission pointed out, potential benefits are properly contrasted with potential harms rather than risks.

The issue is balancing the risk of harm to the subject against the potential benefits that can result from the research for others. While acknowledging that a precise and quantitative assessment is not realistic, the Commission made suggestions for a thorough and systematic accumulation and assessment of the evidence to make the analysis itself as systematic as possible.

The point that I wish to emphasise is that, fundamentally, this is a value judgement. It is a matter of judging the value of research (the potential good) against the negative value (potential harm). Recognising the essential value judgement underscores the broadly political nature of this consideration. It is a question of weighing one set of community values against another. Recognition of the inherent value judgement also raises the issue of who should be making this judgement. Ideally, value judgements of this sort would not be made by persons who have a vested interest in the outcome. This is a concern that is dealt with later in this book in terms of the ideal composition of research ethics committees.

Justice

The third principle outlined by the National Commission was the principle of justice. The notion of justice is rooted in ideas of 'fairness and desert' – people should be treated fairly and disinterestedly, and should be given what they deserve in the sense of what they have earned (Beauchamp and Childress, 1989: 257). A direct application of the notion of justice is the idea that a person injured in research ought to be compensated because the benefit of their volunteering accrues to other people (if not society as a whole) and it is only fair that the burdens of their volunteering ought to be shared. Some suggestions are made about incorporating a requirement for compensation in Chapter 9.

The Commission discussed the principle of justice in terms of treating people equally. Historically, human experimentation has been unjust in drawing on socially and economically disadvantaged people. Abuses of patients in medical research have most often occurred in poorer patients with low status (noted in Chapter 1). The Commission was concerned that subject selection should be fair both to individuals and to classes within society. In its view there should be no bias in favour of 'special' persons in selecting subjects for potentially beneficial research programs and no bias towards selecting 'undesirable' persons for risky research. Between classes of subjects it was suggested that, as a principle of social justice, there should be a preference for using some classes ahead of others. For example, adults should be used as subjects of research in preference to children. In effect, their recommendations mean that some classes of patients, such as institutionalised mentally infirm patients or prisoners, should only be involved in research on two conditions. First, that the research is directly related to their conditions; and second, that there are no alternative people, capable of giving consent, who could serve as subjects.

Criticisms of the National Commission

Most commentators praised the work of the National Commission (see, for example, R. J. Levine, 1979; and Neville, 1979). There were some, however, who criticised the composition of the Commission as being biased in favour of the interests of researchers (for example, Annas, 1980). This prompted a spirited defence of the Commission and the validity of its findings from Jonsen and Yesley (1980), Jonsen being a Commissioner and Yesley being a staff member of the Commission.

Another critic argued that the moral philosophy of the Belmont Report rested on a philosophical mistake (Marshall, 1986). By including both 'benefit' and 'harm' within the one principle of 'beneficence', Marshall argued that the Commission had fused the interests of individual subjects with those of society. The result was an inevitable bias against human subjects of research because research on relatively few subjects may have potential benefits for many others in the long run. In other words, the harm to a few is easily outweighed by the potential benefit to others. This concern emphasises the importance of a commitment to requiring that the interests of subjects should predominate over the interests of those who may benefit from research.

Another criticism was of the lack of a 'systematic theory' for dealing with conflicts between principles (Veatch, 1979). One way of dealing with conflicting principles is to determine which principle should predominate when any conflict arises. A number of commentators have argued that there should be one fundamental ethical principle on which to make decisions about the ethical validity of experimentation on human subjects. Various principles have been put forward in this regard. However, the search for a fundamental principle raises many of the difficulties inherent in experimentation on human subjects, and will be dealt with here in some depth.

FUNDAMENTAL PRINCIPLES OR 'PRIMA FACIE' DUTIES?

Two prominent philosophers to champion a fundamental principle of research ethics were Hans Jonas and Robert Veatch. Jonas argued persuasively that the fundamental principle was 'inviolability of the individual' (1969: 220). For Veatch, the basic principle was that 'persons are to be respected as individuals with rights and interests that take precedence over the greater good of the society'. He described this as 'patient-centeredness' (Veatch, 1979: 27). The issue for Jonas and Veatch was whether rights of an individual should ever be overruled in the interests of society. In Jonas's view there were individual rights which were primary, specific and identifiable. The potential benefits to society were not equivalent. The individuals who might benefit were not normally identifiable and, therefore, benefit to society was an abstract principle.

Jonas reasoned that the emphasis given to consent was a tacit acknowledgement that there was no societal right to subjects' participation. In his view, consent assumed importance because it served to *mask* a difficulty that was not easily soluble in other terms. It was a cover for the virtual conscription of research subjects. In practice, research subjects were under pressure to volunteer simply by being solicited by an authoritative person (Jonas, 1969: 220–1, 233). Jonas suggested that we should see the subject's participation as a sacrifice. The ideal he proposed was self-sacrifice, a form of altruism that 'exceeds that of moral law and reaches into the sublime solitude of dedication and ultimate commitment'. Consent was not sufficient on its own to justify the use of humans as subjects in experiments. There must be an active participation that amounts to a co-operative enterprise between researcher and subject – as 'joint adventurers in a common cause',[5] or perhaps as a 'research participant, who is also a collaborator of the research worker' (Mead, 1969: 371). The issue of concern to these writers was that the subject was asked to participate in a venture that entailed some risk to him or herself and, in many cases, no benefit. For this reason, Jonas considered that those who should be asked to participate in research are firstly the researchers themselves or 'members of the scientific community' and then 'the most highly educated, and the least "captive" members of the community' (1969: 235). In essence, the ideal research subjects would be those who could most easily identify with and understand the situation and identify with the goals: the elite and privileged, including the researchers themselves.

Jonas considered that subjects of experiments should not include the disadvantaged and certainly not the sick merely by virtue of the fact that they are in hospital and available. This was in stark contrast to what happens in practice. As shown in Chapter 1, it is public patients rather than private patients, and the institutionalised, who have been drawn on as subjects of experimentation in greater proportions throughout the history of experimentation.

In opposition to Jonas, it has been claimed that he was taking a catastrophic view of medical experimentation, as if the subject was violated and victimised. Instead, it has been argued that the interests of the individual are not necessarily in conflict with those of society (Dyck, 1970). In another rebuttal, Lasagna (1969: 461) contended that absolutist doctrines like those of Jonas are easy to advance but they do not deal adequately with concrete situations. He did not accept

5. Those who have expressed this view include Ramsey (1970: 5), Edsall (1969: 476), and Fried (1978: 702).

that concern for the individual was any more noble than 'a desire to aid many' suggesting that 'it might be argued that the opposite underlies the democratic process'. In my view, Jonas was idealistic in his notion of participation and suggested an almost impossible standard for consent.

However, it has also been demonstrated that Jonas was not as dogmatic in the application of his ideas as his initial argument would suggest. His stance in relation to the appropriate course in particular cases was much more permissive than his theory (Schafer, 1983). This tends to bear out Toulmin's experience (discussed above) that the National Commission members could agree on practical guidelines but had great difficulty in agreeing on underlying principles or theories of ethics (Toulmin, 1981: 31–2).

Research without consent: research on children

The fundamental differences between the various proponents was brought to a head in the issue of research on children. Non-therapeutic research on children is a difficult area in ethics as well as in law (as was discussed in the previous chapter). Paul Ramsey, a theologian, described research involving children as a 'prismatic case' by which to tell whether we mean to take seriously our ethical commitments (Ramsey, 1970: 35). Jonas and Ramsey both took the view that research on children was excluded by a fundamental and absolute principle. Jonas considered that research that had no therapeutic benefit for children was excluded by their inability to give a valid consent. (This is the same issue that I considered in the previous chapter in terms of whether the law would accept research on children when they are unable to consent for themselves.) Jonas took the view that no other person, including the parents, could ethically consent to a procedure that involved risk and no benefit for the child.

Veatch's concern was that in some areas of research, such as research with children, the comatose, the retarded and the senile, the principle of 'patient-centeredness' had been abandoned 'without inserting the other safeguarding principle of our culture – the principle of self-determination' (Veatch, 1979: 27). Both Veatch and Jonas were grappling with the same problem. Patient-centredness (Veatch) or the inviolability of the person (Jonas) were the ideals and these did not justify research conducted on human subjects without consent. There was no principle that had been developed to justify research outside those principles. Although Veatch did not rule out research under those circumstances, both Jonas and Ramsey did.

The main issue here then is that a fundamental principle which put the rights of the subjects ahead of those of science could mean that research on human subjects is disallowed unless the subjects themselves agree or, for Jonas, are active partners in the research project. This is a deontological position that uncompromisingly puts the duty to protect the individual's rights ahead of the consequences for other people (Fletcher, 1967: 638–9).

The difficulty is that if Jonas and Ramsey's position were accepted then some groups from society would be deprived of the potential benefit from research. Some medical conditions suffered by children, for example, depend on research on children for the alleviation of the symptoms. McCormick, another deontologist, attempted to reconcile the need for scientific research with the requirement for research. He supported scientific research on children even though there might be no benefit to the child and children were not capable of consent. He considered that parents could give a valid proxy consent on behalf of their child without it being construed as the imposition of the will of the parent. His argument developed from asserting that it 'can be good for one to pursue and support' non-therapeutic experimentation and led him to the proposition that 'when it factually is good, we may say that one *ought* to do so' (McCormick, 1974). It is arguable that parents may consent to treatment on behalf of their child if it is what the child would wish had the child been able to consent for him or herself. It does not follow that parents or, for that matter, the child ought to consent. Even if the assertion that it is good to support non-therapeutic research is accepted, there could be no obligation on a child to consent, especially as it exposes the child to risk. Jonas (1969: 221) has labelled this argument as a 'moral claim' not amounting to an obligation. Others also took issue with McCormick. For example, Ramsey (1974: 24) pointed out that McCormick's argument could be applied to all subjects. In effect, the argument would dispense with the need for consent at all.

What I find interesting about McCormick's argument, and I suspect it was what motivated him, was his resistance to the notion of a 'societal right'. He recognised that a failure to reconcile non-therapeutic experimentation on children within 'a genuine ethic of consent' would open the door to a 'utilitarian subordination of the individual to the collectivity' (1974: 15). McCormick attempted to get around this difficulty by construing consent on behalf of the child. In my view, however, the construction was an artifice that could not hide the resulting imposition of someone else's will on the child – the very opposite of consent. When consent is construed on behalf of subjects incapable of giving consent and justified on the grounds of benefits to others, the sense of a societal right persists. McCormick's rationale for research on children was an unsuccessful attempt to reconcile two conflicting interests in research: the need to protect the interests of children as subjects of experimentation and the needs of future children for research which may provide answers to their problems.

In my view there is no escaping the conflict between these values unless one is given predominance over the other whenever they would (otherwise) conflict. Jonas and Ramsey gave unequivocal predominance to protection of subjects. McCormick, in attempting to reconcile both scientific research and protection of subjects within a single principle, proposed a solution that supported science but offered little protection to individual subjects. In essence, his solution was to give predominance to research. If autonomy can be limited by a notion of societal right to put some at risk for the potential benefit of others, then societal rights could be construed as having priority over those of personal autonomy. Although there are few exponents (Howard-Jones (1988: 1440) has quoted one proponent of this view), the extreme would be to argue that the rights of the individual must be subjugated to the claims of research. This construction could mean the conscription of people to experiments – and is clearly not acceptable.

While we should give great importance to what people would wish for themselves, I am not persuaded that we should respect autonomy for its own sake. I accept that concern for the welfare of subjects should take precedence but I do not regard protection of their autonomy, or the broader duty to protect subjects, as an absolute. Nevertheless, there should be a presumption in favour of requiring that research on human beings be conducted with the consent of subjects. Other interests, such as a pressing need for research to alleviate suffering, might be considered to rebut the presumption.

There are ethical positions which might support this view, such as W. D. Ross's 'deontic position' which includes the notion of *prima facie* or conditional duties.[6] Within his theory there may be a *prima facie* duty to protect the welfare of subjects, including their autonomy, but this duty must be balanced against another *prima facie* duty to maximise good (or at least to minimise bad) (Ross, 1930; Sprigge, 1987).[7] When all things are considered, the obligation to protect the subject's autonomy may be outweighed by an obligation to conduct research for the relief of suffering.

This is the position in practice. Autonomy is protected by a requirement for consent and, in cases where consent is not possible, there are some special rules such as those of the United States Department of Health and Human Services Rules and Regulations and the Australian NHMRC Statement on Human Experimentation. These rules are not absolute. They are guides which can help in making a decision. Inevitably though, when an absolute position is rejected and the standard is flexible, there is a need for some person, or group, to have the discretion to decide how to apply the rules in a particular circumstance.

DISCRETION

At the beginning of this chapter I raised the question of whether there is a need for a discretionary function in applying ethical principles and rules of human experimentation. I would argue that the inherent conflict between the need for research and the need to protect subjects of experimentation means that there is a need for a body with the discretion to decide which rule should predominate and in what circumstances. If there are circumstances in which an obligation to protect autonomy may be outweighed by an obligation to conduct research, there is a need for a discretionary body to consider the various *prima facie* obligations, competing interests, and circumstances, and to arrive at an appropriate decision.

There is another reason for discretion. The exercise of discretion is necessary because it is not possible to specify in advance the situations to which a rule should apply. The philosopher Wittgenstein made a fundamental observation about the application of rules to particular situations. He stated that 'no course of action could be determined by a rule, because every course of action can be made

6. I am grateful to Professor Peter Singer for making this point and drawing my attention to the work of W. D. Ross.
7. Beauchamp and Childress (1989: 38-9) have described Ross as a 'pluralist deontologist'.

out to accord with the rule' (Wittgenstein, 1953: 81e). Wittgenstein's dictum has been explained as meaning that 'no rule can specify completely what is to count as following or not following that rule' (Mulkay, 1980). The validity of this dictum has been illustrated by several studies that demonstrate the variable application of rules to fit the exigencies of differing situations. In one of those studies, observations were made of the variable application of the rule 'share your experience with other patients' in therapy groups. It was concluded that 'such organisational rules and rights do not contain instructions which "fit" them to each instance'. An exhaustive list of applications could not be provided 'because such a list would be indefinite' (Wootton, 1977: 341, 347). In another study, researchers observed the variable interpretation and application of the rule 'first come first served' by receptionists assigning interview applicants to caseworkers. Receptionists varied the application of the rule apparently for efficiency. In this study it was concluded that rules cannot be treated as 'possessing stable operational meanings invariant to the exigencies of actual situations of use' (Zimmerman, 1971: 223). The inevitable conclusion was that it was not possible to identify factors that would predict the reinterpretation of the rule in either study (Mulkay, 1980: 116).

This is a feature of rules. There needs to be an authority to define the cases to which the rule applies because it is not possible to specify in advance all the situations to which the rule or principle applies. This is the basis for the argument for discretion in the application of rules.

'Ethics of strangers' and the 'ethics of intimates'

There is another argument for discretion. The exercise of discretion can soften apparent inequalities in the strict adherence to rules. Kenneth Davis, a writer on discretion, has said that in the complexity of our modern legal and political systems, rules on their own are insufficient. They need to be tempered by discretion (Davis, 1969: 25).

Toulmin (referred to earlier in the discussion of the National Commission) took this position even further. In an article entitled 'The tyranny of principles' (1981), he warned of oversimplification that comes from a dogmatic adherence to principle. He considered that 'principles' and 'rules' of ethics need to be applied with a discretion that weighs the particular circumstances of the case in the same manner that the rule of law is tempered by equity. He warned of 'tyrannical absolutism' – that is, denying personal judgement in ethics and insisting on strict adherence to principle and consistency in the application of the rules. He wrote of the 'ethics of strangers' and the 'ethics of intimates'. In a world of strangers, where there is no trust, the insistence is on equality in the sense of every one being treated in like manner. In intimate relationships, however, particular idiosyncrasies are taken into account and people deal with one another differently according to their judgement of what is appropriate in each circumstance. There is consequently more room for discretion. Although Toulmin did not ground his argument on Wittgenstein's dictum, his argument is supported by the observation that discretion is needed to determine the application of rules because the rules themselves do not make this apparent. Toulmin argued that justice results from the application of both the rule of law and equity. The 'ethics of strangers', in the way that Toulmin describes them, are not workable. Rules require at least interpretation and some discretion in their application.

While I agree with Toulmin's argument on the need for discretion, I have misgivings about the point of balance between reliance on rules and reliance on discretion. Toulmin appears to have put greater confidence in the 'ethics of intimates' and in discretion. In my view discretion can also lead to tyranny. Davis warned that 'the exercise of discretion may mean either beneficence or tyranny, either justice or injustice, either reasonableness or arbitrariness' (1969: 3). The 'ethics of intimates' can rely entirely on discretion and support a *tyranny of the powerful*. This is as objectionable, if not more so, than the 'tyranny of principles'. The ethics of intimates within a family, for example, can result in the abuse of the physically weaker members – most often women and children.

The point needs to be made that the 'ethics of intimates' depends on the magnanimity of the powerful for its equity. The assumption is usually made that parents have the better interests of their children at heart in the exercise of their discretion. Such discretion can be withdrawn by government agencies when parents do not act in the interests of their child. In other relationships, the assumption may not be warranted in the first place. It is simply not appropriate to rely on the discretion of those in power when their interests are in conflict with the interests of those that they are required to protect. As I have stated already, it cannot be assumed that researchers will put the interests of subjects ahead of their own needs. The assumptions of the 'ethics of intimates' in these circumstances have been shown by many instances in the history of human experimentation to be a 'tyranny of the powerful'. Discretion then, needs to be constrained by some rules and principles. Annas, an American professor of law and ethics, warned that without substantive principles and rules, medical law and medical ethics would become 'simply the arbitrary exercise of power' (Annas, 1988: xiii). The suggestion is sometimes made that, because of the underlying difficulty in agreeing on principles, we should put our confidence in discretion. In response to this, Annas made a plea for developing substantive rules for decision-making. Even though this may be a complex and frustrating task it is 'one that is worthy of law and social policy' (p. xiii).

I have canvassed the arguments for substantive principles and rules on the one hand, and the arguments for discretion in applying rules on the other. If we accept that some research on human subjects is acceptable in some circumstances then there needs to be a balance. Davis (1969: 42) concluded that 'elimination of all discretionary power is both impossible and undesirable. The sensible goal is development of a proper balance between rule and discretion'. I acknowledge the need for substantive principles and rules for the protection of subjects of experiments. I also acknowledge the need for discretion in applying those principles and rules. We need both clearly defined rules and principles and an unbiased authority with the discretion to apply the rules to particular situations.

In human experimentation, research ethics committees are ideal candidates to exercise discretion in the application of principles and rules to particular research proposals. This discretionary function is their *raison d'être*.

Discretion and consistency

Davis was of the view that there should be an *appropriate degree* of consistency in the exercise of discretion (Davis, 1969: 106–7; also Stewart, 1975: 1699–1700). On the one hand, consistency leads to greater equality and is a limit on arbitrariness in decision-making. On the other, however, a requirement for consistency has the effect of making binding precedents and can lead to rigidity in decision-making and an inability to take advantage of changing circumstances and improved understanding (Davis, 1969). The High Court of Australia has stated that the 'point of preserving the width of discretion . . . is that it maximizes the possibility of doing justice in every case. But the need for consistency . . . provides an important countervailing consideration.'[8] This is the issue for research ethics committees.

Research ethics committees in most countries exercise broad discretion and are free to come to different decisions on the same issue. In Australia, the NHMRC has stated explicitly that the decisions made by a committee in one institution could be quite different 'from ethical judgements being made about the same matter' by a committee in another institution. This would allow for differences in 'cultural and social attitudes' between one locality and another (NHMRC, 1986a: 236). In my view this is overstating the importance of differences in attitudes between local communities. Hospitals are not necessarily local in their operation; similarly, research institutes and universities are not tied to their locale, instead drawing their staff and students from across the nation and abroad.

The real concern, I believe, is that some form of control would necessarily accompany a demand for consistency. It would establish a need either for binding precedents or for some form of national control and lead to rigidity in decision-making. However, the present lack of consistency can lead to inequality between different researchers in that one researcher might have a research proposal accepted by one committee whereas another researcher may have the same project rejected by a different committee. The lack of consistency can, and does lead to researchers 'forum-shopping' for an agreeable committee, and to difficulties in gaining consistent approvals for multi-centred studies. Some balance is needed between the extremes.

In my view there is a need for a specified minimum standard of research ethics. Davis referred to the 'confining and structuring of discretion' (1969: 225). The degree of discretion exercised by committees should not mean that some committees can approve research on human subjects that is below the minimum ethical standard for such research. This position highlights the need for education of committee members and for researchers to establish those minimum standards in practice. It also requires an active national body to oversee the system of review and provide specificity in research guidelines.

8. *Norbis v. Norbis* (1986: 519) per Mason and Deane JJ.

Specificity in guidelines

In the United States and in Australia the criticism has been made that too much emphasis is given to discretionary decision-making. One of the criticisms made of the early development of review by committee in the United States was that too much faith was placed in peer review and not enough in developing substantive rules (Katz, 1987: 3). In Australia a similar criticism was made early in the development of review committees about the failure of the NHMRC to develop principles and its reliance on 'administration of ethics' (Osborne, 1983a).

Although there are substantive rules incorporated in the regulations and national codes in most countries, these rules still leave a great deal to the discretion of committees and there are areas which still need the development of substantive rules: for example, compensation and treatment for subjects harmed in the course of an experiment; and rules about the guarantee of continued treatment for subjects, such as persons with HIV/AIDS, who have been included in drug trials. The development of rules for the ethical conduct of research should extend beyond the relevant authority and seek advice from consumer groups (for example, the Consumers' Health Forum in Australia). This process should be part of a public debate. The purpose is to enunciate clear principles and rules that give priority to the interests of subjects of experiments, while making more explicit the extent to which research with any potential for harm would be allowed. The debate generated by this process would have a positive educational impact both on researchers and on potential subjects.

Discretion, beneficence and autonomy

Committees are acting for subjects in a beneficial role to ensure that risk of harm is within reasonable limits. Part of their consideration is whether risk of harm to subjects is justified by potential benefit to others. The potential beneficiaries in this case are 'future persons' except in the case of so-called 'therapeutic research'. Even in therapeutic research, the major justification is the potential benefit for future patients. Subjects are therefore protected from potentially harmful experiments by a committee and are only asked to take part in an experiment after a committee has decided that there is a potential benefit to be had from the study.

One commentator has argued against such paternalism because it deprives subjects of the opportunity to volunteer for risky experiments or even death in an altruistic sacrifice for the benefit of others (Battin, 1985). Given the history of exploitation of research subjects and the potential for abuse, I believe her argument is naïve. It fails to take into account the exploitation of the altruism of volunteers by experimenters. The argument rests on an assumption that research is simply motivated by a researcher's desire to help others. It ignores the conflict of interests created by the researcher's personal interest in the research. It also assumes that research can be equated with benefit to others. This is a potential that needs to be established by more than the optimism of the researcher to justify subjects being put at risk of harm.

Nevertheless, the issues arising from HIV/AIDS research and research on Aborigines (discussed in the following chapter) suggest that research ethics committees need to consider the interests of subjects from their point of view. It may be that subjects, or their representatives, consider that their interests are best served by volunteering for 'risky research'. For this reason I have argued that an appropriate balance between the interests of researchers and subjects can best be found by equal representation of researchers and subjects on committees of review. I also consider that this is an appropriate mechanism for deciding whether the principles of bene-ficence or autonomy should predominate in any particular case.

CONCLUSION

Society has a role in delineating the extent of scientific investigation on human subjects and for ensuring that there are mechanisms in place to give some assurance that those limits are adhered to. Having identified the principles and rules, there is still a role for discretion in applying them. This discretion is necessary because rules need application and rules and principles conflict with each other. It is important that this discretion be exercised in a manner that is balanced between the interests of science and subjects. Researchers are not sufficiently impartial to be relied on for the protection of subjects according to abstract rules and principles. Ideally, there would be a body of impartial decision-makers to define the appropriate limits in each case and to ensure that these limits are adhered to. Impartiality is an ideal that may not be achievable because scientists and researchers are needed by 'non-scientific' decision-makers to help them understand the ramifications of the research being considered. In the remaining chapters of this book, I develop the suggestion that an alternative is to require that ethics committees be constituted so that they are collectively balanced between the interests of science and the interests of subjects.

PART FOUR

Politics of Review by Committee

CHAPTER 7

A Political Balance between Science, Society and the Subject

This chapter explores the various interests involved in experimentation on human subjects. Essentially, these are *science, society* and the *subject* which have been described as the 'three major social interests or values' in human experimentation (Curran, 1968). In order to reconcile these interests it is necessary to understand the values and motivations represented by each. Ultimately a balance has to be struck between these interests – and this is essentially a political process.

The obvious conflict of interest in experimentation on human subjects is that doctors conducting research are caught between their role as healer and their role as dispassionate researcher. In a 1990 judgment of the Supreme Court of California, it was stated that 'a physician who treats a patient in whom he also has a research interest has potentially conflicting loyalties'.[1] The reason for this is that the goal of research is the 'production of generalizable knowledge, not primarily the promotion of individual health' (Appelbaum, Lidz and Meisel, 1987: 238). In research on human subjects, many have commented on a tension between the researcher's commitment to the welfare of the research subject and a competing commitment to science and society.[2] Jonas (1969: 220) has referred to this polarity as the 'individual versus society' and as a perceived tension between private and public welfare. Others have referred to 'individual rights versus societal rights' and the favouring of 'future over present lives' (McDermott, 1968: 29; Capron, 1983: 391).

Implicit in both the Declaration of Helsinki and the Australian National Health and Medical Research Council (NHMRC) Statement on Human Experimentation is a conflict between the interests of

---

1. *Moore v. Regents of the University of California,* p. 484.
2. See, for example, Katz (1972: 728–33), Churchill (1980), Capron (1986: 217) and Delgado and Leskovac (1986: 97–8).

the subject and the interest of science.[3] Both dealt with the conflict by giving priority to the rights of the subject, and both are representative of the view that the subjects of research require protection above and beyond the conscience of the individual investigator (as compared with Beecher, 1966b).

TENSION BETWEEN SCIENCE, SOCIETY AND THE SUBJECT

There is a difficulty in representing the conflict as being between two widely divergent elements: science and society at one extreme and the subject at the other. As shown below, the assumption that the interests of the scientist and society coincide is open to challenge. This view of the scientist derives from an ideal view of science as a disinterested and objective activity. The assumption is made that experimentation and science are for the good of society. However, scientists are not necessarily motivated by the good of society.

The motivation for research may be a desire for knowledge or a desire to 'help others'. However, research is also motivated by a desire to 'add to the scientist's reputation and academic standing' (Delgado and Leskovac, 1986: 97–8). The latter underscores the scientist's personal interest in the outcome of scientific activity quite apart from any noble societal goal. Researchers, in common with all human beings, are susceptible to the distortions that accompany self-interest. In addition, researchers are usually supported by institutions that gain in reputation through the success of their research staff in attracting funds and publishing research results. These institutions can be characterised by particular values. Accompanying scientific activity is a world-view and a set of values that measure success in terms of scientific output. These values are not necessarily shared by other members of society (Albury, 1983).

Furthermore, some research on human subjects has a commercial potential. For example, drug trials to establish the efficacy of a therapeutic agent and experimentation with recombinant DNA both have the potential for large profits. In the case of *Moore v. the Regents of the University of California* it was claimed that the market for a patented cell line would exceed 3 billion dollars. Moore

3. Declaration of Helsinki (1983, Principle I.5); NHMRC Statement on Human Experimentation (1992, Supplementary note 1.6 (ii)) [see Appendix 2].

unsuccessfully claimed in the Supreme Court of California that he was entitled to some of the royalties or profits from the cell line developed from hairy-cell leukaemia tissue taken from his body.

A great deal of research is carried out by, or sponsored by, large international drug companies. The potential profit from research activities obviously places additional pressure on researchers. It is therefore naïve to view the scientific activity as purely objective and disinterested, operating simply for the good of others and sharing the same goals, attitudes and values as others in society.

The relationship between science, society and the subject is more complex than can be represented by considering science and society on the one hand and the rights of the individual subject on the other. Each of the interests represented by science, society and the subject represent different values, claims, interests and needs.

SOCIETY

It has been observed that 'surprisingly little attention is paid to the general justification for involving human subjects in research' (Beauchamp and Walters, 1982: 503). In many of the codes of ethics for research, there is an assumption that the interests of science coincide with the interests of society. The Declaration of Helsinki refers to 'the interest of science and society'. The Royal College of Physicians guidelines for research state that 'research benefits society' (1990a: 3). However, the assumption is open to question.

Hans Jonas, a philosopher writing on the ethics of human experimentation in the 1960s, challenged the view that 'science benefits society'. He challenged the polemical use of the term 'society'. Implicit is an assumption that the benefits of research are experienced by the whole of society whereas the burdens are suffered by individual subjects. The assumption wrongly casts the issue as 'public interest' against 'private interest' and as 'the common good against the individual good' (Jonas, 1969: 227). It is not society as a whole but some individuals who may benefit from research into particular diseases. The issue then is the conflict between the search for potential benefits for individual sufferers of a disease as against the potential harms, or the risk of harm, to individual subjects of research. In experimentation on human subjects, society cannot be assumed to be aligned with the interests of either science or the subject. It presumably has an interest in both.

Justifications for research

Many of the justifications offered for research are in terms of obligations or benefits to society. The grounds for societal justifications are examined as follows.

Social contract

One justification for experimentation on human subjects is that a 'social contract' between the individual and society carries with it certain obligations such as the obligation to contribute to research from which all members of society benefit. Jonas (1969: 224) referred to this as a 'fiction of political theory' which took individual freedom as fundamental and justified the limitation of this freedom (or the imposition of an obligation) by some benefit to all. The 'contract' metaphor, however, implies a reciprocal relationship. It may be appropriate when one's rights or freedoms are forgone in the anticipation of a benefit: for example, giving up individual choice over the 'rules of the road' promises the benefit of relative orderliness on the roads; paying tax is an obligation on the individual who benefits by the services provided. But giving up one's rights to inviolability in a non-therapeutic experiment carries with it no corresponding benefit. In this situation, the contract metaphor is not appropriate. There is no valuable consideration – an altruistic pleasure perhaps (such as the pleasures of contributing mentioned above), but this is more like the pleasure from giving than from exchange. For this reason the philosopher May prefers the term 'covenant' rather than 'contract' to describe the voluntary 'donative' element in a doctor's relationship with a patient and the corresponding giving by the patient in return (May, 1977).

The war analogy

Another justification for the right of society to enlist the support of volunteers in experimentation on human subjects has been drawn from a war analogy. Jonas discussed the extremes of war during which individual rights are abrogated in favour of communal rights. Society is perceived to have the right to require the young and fit to put their lives at great risk by going to war. In this situation, consent is not relevant. Young men are conscripted whether they like it or not. It may be possible to establish a claim for exemption on the grounds of conscientious objection but this does not imply that all those sent to war have consented (Dyck, 1970: 35). Few in this society would regard participation in medical experimentation as an obligation of the sort that might justify conscription in time of war.[4]

War has been used to justify much gratuitous cruelty in the name of science (see Chapter 1). However, there is no good reason for exempting experiments on human subjects in wartime from the same principles that apply in peacetime. The issue is whether the risk of harm to these particular subjects can be justified by the potential benefit to others. Injuries to Australian soldiers in the mustard gas experiments could not be justified by any potential benefit to Australia in having an effective chemical weapon. In my view, even the exigencies of war do not vindicate the deliberate and knowing exposure of human subjects to extreme risks of harm in an experiment designed to test the effectiveness of weapons.

For Jonas, there would have to be an 'extraordinary danger' affecting the whole community to justify suspending otherwise inviolable rights (1969: 228). Once the danger was past there could no longer be any justification for this abrogation of rights. A similar argument for the abrogation of people's rights has been advanced for the quarantine of those with HIV and AIDS on the grounds that the threat of AIDS is so extreme that sufferers should be isolated to stop the spread of the disease. The argument has been rejected on account of it being both unethical and impractical. Few have been willing to justify the suffering which would be caused to those with the disease. The same rebuttal applies to suggestions that rights of persons with HIV/AIDS be abrogated in favour of the need for research. People with HIV/AIDS may become unco-operative and withdraw from voluntary treatment and reject behavioural change programs if there was a possibility of enforced participation in research. Any abrogation of research subjects' rights in favour of research would have to be justified in terms of the value of the information far outweighing the potential suffering or loss of rights to the subjects. It is accepted by many that non-identifying epidemiological research is justified on this ground.[5] In my view,

4. An exception is Carmi who argued that there should be 'compulsory experimentation' on the ground that more deaths result from disease than from war (reported in Howard-Jones, 1982: 1440).
5. See, for example, Bayer, Levine and Murray (1984) and Bayer, Levine and Wolf (1986). In addition, an edition of *Law, Medicine and Health Care* (1991, vol. 19, no. 3–4) is devoted to 'Research on human populations: national and international ethical guidelines' and contains good discussion of this issue.

however, this concession to epidemiological research should be made with caution – particularly in relation to the practical implementation of the requirement for non-identification.

Progress

Another justification for experimentation on human subjects is that it is necessary for the improvement of health and the progress of medical science. The Declaration of Helsinki states that: 'Medical progress is based on research which ultimately must rest in part on experimentation involving human subjects.'[6] The Australian NHMRC Statement on Human Experimentation (1992) includes the assertion that: 'Planned experimentation on human beings is necessary for the improvement of human health.' Implicit in this is an argument that we should improve the conditions in which we live, both for those among us in need, and for those who will follow. This includes finding means for reducing disease and disability. Experimentation is necessary to achieve this goal and is therefore in the interests of society.

For Jonas, however, this was not a fundamental obligation. The goal of science in this sense is melioristic and gratuitous. Progress is an expansive goal not dissimilar from the economic imperative to produce more and improve our standard of living. It does not seek to preserve the 'existing good'. Jonas argued that there are more fundamental obligations to fulfil. For example, 'our dependants have a right to be left an unplundered planet; they do not have a right to new miracle cures'. This is a theme which is common to both science and economics. Jonas claimed that progress is an 'optional goal' and slower progress does not threaten society. What is more threatening to society is the erosion of fundamental values. Society cannot afford the loss of virtue, compassion or justice. Experimentation on human subjects should not put the fundamental values, such as the inviolability of the individual, at risk. These values are more important than the goal of prolonging life (Jonas, 1969: 229-31, 245).

To put the argument in its most extreme form, Jonas contended that we do not need medical progress to stave off death. In his view, society 'is built on the balance of death and birth decreed by the order of life'. While not being insensitive to human misfortune, each of

6. Introduction to the Declaration of Helsinki as amended in Venice, 1983.

us has to die from 'some ill or other'. He added that it 'cannot be the aim of progress to abolish the lot of mortality' (1969: 228, 245).

Establishing efficacy of treatment
Contrary to Jonas and other critics of medical research who were concerned about the harm to an individual, Eisenberg, a professor of psychiatry at Harvard, considered that greater harm was done by a failure to carry out research. In his view, critics failed to appreciate the extent to which common forms of treatment rest on custom rather than on scientifically established evidence. Consequently they failed to understand the need for properly conducted trials to establish the efficacy of accepted remedies. He cited bloodletting as an example of a harmful practice adopted by the most respected of physicians of the day, only to be effectively challenged by careful experimentation. He claimed that medical practice needed 'exacting scrutiny' which would result in gains to public safety that would far outweigh any gains from a 'restrictive approach to medical research'. In Eisenberg's view it is everyone's responsibility to enhance the quality of life by 'sharing in the risks of the search to diminish human suffering' (Eisenberg, 1977).

Eisenberg's response does not deal directly with Jonas's point that progress is assumed to be a good thing. He has simply restated a belief in progress. Nevertheless, the argument that risks of harm to human subjects are justified by improvements to health and living standards appears to be the only acceptable justification from a societal perspective. This justification is not sufficient in all situations. It needs to be considered in relation to other interests which may be regarded as important.

Society's dual interest

Any assumption about the views of 'society' is clearly a simplification. Society is not an amorphous whole – there are many voices. There have been times when the predominant voices have been on the side of medical progress. There have also been many revelations of unethical research in this century that have led to an outcry against abuse of subjects of experimentation. During the Second World War, for example, the interests of science predominated. After the war there was a resurgence of concern for the subject. There were also changing attitudes expressed toward human experimentation by the courts. As discussed in Chapter 5, prior to 1930, English and American courts were opposed to experimentation. This attitude has shifted to cautious acceptance of human experimentation (within certain limits).

Society then, cannot be assumed to be aligned with the interests of either science or the subject. It is like a swinging voter in an election who may vote for one or other party depending on the issues of the time. Groups with different interests in society may swing the balance toward or away from support for research on human subjects. For example, those desperately seeking relief from the consequences of HIV infection may urge a 'pro-research' attitude, while those affected by an unethical research program, such as the women deprived of treatment in the New Zealand cervical cancer case (discussed in Chapter 3), may promote a cautionary attitude to research. This perspective gives recognition to the inevitable political nature of a balance between the interests of science and subjects.

SCIENCE

There are three distinct elements in the interests of science in human experimentation: first, science as a disinterested pursuit of knowledge; second, science as potentially yielding benefits to others; and third, the scientist as a human being in need of achieving personal goals and ambitions (Curran, 1969; also Fletcher, 1967: 628).

Science as a pursuit of knowledge

Curran, a respected Harvard professor of health law, considered that the promotion of science served the interest of society and deserved support in much the same way that industry is regarded as having a right 'to operate and to prosper in the general interests of the community' (Curran, 1968; reprinted 1977: 297, 300). This defence of research is in general terms and not necessarily dependent on there being a directly applicable outcome. Although some research may lead to benefits to others, much research is exploratory without any identifiable application. Classical experiments, such as those of William Harvey in the seventeenth century which demonstrated the blood circulatory system and showed the heart to be like a pump, were prompted by a desire for knowledge rather than a desire to benefit others (Ackerknecht, 1982: 113–16). Admittedly, most of these experiments were on animals and cadavers. However, they illustrate the fact that in medicine, as in all science, the pursuit of knowledge has been regarded as important, in and of itself (Churchill, 1980: 216). One of the needs of science as a disinterested pursuit of truth is said to be 'freedom of scientific inquiry'. As Australian philosopher Singer has pointed out, this demand must be accepted in a free society in so far as it means the freedom to ask questions. In his view it cannot substantiate a claim for scientists to experiment on their subjects in any way in which they see fit (Singer, 1989: 10; also Fried, 1978: 699). Science still needs to be conducted in a manner that is not harmful to other people. The pursuit of knowledge is only one of the interests to be taken into account. In experiments on human subjects the welfare of the subject is also regarded as very important.

Science as yielding benefits to others

Most commentators accept that research which yields no obvious benefit to society should not be allowed to put its subjects at risk of harm (Capron, 1986: 223). For this reason the Nuremberg Code required that the 'experiment should be such as to yield fruitful results for the good of society' and the Declaration of Helsinki required that 'the importance of the objective is in proportion to the inherent risk to the subject'.[7] These research codes reflect the importance placed by society on the welfare of the subject. Thus, while research as a contribution to knowledge is a worthy goal in and of itself, this justification can only be relied on where there is no likelihood of harm, or where any minimal harm which might result is of little concern to potential subjects.

Needs of the researcher

It is acknowledged that science would not exist apart from the activity of scientists. However, separate consideration of the interests of science and scientists highlights the human aspect of scientific interest and places it in perspective with other interests in human experimentation. While society, or at least some individuals within it, *may* benefit from research, there are very direct and tangible

---

7. Declaration of Helsinki as amended in Venice (1983: Principle, I.4).

benefits for the researcher. The theologian Ramsey wrote that 'it is not only that medical benefits are attained by research but also that a man rises to the top in medicine by the success and significance of his research' (Ramsay, 1970). For this reason the scientist cannot be regarded as a disinterested party.

The researcher's interest in his or her own advancement and standing may be an added pressure to cut corners and act in ways that are unsafe. The case of Janet Parker is an unfortunate illustration of the forces that can operate to push research beyond safe limits. Parker was a staff photographer assisting research into smallpox who died after being infected with smallpox. It was not stated how she contracted the disease but it was known that the laboratory where she worked was under threat of imminent closure. Cheston and McFate (1980), who analysed this case, considered that 'dual pressures of the desire for scientific success and humanitarianism' led to 'elementary safety precautions [that] were either wilfully or accidentally ignored'. This neglect also cost another life. The scientist who was head of the laboratory committed suicide shortly after Parker's cause of death was confirmed.

Instances of blatant disregard for subjects' welfare have understandably gained the most attention. However, it is likely that more harm has been caused (in total) by researchers who mean no harm but are unaware of the extent of risk to their patients. Their bias toward achieving the goals of their research may lead them to minimise, in their own thinking, the risks inherent in their research and give a disproportionate value to the research enterprise. It has been observed that 'researchers are "true believers" ' who think that a 'true contradiction cannot exist between the protection of human subjects and the advancement of . . . medicine' (Ramsey, 1974; and Churchill, 1980: 217).

Scientists are as capable as any other interest group of pursuing their own interests to the exclusion of the interests of others. The psychiatrist Eisenberg, writing on the ethics of experimentation, argued that medical researchers are no worse than 'lawyers or philosophers' nor are they any better. In his view researchers 'are simply human; that is to say, fallible' (Eisenberg, 1977; reprinted 1982: 520). What makes the issue so much more stark for medical researchers than for lawyers or philosophers, however, is that the consequences of human fallibility in medical research can be extreme.

SUBJECTS

Identifying the subject's interest

While it is apparent that the researcher may have much to gain through engaging in research, it is not readily apparent what the subject has to gain. This is more obviously true in research that has no therapeutic potential for the participant volunteers. Delgado and Leskovac (1986: 97–8) have made this point succinctly in stating that the subject 'ordinarily has little interest in the researcher's professional reputation, academic advancement, or ability to obtain new grants'. Although subjects may have no interest in the researcher's advancement, it must be assumed that they have an interest in their own welfare.

There have been various answers given to the question 'what does the research subject get out of it?'. These include 'the privilege of volunteering for medical studies'; and 'prestige and satisfaction of having made "a contribution to the advancement of knowledge" '.[8] The National Commission study in the United States found that the desire to help science, or the desire to help people with similar problems, was the second most common reason given by subjects for volunteering for medical research. The most common reason was that there could be some benefit for them medically, psychologically, or educationally (National Commission for the Protection of Human Subjects, 1978c: 1–84). An important finding is that patients tend not to distinguish between research and treatment, and hold out hope for an improvement in their condition from a research procedure even when they are told it is not beneficial to them (Fletcher, 1967: 635). Appelbaum, Lidz and Meisel noted that there are difficulties in adequately informing patients about research in medical-care settings where patients expect that procedures are carried out for their personal care (1987: 246–7). An example of this is a study in the United States based on interviews with women in early stages of labour, who were subjects in a study of a new drug to induce labour and childbirth (Gray, 1975). It was found that 39 per cent of them did not know that they were subjects in a drug trial; another 43 per cent knew that a drug was being tested but mistakenly assumed that it was the best one available even though

8. For example, McDonald (1967), Hodges and Bean (1967) and Parsons (1969: 339–40).

the point of the research was to test the effectiveness and safety of the new drug. I am not suggesting that these figures are typical of research on human subjects. What the study highlights are the difficulties and inappropriateness of relying on consent from patients for protection of their own interests.

Patients' acceptance of the request to volunteer does not appear to depend on a careful assessment of the proposal. In another study it was found that 71 per cent of patients had made their decision to participate in research before being given the relevant information (Benson, Roth and Winslade, 1985: 1337). Even when there are potential benefits to subjects there may be some unanticipated loss for the patient in volunteering, such as the loss of the right to select among treatments in a randomised trial (Appelbaum, Lidz and Meisel, 1987: 239).

Subjects may also be motivated by money. In Australia, as in other countries, the guidelines on research state that payment should not be so high as to amount to an inducement (NHMRC Statement on Human Experimentation, 1982: Section 13). However, some studies offer money which does act as an inducement. A personal experience illustrates this point. In October 1991, I received a long-distance telephone call from my daughter in London who had run out of money on her travels. She was contemplating 'volunteering' for drug trials and had been offered £250 for three days (10 a.m–6 p.m) or £1,300 for ten days in a live-in study. Both offers related to the testing of drugs. I sent her the money she needed. Clearly, the reimbursement offered by the drug company acted as an inducement. Dooley (1991: 20) has reported that in the Republic of Ireland the majority of volunteers for non-therapeutic drug trials are students and the unemployed. He considered that this was 'potentially coercive because of the poverty of the participants'. The National Commission study in the United States found that 17 per cent of subjects gave financial reimbursement as the main reason for volunteering (1978c: 1–84). For many, such as impecunious students, the unemployed, young travellers and many other 'volunteers', money is the major reason for their volunteering (Robertson, 1986).[9]

While research may have a potential benefit for subjects, all experimentation has some unpredictability and risk associated with

9. The case of *Halushka v. University of Saskatchewan*, which involved a university student who volunteered for money, is discussed in Chapter 6.

it. It is the subject who bears the risk, and the benefits claimed for their participation are intangible and not commensurate (in most cases) with those risks. Two American studies found that the risk of harm to subjects was slight,[10] but Annas (1980) has disputed the findings on the grounds that they depended on researchers' reports on subjects harmed. A report of six studies 'that could predictably be expected to cause harm' from the editors of the journal *Laboratory and Clinical Medicine* is of concern although the editors note that these were only a 'tiny fraction' of the papers received (Daniel et al., 1988). Even if it is conceded that the risk of injury is very low, the outcome could be catastrophic for the subject injured. Often there is no guarantee of compensation unless the harm can be attributed to the researcher's negligence. As shown in Chapter 5, this is often difficult to establish.

Jonas contended that the interests of the subject and the interests of society are in no sense equivalent. From the point of view of the experimenter, the subject is a token – a symbol from which to generalise. But procedures carried out on experimental subjects are also definitive actions taken in a real person's life and 'not even the noblest purpose abrogates the obligations this involves' (Jonas, 1969: 220, 235). For the researcher, the relationship with the subject is impersonal and instrumental in serving the ends of the research whereas for the subjects it is a personal experience. This is conveyed in a poem (see next page) which was written by a young woman who participated as a subject in a drug trial for treatment for a chronic viral illness. The drug regime required treatment in hospital for 48 hours on three occasions. Volunteering for an experiment had several unforeseen adverse consequences for this subject including a loss of income. It had been necessary for her to return to hospital for treatment as she had been randomly assigned to the control group and her first three stays in hospital were to satisfy research (but not treatment) requirements. Some of the adverse consequences could have been avoided by a more rigorous review by the relevant ethics committee. Some of them, however, as the poem conveys, were the result of the impersonal way in which the trial was conducted.

Vulnerability to exploitation is a part of the reason that codes of ethics for experimentation on human subjects recognise a primacy

---

10. Cardon, Dommel and Trumble (1976) and The National Commission for the Protection of Human Subjects (1978b: 63).

of the rights of the subject. In the Declaration of Helsinki it was stated as a 'Basic Principle' that 'concern for the interests of the subject must always prevail over the interest of science and society' (1983: Principle I.5). Similarly, the Australian NHMRC Statement on Human Experimentation has given precedence to the rights of subjects of research (1992: Suppl. Note 1.6(ii)) [see Appendix 2].

Subject

I feel the blankness of meaningless combinations
of letters and numbers
Which say who I am according to them
No woman
No person
A count
A number of cells
A lack of antibodies
A statistic
A textbook case

No one wants to help me
To me to help
To help
They want me
To help
Them
To make discoveries
To write research papers
To make them famous

They don't even want
to know my name
To know me
To know at all
That those counts of cells
Belong to a body
Who is a person
Who has suffered and is tired
Tired of all this poking and testing and number counting
Who is just tired

Anonymous, August 1987

Until recently, the main interest of subjects was seen to be protection from harm. However, claims from two groups of subjects have made it apparent that the interests of subjects may be much broader than protection from harm. These groups are subjects of anthropological research, and subjects of HIV and AIDS studies.

Australian Aborigines

In 1988, the NHMRC published a report containing the concerns of Aborigines about research (NHMRC, 1988b). The main concerns were that researchers had been insensitive to the differences in cultural mores, customs, beliefs and attitudes between Aboriginal and other Australian communities. For example, medical researchers have (in the past) taken biological samples from the bodies of Aborigines, and anthropologists have published photographs of Aborigines who have later died. Both the taking of biological specimens and the depiction of deceased persons are contrary to Aboriginal mores.

Aboriginal representatives considered that research aims, methodology, and the use made of research results, took insufficient account of Aboriginal perspectives. It was claimed that there had not been enough consultation between researchers and Aborigines and that they had consulted inappropriate Aboriginal representatives. There had also been insufficient research on issues of concern to Aboriginal communities.

The report on Aboriginal research dealt with six major issues: the process of consultation; social and gender issues; communication and consent; community benefit and employment of local people; ownership and publication of materials; and exploitation of community resources. The NHMRC responded by suggesting that research ethics committees should require evidence from researchers that they had conducted a proper process of consultation with Aboriginal communities. Committees also need to ensure that research is monitored to make sure that it complies 'with ethical commitments' (NHMRC, 1988b: 9).

Some of the matters discussed in the report had not been agreed upon by the Aboriginal community and remained contentious. For example, the NHMRC considered that researchers have a duty to publish material that is accurate and helpful. Aboriginal representatives on the other hand, considered that material relating to their culture is sensitive and should only be published by agreement with Aborigines themselves. In effect, they saw the ownership of that material as lying with Aborigines and thus demanded the right to withhold publication. Clearly, this is an example of scientific and academic values being at odds with traditional Aboriginal values.

This report recognised that the aims of scientific and anthropological research may be in opposition to the interests of Aborigines. The purpose for which the research is conducted and the use to which the results will be put is not purely a scientific question but is also political. The report foreshadowed a significant concession by the NHMRC, namely that the interests of scientists in these circumstances may have to take second place to the beliefs and customs of Aborigines. More recently, interim guidelines have been approved by the National Health and Medical Research Council in consultation with Aboriginal and Torres Strait Islanders which state that 'the ownership of raw data or the rights to publication of research findings . . . must be discussed and negotiated . . . before the research begins' (NHMRC, 1991a). At the time of going to press, the guidelines were awaiting approval by the Aboriginal and Torres Strait Islander Commission before they would take effect (NHMRC, 1991b). It is still open to representatives of the Commission to require greater control over publication.

The Aboriginal people have challenged the right of scientists and anthropologists to define their reality within scientific terms and the right of researchers to assume that truth, from a Western perspective, has a superior claim over the rights of Aborigines to define their own reality and be free from interference and exploitation by researchers.

Aborigines have also challenged the right of researchers and ethics committees to decide the issues by their own processes. The 'Advisory Notes on Aboriginal Research' observes that the 'style and process of decision making' in Aboriginal communities is different because of 'major social and cultural values underpinning them' (NHMRC, 1988b: 13). In other words, it is not just substantive issues of research ethics that are at stake. There is also a difference between cultures in the manner of resolving differences and a reluctance on the part of Aboriginal representatives to accept decisions made by others on behalf of Aboriginal communities.

The political reality is that the demands of Aborigines have to be accommodated by the representatives of science. The concern of researchers is that any concessions could have far-reaching consequences. It could be a challenge to suggest that both the purpose and methodology of research on Aborigines has to change to conform to Aboriginal concerns. Researchers argue that there has to be a limit to any trade-off because, at some point, the concessions demanded could endanger the nature of research itself – the research methodology, for example, may have to be so modified that the questions it sought to answer have to go unasked, or the findings have to be so specific that they would have no generalisable application.

HIV and AIDS research

Representatives of people with HIV and AIDS are claiming an active role in determining the way in which research is conducted. This is especially so in relation to research into new pharmaceutical treatments for these diseases. Those affected with AIDS, and many of those who are HIV sero-positive, are not likely to benefit from treatments that take a long time to be developed. Many hope to have the opportunity of possible benefit from the testing of new drugs at an early stage in the development process. They consider that they have little to lose by being research subjects. This claim could be seen as undermining previous assumptions about the need to protect subjects from harm in that some of the remedies to be tested may be extremely toxic. In my view it is simply an illustration of another important principle: that subjects ought to be able to participate in decisions affecting their own lives.

The same activists have opposed the use of control groups in HIV drug trials because it means that there is no possibility of therapeutic advantage for those research subjects. These arguments have been challenged as a 'therapeutic misconception' (Appelbaum, Roth, Lidz et al., 1987) but the political reality is that AIDS activists are demanding (and have been given) a say in the conduct of research. For example, in the United States, members of ACT UP (AIDS Coalition to Unleash Power) negotiated with a drug company and the Food and Drug Administration over the testing of DDI (dideoxyinosine) and took part in the design of the protocol and monitoring of drug trials (Spiers, 1991c: 4). There may be some advantages for the researchers in that the process of consultation can lead to committed subjects (C. Levine, 1988: 173). There are, however, concerns that the 'politicising' of drug testing with treatments for HIV/AIDS undermines scientific validity and efficacy. Spiers, a philosopher and AIDS activist, has claimed that community consultation should have a greater role. He added, however, that he did not believe that AIDS activists wanted to see 'the scientific integrity of drug trials compromised' (Spiers, 1991c: 5). Nevertheless,

Spiers was critical of 'adhering slavishly' to rigid scientific standards that had more to do with 'abstract and abstruse' ideas on scientific procedure than with the needs of people with HIV or AIDS. He referred to a distinction between 'fastidious and pragmatic clinical trials' in suggesting that a compromise could be arrived at between 'pure' scientific research and the needs of 'sick people living (and dying) in the real world' (Spiers, 1991: 8). He acknowledged that this was a challenge to traditional notions about science and scientific methodology. From that perspective the politics of drug testing had little to do with scientific epistemology. While admitting that 'community consultation is a desirable, but not a critically important element' in the scientific process, Spiers pointed out that, because of suspicion toward the medical establishment among people with HIV/AIDS, consultation was politically essential for the success of trials (1991a: 9–10).

RECONCILING SCIENCE, SOCIETY AND THE SUBJECT

Given that the interests of science, society and subjects do not coincide, some reconciliation between competing interests must be sought.

Political balance

Many have written of the need for a balance between the need for research and the need for protection of the individual who serves as subject.[11] Among these writers, Curran (1968) stated the need for a 'balance between the rights of the individual and the needs of society', and American philosopher Toulmin referred to a 'balance that has to be struck between different rights and claims, interests and responsibilities' (Toulmin, 1981: 32, 37).

Researchers may wish to treat any concessions made to subjects of anthropological research and research on HIV/AIDS as exceptions to the general rule which requires thoroughly validated scientific studies. In my view, however, these two areas make it obvious that finding a balance between the interests of science, subjects and society will always be a political process. What has made the political dimension more obvious in the case of research on Aborigines

---

11. For example, Katz (1972: 727), The National Commission for the Protection of Human Subjects (1978b: 1) and Woltjen (1986).

is that this group has been subjected to so much research that the people are no longer willing to be treated as passive objects in the process. In the case of those with HIV and AIDS, their health situation is so desperate and their number so large that they also have not been content to be treated as objects of investigation. A major factor is that in each case the research is of concern to groups with some political power. Both HIV/AIDS activists and Aborigines can draw on support from previous political activities in gay rights and land rights respectively. The research issues have affected people who not only have a cohesive group identity but who are able to mobilise themselves to take political action.

Both groups have demanded, and been given, active roles in negotiation over the form of research, its objectives and its methodology. This clearly involves more than autonomy (in the restricted sense of consent). It directly affects the practice of science and demands that science is not allowed to dictate what issues are studied and what methods are employed. Society has always accepted (as indicated by decisions of courts and actions of governments and professional associations) that some forms of scientific research, conclusive as they might be, are not acceptable and should never be employed. Clearly, there are both legal and ethical limits to science. The concern is to balance between research issues (such as the need for scientifically valid research) and the values, needs and aspirations of the human subjects of experimentation (Spiers, 1991c: 7).

In considering the relative importance of the interests of science, society and the subject, it still needs to be recognised that human subjects are particularly vulnerable in many areas of research. Their protection must be regarded as a *prima facie* duty. However, as the discussion of the situation concerning Aborigines and persons with HIV/AIDS shows, the interests of subjects may extend beyond protection. It involves a balancing of priorities between groups (subject populations and researchers) for whom the priorities may well differ.

In the following chapters, a rationale for the functioning of research ethics committees is proposed and practical suggestions are offered for achieving some balance between the interests of science and subjects.

CHAPTER 8

Power, Status and a Rationale for Committee Representation

Committees in most countries engage members experienced in research to consider the ethics of proposed research from the perspective of their expertise. The difficulty is that the experts have a unique commitment to research that favours the interests of science. The means for overcoming this bias has been to include lay members on review committees. This chapter considers whether committees, composed of professional and lay members, are capable of fulfilling their function. Three aspects in particular are considered: first, the rationale for such a committee; second, the relative difference in power and influence between professional and lay members; and third, the recognition that representation on ethics review committees, in its present form, is effectively self-regulation devised and supported by powerful research bureaucracies. An alternative rationale for the composition of committees (based on representation of the interests of science *and* subjects), is proposed – and, in the following chapter, is expanded as a 'democratic' or 'participatory model'.

PROFESSIONAL OR REPRESENTATIVE COMMITTEES

In 1975 the philosopher Robert Veatch claimed that there was no rationale for ethics review committees composed of expert and lay members. His criticisms have yet to be adequately addressed.

'Professional review' or 'jury' models

Veatch considered that research ethics committees fell between two models of review committees. These two models were the 'interdisciplinary professional review model' and the 'jury model'. The interdisciplinary professional review panel is made up of experts from various areas and has been employed particularly in areas where scientific and technological issues present complex problems that require a variety of expertise to resolve. The jury, on the other hand, has the task of reflecting the common-sense view of the reasonable person. As Veatch (1975) pointed out, in this situation 'expertise relevant to the case at hand is not only not necessary, it often disqualifies one from serving on the jury'. Research ethics committees fall between the interdisciplinary professional review model and the jury model in that they are composed of some members who are there because of their expertise and other members who are there as representatives of the community without special expertise. For Veatch, this mixture represented a conflict in the premises underlying these committees.

The history of the development of committees as a mixture of professional and lay members was outlined in Chapter 3. Originally, committees were 'peer-review' panels rather than interdisciplinary committees in that most of the members were medically trained or were biomedical researchers. In most countries the membership of peer review panels has been expanded to include members of other professions (notably lawyers and the clergy) and, in some cases, members of the community. It is in this broadening of the membership of committees to include both those with professional expertise and those who are representative of the community that Veatch identified a basic schism in the committee structure. In his view, this split reflects the lack of any clear rationale 'of what these committees are supposed to be able to do, of what purposes they are to serve, [and] of what skills their members ought to have'. He considered that there was a need for a theory to clarify the ambiguities and for structural changes to be made to committees to make them consistent with that theory. Without these changes he believed it would be impossible for research ethics committees to fulfil their task successfully although he acknowledged that subjects were better protected by committees, even as presently constituted, than by reliance on a researcher's judgement alone.

In my view, the schism described by Veatch is still apparent in committees all over the world. Interviews with members of committees in Australia and the United States have indicated that it is not clear to members whether their committee should function as a panel of experts (as in the interdisciplinary professional review model) or as committees expressing a community morality on the desirability of particular research projects (as in a jury model). In the main, committees appear to function as panels of experts with some small input from the lay members. The only countries to give equal representation to lay and professional members are New Zealand and Denmark (as outlined in Chapters 3 and 4).

Our study of Australian committees and a study in the United States (discussed in Chapter 4) together show that the medical and research members participate more actively on committees and are generally regarded by all members of committees as more important in the decision-making process. The non-medical and non-professional members become marginal in a number of ways. The use of language and technical terms which presume medical (and other technical) knowledge is one of the factors edging them to the margins (Glantz, 1984). Lay members may feel comfortable in offering an opinion on matters within their comprehension (such as the understandability of the consent form) but seldom speak on other issues. I suggest that this is one of the reasons why invasive, high risk research may be passed without question while relatively harmless research may consume a great deal of the committee's time and be disapproved by a committee (Shannon and Ockene, 1985). For example, many committees spend time on the wording of questionnaires (which have relatively low risks of harm) and relatively little time on technical protocols that are difficult to understand by members without the relevant expertise. Yet the technical and difficult studies are more likely to involve invasive procedures or drug research which have a higher risk of harm.

The non-professional members must rely on the professional members for assistance in understanding the technical issues which may give rise to ethical problems (Bailey, 1977: 70). In the case of medical research, the non-medically qualified (including the other professionals) are dependent on medically qualified committee members to explain technical terms, implications of various research options that might be proposed, and the likely effect and experience of subjects. Yet these doctors, especially medical researchers, 'by definition have a unique commitment to the value of research' (Veatch, 1975: 37). The biases of such a specialised group are likely to be very different from those of a committee such as a jury or a representative group from the community.

Veatch considered that a 'dominance of the committee by scientific professionals' would produce a 'risk-shift in the direction of the researchers' values – normally in favor of research'. 'Risky-shift' is based on the observation that groups make riskier decisions than individuals (Douglas, 1985: 66–7). The presence of community members is not likely to overcome the shift toward accepting risky proposals – at best it can dilute it. Veatch goes further in suggesting that 'even a feisty member of a minority will find it extremely difficult to withstand the psychological pressure to cooperate in forming a consensus'. He argued that as long as one researcher was on the committee it would still be influenced in the direction of research values compared with a committee composed on a 'jury model'. Riis, a medical researcher himself with experience on committees in Scandinavia, stated that 'even if lay representation is based on parity, the balance will still be skewed' (1983: 125). For this reason Veatch (1975: 37) considered that 'the subject would be much better served – at least in theory – by a committee of peers of the subject rather than peers of the researcher'.

Veatch's solution to the conflict between the 'professional review model' and the 'jury model' was to have two committees. One of these would be composed entirely of professional members and would consider the acceptability of research proposals on the basis of scientific and professional criteria. The other committee would be composed entirely of community representatives who would consider the acceptability of research proposals in terms of community morality. In our study, we found that 36 per cent of Australian institutions had two committees (McNeill, Berglund and Webster, 1990: 290). One was a scientific committee to evaluate research from the perspective of scientific validity. The other was an ethics review committee that considered the ethics of the research. However, the membership of these research ethics committees differed from the constitution of committees suggested by Veatch. In every case, the ethics review committee still had a majority of scientific and medical members.

The difficulty with Veatch's solution is that it fails to take account of the difference in power and status between the professional and the non-professional members. A committee composed entirely of community representatives would not be taken seriously by researchers or their institutions. I would anticipate that the professional committee would be regarded by the institution as the important committee. The community representative committee would not have any of the power and influence of the professional committee. This difference in the power and status of professional and non-professional members is critical and is an issue I shall explore further before considering alternative committee structures.

UNEQUAL POWER RELATIONS BETWEEN COMMITTEE MEMBERS

The difference in power between professional and lay members on committees is part of a general difference in the power and status between professionals and non-professionals in society (Forester, 1984). A power difference on committees of review means in practice that those with a vested interest in research are the most influential in decision-making. Walters, a senior medical researcher and clinician, and a member of two Australian research ethics committees, stated that some committees are 'dominated by members of the medical staff of the institution' (1986). Meyers, in a letter to the *New England Journal of Medicine*, made the same point about American Institutional Review Boards (IRBs). She said they are 'governed by the dynamics of power'. This is not surprising in that those with relevant knowledge have more power and status, are often employed by the institution, and have greater interaction with each other. The committee members who are not a part of this group 'perceive themselves as low-power persons and act deferentially toward the higher-ranking members'. She went on to say that this power dynamic needs to be recognised so that the views of all parties can be given equal consideration (Meyers, 1979).

Power and expertise

Most research considered by ethics review committees is medical. In the United States this represents 66 per cent of studies and in Australia 80 per cent. An examination of power differences between the expert and non-expert members on review committees would not be complete without looking at the differences in power between members of the medical profession and lay members. There are differences in power between most professionals and lay people but they are greater between the medical profession and laity (Arney, 1982; Willis, 1983). This difference in power can be misused and heightens the concern about conflicts of interest.

Freidson, in his sociological treatise on medicine, considered that the power of the medical profession and the power of experts generally was a problem for society as a whole. He believed that the role of the expert in society limited the extent to which 'ordinary men can shape the character of their lives' and challenged the basis of democracy. He argued that a distinction should be drawn between expertise, or 'knowledge itself', and the practice or application of expertise. He stated that knowledge is 'a body of putative facts ordered by some abstract ideas or theories' and argued that there was no link between such knowledge and the activities of the expert in the work of consulting, treating and advising. There was a 'lack of equivalence between knowing and doing'. Experts in his view should be confined to their expertise in this technical sense. Wherever decisions needed to be made that were not purely dependent on medical expertise, but touched on social and ethical considerations, then Freidson would limit the experts' autonomy by requiring more lay participation in decision-making (Freidson, 1970a: 336–7, 372).

I do not accept that expertise can be separated from social and ethical issues as Freidson proposes. This division between knowledge and action, or science and its application, derives from an idealistic view of science that was current in the earlier part of this century. It mistakenly assumes that the activities of research and scholarship are, in some way, more pure and free from the normative and evaluative influences which affect the application of this knowledge in the 'real world' (Rose and Rose, 1971; Barnes, 1985). Nor do I accept that confining doctors to their realm of expertise, and excluding them from evaluative or normative decisions is either realistic or an effective counter to the power of the medical profession. It is not the most desirable solution. It presents doctors as technocrats and confines them to purely technical concerns at a time when the community and the profession are attempting to 'humanise' the medical profession.

Part of the difficulty is that Freidson dealt with the power of the profession only in the sense in which power is something won from the State. He believed that occupations gained 'professional status of self-regulative autonomy' through a process of political nego-tiation and persuasion (1970a: 83). Power given by the State could be taken away by the State. However, authority is only partially attributable to the State. The dispute between the Australian Federal Labor Government and medical specialists in 1984 and 1985 was a telling demonstration of the fact that the State had very little ability to resist the power of the medical profession (Adams, 1986).

The French philosopher Michel Foucault analysed power in a way that accounts more fully for such events. In his view, power is intrinsic to the recognition of expertise. His focus was on power relations between persons and between groups in society rather than on power as something delegated, or won from the State. He wrote of power as being ubiquitous – infused or at least interspersed throughout society. The image Foucault used to portray this relation was Jeremy Bentham's 'panopticon' – an ideal prison in which the prisoners, conscious that they were always able to be seen, would act as if they were being observed by the warders. In so doing, they gave effect to the automatic functioning of power. Power became effective because it was internalised. The prisoner 'assumes responsibility for the constraints of power . . . he becomes the principle of his own subjection'. Foucault used the panopticon as a metaphor for 'defining power relations in terms of the everyday life of men'. It was a model for understanding the 'disciplines' as a machinery of power. The disciplines included the military, education and medicine. They were hierarchical. For Foucault, power exerted through the disciplines was the underside of democracy (Foucault, 1979: 203–5; 216–22). By contrast, there was no necessary relationship between power and knowledge for Freidson. As power was independent it could simply be taken away. For Foucault, however, medicine was part of a system of 'furtive power'. He thought it was a mistake to see power purely in terms of the legitimate authorities such as parliaments and courts because such a model could not fully explain the workings of power. In his introduction to *History of Sexuality*, Foucault developed the notion of power relations inherent in knowledge. Foucault's point was *not* that there was some property in sex that created this knowledge-power relation. Rather, it was created 'by virtue of the tactics of power immanent in this discourse' (Foucault, 1981: 57–70). Power then was to be understood as a multiplicity of force relations which are inherent in the relations between people.

Foucault's conception of power was that of a dynamic system in which the inequalities were likely to continue. If we wish to recognise expertise then we are stuck with the consequences of inequalities in power and knowledge. On Foucault's analysis, the recognition of medical expertise was in itself the recognition of a power relationship. Acknowledging expertise was to acknowledge an inequality in power between the expert and the lay person. Given this inequality, there was no structural change that could simply take it away.

For Foucault the role of the intellectual was to expose the mechanisms of the disciplines, not to change them. He believed that the purpose of an analysis in terms of power was not to engage in an ideological struggle with those in power but to make visible and intelligible the power relations involved. It was for the revolutionary to fight the on-going battle against inequalities. The battle front would continually move and the fight would never be won. It was illusory to believe that there was a solution to the problem that could be effected by a change in structure (Foucault, 1980: 236-7; also Bouchard, 1977: 207-8).

The appeal of Foucault's analysis is that his view of power as immanent within relations and inherent in the recognition of expertise fits my own experience. As a non-medical graduate in a medical faculty, I see the medical profession as very much concerned with power and status. Even within its ranks, it is as hierarchical as the military. I conclude that it is too simplistic to accept a model of power as a delegation of government. Doctors have power and status that derive, at least in part, from the recognition of medicine as a discipline with significant knowledge and expertise. Neither is it sufficient to see power in the medical profession in terms of bureaucratic hierarchies and Machiavellian characters within professional medical associations. There is something pervasive about the power of the medical profession. I think it is inherent in the relation between the medical profession and the rest of us who, as lay people, recognise their field of expertise. It is not separable in the sense that Freidson proposed. The point of this recognition of the relationship between power and knowledge is that it demonstrates that there is no structural alteration that will simply correct the imbalance of power between a medical professional and a lay person.

Nevertheless, the approaches of Freidson and Foucault are complementary to some extent. While Foucault has given a more satisfying analysis of the relation between power and expertise, he can not be taken to support any structural change. Freidson on the other hand has drawn attention to the normative and evaluative strand within expertise and strongly advocates the need for lay participation in decisions which are inextricably evaluative. While the separation between knowledge and its application is not as simplistic as Freidson proposes, one can make some distinction between matters of fact and value-laden assumptions in science. Scientific assumptions, values and interests can then be considered in relation to other interests and values such as the interests of subjects.

Inevitably, medical researchers and medical practitioners are needed in the evaluation of the ethics of medical research. By virtue of their expertise they are in a powerful position relative to subjects of experimentation. It has been observed that ethics review is 'intended to equalize the power imbalance between researcher and subject'[1] In my view, however, the present systems of review fail to achieve this, with the possible exception of review committees in Denmark and New Zealand.

Lay members of research ethics committees have a potential role in reducing this inequality and acting in the interests of subjects – yet there are limits to the effectiveness of this role. These members, like the subjects of the research, are dependent on the profession and may never achieve the goal of egalitarian relations between themselves and the expert members of committees. Nevertheless, the inclusion of strong subject representatives who are capable of identifying inherent conflicts of values and representing the interests and values of the subjects of research may go some way toward balancing the power of expert members. In Chapter 9, I make some suggestions about the appointment of subject representatives by appropriate community groups – suggestions which should strengthen the position of the subject representatives.

The role of self-regulation

The power of scientists and researchers in the review process raises the issue of self-regulation. The issue is highlighted by the fact that researchers' power is augmented from a network of powerful institutions that includes universities, hospitals, research institutes and commercial laboratories. Self-regulation, when adopted by funding bodies and put into effect by institutions responsible for research, may be no more than an exercise in public relations. This phenomenon can be readily understood in terms of sociological theories of the functioning of bureaucracies and the power of oligarchies within bureaucracies.[2]

1. Professor Abbayann Lynch, reported by Miller (1989: 518–19).
2. See, for example, Michels (1959), Mouzelis (1975: 9–26) and Weber (1978: 987).

In Australia, representatives of the National Health and Medical Research Council (NHMRC) have maintained that review by research ethics committees is not self-regulation in that lay members are included in the review process.[3] However, my conclusions about the relative power and influence of the professional and researcher members of committees underscore the self-regulatory nature of this system. I conclude that in spite of the presence of non-medical and non-research lay members, ethics review by a committee is, in effect, self-regulation.

Self-regulation has been described as a set of activities ranging from mere 'window-dressing' at one end of the spectrum to a system of regulation that is thorough and carries with it 'formidable sanctions' for non-compliance at the other. Australian legal scholars Moore and Tarr have stated that the reasons that businesses and occupational groups adopt self-regulation are first 'to demonstrate their sense of social responsibility' and 'promote their public image'; and secondly 'to adopt some form of self-regulation to accommodate the public interest' and to avoid 'the threat of more restrictive statutory intervention' (Moore and Tarr, 1988: 9–11). This analysis is equally applicable to regulation of experimentation on human subjects.

Moore and Tarr outlined the advantages and disadvantages that were claimed for and against self-regulation. On the one hand, self-regulation was claimed to be more efficient than legislation; to be more flexible; to have the potential for quick and easy revision and be more responsive to public pressure; to be able to take into account the idiosyncratic problems of the particular situation; to be more susceptible to common sense application than legislation; and to be able to employ systems for the speedy resolution of problems and complaints. They also suggested that those adopting self-regulation are more likely to comply with the spirit of the self-regulatory code than those obliged to conform with statutory regulation. On the other hand, self-regulation was often said to fall short on enforcement and sanctions; that members of an association were reluctant to take action against other members of that association; and that self-regulatory systems usually had insufficient legal powers to enforce any sanctions that may have been declared. The strongest case against self-regulation is the argument that 'no person should be judge in their own cause' (Moore and Tarr, 1988: 10–11).

3. *Hansard Report of Select Committee*, 1986, pp. 313–18.

In Moore and Tarr's view, self-regulation would fail wherever it impinged 'to a large measure on profits' even when it is obviously 'socially desirable that occupations restrict their activities in the public interest'. This warning applies to the regulation of both commercial and non-commercial experimentation on human subjects. As stated in the previous chapter, a great deal of medical research is drug research, some of which has potential for developing commercially viable drugs – and large profits. Self-regulation, under these circumstances, can be a cover for unethical (if not illegal) activities (Braithwaite, 1984). Non-commercial research has similar pressures. For universities and research institutes, the prestige associated with being awarded grants serves in much the same way as profit for a commercial venture. Research grants are the currency of research institutions. As one commentator pointed out, a committee can be much more demanding of a research proposal with no potential funding than with a 'proposal for $2 million that is going to support forty people' (Glantz, 1984: 131). Regulation adopted by granting agencies and put into effect by researchers and institutional administrators may be no more than 'window-dressing'.

The self-regulatory nature of ethics review is very apparent in some committees. The chairpersons of many committees are themselves committed researchers. Other committees include deans of faculties who actively encourage their academic staff to apply for grants and who measure the success of their faculties by the amount of research funding that is attracted.

In my view there is conflict of interest in research ethics committees making decisions on the ethical acceptability of research proposals when the institution in which they are based stands to gain from research it conducts. It must be assumed that there is a pressure on research ethics committees within research institutions to approve research and attract funding and kudos to their institution.

REPRESENTATION

In the previous chapter there was an examination of the three major interests in experimentation on human subjects: those of science, society and the subject. Each of the interests was said to represent different values, claims, and needs.

Science

The point has been made throughout that the interests of science are well represented at all levels of the system of review. Ethics committees have members who are well aware of the needs of science. The system of review itself has been formulated by institutions that have an investment in science and the review of the ethics of research is conducted within institutions that support scientific research. Clearly, the adequacy of the representation of some committees to consider particular fields of research must be questioned. Australian committees, for example, do not appear to be adequately equipped to deal with the large volume of drug research evaluation. Relative to the representation of the interests of subjects, however, members with a commitment to science and the research enterprise are in the majority.

Society's interest

The interests of society are not as well represented. Ethics committees in most countries include lay members. It is sometimes assumed that these members are there to represent the community. Even if we accept for a moment that lay members represent the community, they are typically in the minority, participate less in the committee dis-cussion, are seen (and see themselves) as relatively unimportant and have consequently less influence in the decisions reached by the com-mittees. (The basis for these assertions was presented in Chapter 4.)

However, the evidence does not support the assumption that lay members do represent the community. In Australia, as elsewhere, the majority of appointments of lay members are made from the recommendations of people known to staff of the institution or to committee members. We found in Australia that 76 per cent of lay members on research ethics committees were appointed on recom-mendations from within the institution or on recommendations from committee members themselves. It is inevitable that institutions, or committees, will 'select compatible people for the committee' (McNeill, Berglund and Webster, 1990). Such people are much more likely to have characteristics in common with other committee members. The prime motivation of the institution for including community members is to conform with the rules for membership and to give the committee credibility in the eyes of society (Mannisto,

1985: 19). It may not be prompted by a genuine desire to incorporate a community perspective.

This does not necessarily disqualify the appointed lay members from representing the attitudes of the community, but it suggests that members appointed in these circumstances will give allegiance to the institution or to the committee rather than to 'the community'. For these lay members, 'the community' is an abstract concept relative to the concrete reality of the committee.

To sum up this argument, lay members cannot be expected to be truly independent of the institution when they are appointed by the institution. In our study (McNeill, Berglund and Webster, 1990), few Australian committee members saw any of their committee members as 'representative' of a 'particular community' or saw any of their committee members as 'representative' of a 'community interest group'. Porter (1987) noted that there was no agreement among members of American institutional review boards (IRBs) on whether lay members represented the community. It also became apparent from her study that community members on IRBs in the United States are not representative in the sense of being typical of the community. It was found that a high percentage of lay members were graduates with 32 per cent holding doctoral degrees (Porter, 1986).

Society is not an interest group in the sense in which the supporters of science might be said to be an interest group. Obviously society includes all the interests of its members. The suggestion that science and society's interests were in common was rejected in the previous chapter. This was seen as part of the polemic in favour of science. A broader view is that society has an interest in the benefits that might flow to some of its members as a result of experimentation on human subjects. It is also concerned that subjects are not harmed in the course of experimentation. The reaction of the public and politicians to instances of abuse of subjects is the evidence for this concern. Society might also be said to be interested in finding a balance between the potential for positive outcomes from experimentation and the need to protect subjects from harm. None of these statements about society is literally true in that society is not a corporate being with intentions and concerns. 'Society' is a term for the totality of relations between humans. To project intention onto 'society' is to take the word beyond its usual meaning. The point of considering society in this way is that I wish to stress the multiplicity of interests that the term 'society' might represent.

The assumption that society (or the community) should have a voice on ethics committees is based on a notion about the role of the lay member. The first committees to incorporate non-medical and non-research members did so out of recognition of the bias of institutional members. The perception that the institutional members were biased toward the interests of researchers was, I believe, accurate. The solution for countering the bias was simply inadequate. There is no possibility that a single lay member (or even two plus a minister of religion and a lawyer, as in Australian committees) can overcome the bias of an ethics committee composed of a majority of members from the institution (Capron, 1985: 426). Nor has there been a clear description of the role of lay members that would indicate this intention to those members. In my view, society's concern is that there should be an equitable balance between the interests of science and subjects. This concern is best dealt with by providing mechanisms that are appropriately constituted for achieving this balance. This is a point that I shall return to in Chapter 9.

Subjects' interests

While the interests of society are under-represented, the interests of subjects of human experimentation are not represented at all. They may receive support from members within ethics committees but subjects have no direct voice or nominated representatives on those committees. The main function of ethics committees is said to be the protection of the subjects of experimentation, yet the subjects themselves have no access to this process. Of the three interests therefore, science is well represented, society has limited and ambiguous representation, and subjects have no representation.

It might be assumed that lay members are there to represent the subjects of experiments. Indeed, Australian research ethics committee members saw the lay member as especially concerned with the welfare of subjects of research (McNeill, Berglund and Webster, 1992b). However, they are not appointed as representatives of subjects. It is quite possible for lay members to be blindly supportive of science and not sympathetic to the interests of subjects of experiments. One commentator observed that 'community representatives sometimes become enthralled with the importance of the research and at times become more pro-research than the scientists' (Glantz, 1984: 132).

Lay members are generally not given any rationale for their inclusion that would indicate that they should identify with subjects of experiments. This lack of a clear rationale serves the interests of science. If the non-medical, non-scientific and non-institutional members are unclear as to their role, they are unlikely to challenge research effectively when it is obviously supported by the majority of other members of the committee. The other members, unlike the non-institutional members, have much less doubt about their role.

A bias toward the interests of science

In my view, systems of review by committee in most countries (with the possible exceptions of New Zealand and Denmark) are systems for allowing research on human subjects with a minimum of interference. They do not give priority to the interests of subjects of research in spite of statements to this effect made in guidelines such as the Helsinki Declaration and the Australian NHMRC Statement on Human Experimentation. In practice, committees are composed as if the priority is the creation of optimal conditions for research on human subjects with a minimum of interference. In a sense, the British Royal College of Physicians guidelines are more open about the actual function of ethics committees. Their objectives state that research ethics committees are to 'protect subjects of research from harm'; to 'provide reassurance to the public that this is being done'; to 'protect research workers from unjustified criticism'; and to 'facilitate good research' (Royal College of Physicians, 1990a: 3). There is an ambiguity in this role between facilitating research and protecting subjects but the emphasis appears to be on furthering research while reassuring the public that subjects are being protected from harm.

This is the key to understanding the function of research ethics committees. They are to protect subjects as long as the protection does not interfere too much with research and, in the process, they are to 'provide reassurance to the public'. In my view, these statements make it clear that the principal purpose of research ethics committee review is not protection of subjects but reassurance of the public so that the research enterprise can continue relatively unhindered. This assessment fits neatly into the role that Moore and Tarr saw for self-regulation. They stated (see the quotation given earlier) that self-regulation was adopted by enterprises to demonstrate a sense of social responsibility, promote a public image, be seen to accommodate the public interest, and to avoid the threat of more restrictive statutory intervention. While this sceptical view may be easier to justify in relation to British committees, I believe it is a valid perspective on committees elsewhere in the world.

Argument for representation of subjects

The claim for representation of the interests of subjects rests on an argument from democratic theory. The argument in its simplest form is that subjects should have a right to participate in the process of review in order to protect and advance their own interests. In this theory 'participation' means to contribute equally in the process of making decisions. It also means having equal influence and power in determining the outcome of decisions (Pateman, 1970: 23–4, 37–43). This is a position that is consistent with and closely allied to ethical principles of research. Associations between the ethics of research and principles of democracy have been made by others. Senator Edward Kennedy, for example, linked the ethics of medical research with the 'essence of democracy' (Sobel, 1977: 61–3). This is not surprising in that both applied ethics and democratic philosophy have a similar genealogy. The principles of research ethics and 'participatory democracy' are normative foundations for the view that research subjects should participate in decisions on the acceptability of proposals for research projects on human subjects.

Appropriate representatives of subjects

'Participatory democracy' is, however, an ideal that may not be achievable in research ethics decision-making. Subjects themselves, in the sense of the pool of subjects who may serve in any research under consideration, are not able to be present. Indeed, even if it were logistically possible, their presence at meetings of ethics review committees (where the project in which they are to play a part is being discussed) could, in some experiments, distort the research findings. Representation is needed when an interest is in competition with other interests, when the views of that group need to be put forward in order to arrive at consensus and when those people could not conveniently be present themselves (Diggs, 1968: 36). All three conditions apply to the interests of research subjects in decisions made by research ethics committees and in policy decisions arrived at by national bodies. Some form of representation in the interests of subjects is clearly necessary.

The notion of representation contains the idea that something is 'made present' or 'presented' by an intermediary. A representative could mean someone who is representative of a group (in the sense of being typical of the group) or it could mean someone who represents the group by putting its views without necessarily being from that group or typical of that group (Pitkin, 1967: 59; Diggs, 1968: 36). I would argue that representation is needed in the second sense. Members representing the interests of subjects would not be effective if they were typical of subjects even assuming it was possible to find such people. Subjects are typically in a relatively powerless position in relation to researchers. Ideally, subject representatives on research ethics committees would be people with as much power and influence as the representatives of science and the research institution. Appropriate people would be able to make use of the knowledge of experts without being unduly deferential. They would maintain a commitment to representing the interests and values of human subjects of research in negotiating a balanced position with research representatives.

Representation and community group support

The objection to this argument for representation of the interests of subjects has been that representatives are not acting as individuals and they are not open to persuasion. For this reason the Department of Health guidelines from both Britain and New Zealand stress that members of ethics committees are present on the committees as individuals and not as representatives of any outside interest or group.[4] This restriction operates to disempower the lay members on committees without having a comparable effect on scientific members.

The scientific researchers and medical professional members of committees already have a shared view about the value of science and the importance of research. They have scientific and professional associations and networks that support this view. They are part of an institution with formal and informal support networks and many

---

4. UK Department of Health, 'Local Research Ethics Committees' (1991); New Zealand Department of Health, 'Standard' (1991).

opportunities to consult formally and informally among themselves. Furthermore, they gain authority from their positions and status within their institutions. Although they may see themselves as being present as individuals, they are easily recognisable as persons within a scientific (or professional) and institutional hierarchy. They are likely to be introduced in terms of their work (which implicitly indicates their qualifications) and position as, for example: 'Dr Jones, a nephrologist researcher', or as 'Professor Smith, Head of the Department of Cardiology'. The use of titles such as 'professor' and 'doctor' only emphasises the point that these members are part of, and recognised by, a scientific–professional establishment. These institutional connections are sources of strength denied to community representatives. Furthermore, the researcher and professional members of committees are accountable to their peers. If they disallow research proposed by one of their colleagues they can expect to be challenged by that person. In every sense these members are representative of science, research and the research institution. They might not be appointed as advocates but they are representative in the sense of having a research understanding and perspective, and being accountable to scientific researchers.

Lay members or community members on the other hand are required to be present as individuals and are not accountable to anyone beyond the committee itself. This means that they have no support for their position from outside the committee and no shared perspective or understanding of their role. Nor is there any requirement that they should take a particular interest in the welfare of subjects of research. Furthermore, they may have no experience in health or research issues (one of the conditions of lay membership of committees in Australia and New Zealand) and they may be unable to understand the issues. They may have no understanding of the institution's system, including the way in which decisions are made and carried out, or the hidden agendas of other members.

The distinction I am drawing is between 'lay' or 'community' members and 'subject representatives'. I argue that subject representatives should ideally be members of committees as representatives not as individuals. They need to be informed of the issues from the perspective of all the subjects that they would be representing, and would be accountable to an appropriate community group that can represent the interests of the human subjects of experiments.

This distinction drawn between community members and subject representatives is similar to the distinction between lay members and consumer representatives made by consumer health groups in Australia and New Zealand. Lay or community members are individual members of the public while consumer representatives are accountable to the community through a group.[5] Consumer groups point out that an individual member of the public is not accountable to anyone, and expresses an individual opinion. In addition 'they have neither the benefits nor the responsibilities of consultation' (Consumers' Health Forum of Australia, 1990: 11). A 'consumer representative' on the other hand is accountable to a consumer group for representing the diversity of interests served by that group; and the representative gains support, knowledge, experience and strength from the network provided by that organisation.

The term 'consumer' representative is not appropriate in relation to a representative of subjects of experimentation. Nevertheless, the distinction between lay members and accountable representatives is valid. I am advocating that representation, in the sense of being representative of a community group, is needed to give the representatives some ground and support for their views. I also believe that it is in the interests of committees to include people who are representative of a number of others. To illustrate this point, student representatives on the medical faculty of my university are representatives of the Medical Students Association. They are not students chosen by the faculty who act in an individual capacity. Nor would individual students be as useful. There are many occasions in which it is helpful to have a representative who can speak for a number of students rather than a student member who can give only an individual opinion.

This comes back to the point of concern about whether representatives would be open to persuasion or would tend to block proceedings. In my view this concern is based on stereotypes of 'single-issue' protest groups taking extreme action to gain media attention. It is not typical of community representatives who see their role as working within the system for equity between the interested groups. Representatives, chosen and supported in terms of recommendations by groups such as the Consumers' Health Forum of

5. Auckland Women's Health Council (1989), Working Party (of the Maternity Services Task Force) (1989) and Consumers' Health Forum of Australia, 'Guidelines' (1990).

Australia, are not likely to adopt an adversarial and difficult demeanour. The representative ideally needs to be skilled in communication and the art of negotiation. Representatives are counselled to maintain good working relationships with other committee members and to see other members as 'colleagues you are working together with on a problem'. They are advised to avoid the role of complainant or opponent (Consumers Health Forum of Australia, 1990: 26, 28).

Such people can be expected to serve the community rather than hinder its processes. Subject representatives would assist the committee by being knowledgeable about subjects' experiences and able to analyse the likely effects of research on research subjects from the proposed population. Furthermore, they are in a position to contribute constructively to a debate on the underlying issues in terms of balancing between the interests of researchers, the community, and the interests of subjects.

The beginnings of subject representation

In the official guidelines and regulations of various countries the need for representation of subjects is beginning to be recognised. The United States regulations require that IRBs should include one or more members who are 'knowledgeable about and experienced in working with' vulnerable categories of subjects (such as 'children, prisoners, pregnant women, or handicapped or mentally disabled persons') when the committee regularly reviews research in these areas. The requirement is now part of the 'common rule' for the sixteen government departments with regulations on research on human subjects in the United States.[6] The US Department of Education has taken this even further by insisting on the inclusion of a member whose primary concern is the welfare of handicapped children, or mentally disabled persons, for IRBs reviewing research (in education) on disabled persons (Porter, 1991).

There has been a move toward including patient representatives (rather than subject representatives) on research ethics committees in other countries also. New Zealand ethics committees have been required to include 'patient advocacy' since 1988, and a Danish Commission recommended in 1989 that there should be an additional

6. US Federal Policy for the Protection of Human Subjects; Notices and Rules, *Federal Register*, Part II, Vol. 56, No. 117 (Tuesday 18 June 1991), pp. 28002-32, at p. 28015, Section 107(a).

lay person on Danish research ethics committees who would be nominated by 'patients' associations'.[7] As far as I know, the Danish proposal has not been enacted. The UK Department of Health guidelines (1991: 7–8) require that lay members are to be appointed by consultation with the relevant Community Health Council. These suggestions, like the United States requirements, are significant moves toward representation. I have taken these suggestions one step further and recommended that the people nominated be present as representatives of relevant community interest groups.

In the previous chapter, the analysis of HIV/AIDS research and anthropological research on Aborigines in Australia drew attention to the particular concerns of research subjects from these groups. As in these cases, the need for representation is much more obvious when the relevant community of subjects has particular needs. Given this perspective it is not surprising then to find that both groups have called for consultation on the acceptability of research proposals.

Representatives of Aborigines in Australia insisted on consultation between researchers and the relevant Aboriginal community throughout the 'entire process of research from initial discussions through implementation to publication of research reports' (NHMRC, 1988b: 12). In the United States, Spiers, a philosopher and AIDS activist, suggested that IRBs should actively consult with the HIV/AIDS community prior to approving HIV/AIDS research (Spiers, 1991c: 5). He took this further by advocating that IRBs which regularly review HIV/AIDS research should include 'representatives from relevant AIDS communities'. In a 'consensus' policy document for clinical research on HIV/AIDS drawn up by a diverse group including academics and AIDS activists, it has been recommended that IRBs should 'seriously consider including . . . representatives of or advocates for populations of prospective subjects and intended beneficiaries' (Levine, Dubler and Levine, 1991). This call for representation of potential subjects on research ethics committees could herald a change in rationale for committee review.

A RATIONALE FOR COMMITTEES

At the beginning of this chapter I presented Veatch's argument that there is no rationale for research ethics review and no clear theory about what the committees are supposed to do – which means that

7. New Zealand Department of Health (1991) and Denmark, Ministry of Health, (1989: 77–9, 90).

there is no clear statement about how they should be composed and what they should do. I propose the following rationale for committee review. Research ethics review committees are discretionary bodies with the power to apply the principles of research ethics, and the rules relating to particular fields of experimentation on human subjects, to research proposals and research in progress. In conducting this function, review committees need to be balanced between the interests of science and the interests of subjects.

This is a very different formulation from the notion of balancing between the interests of science and the need to protect subjects. Protectionism has been the paradigm until recently. Carol Levine (1988: 167) described ethical review as having been 'born in scandal and reared in protectionism'. Ethical review, to continue the metaphor, is now an adolescent and showing signs of rebellion against parental protectiveness. Subjects of research are demanding a say. As was discussed above and in Chapter 7 (particularly in relation to HIV/AIDS research and research on Aborigines), subjects have an interest in suggesting the direction of research and the manner in which research is carried out. Protecting subjects against harm may still be the fundamental concern but subjects must be allowed to represent *all* their interests. They have many concerns and interests including interests in research methodology, the basis of selection of subjects, publication, ownership of the research data, access to research results, privacy, the manner of arriving at conclusions and the conclusions themselves. The discretionary function then needs to take into account the interests of researchers and subjects. As was suggested in the Introduction, the paradigm has moved from protectionism to consultation and consensus.

The model for the functioning of committees within this paradigm is a representative model. Representatives of both interests would be included on the committee. This is to be distinguished from the representative model mentioned by Veatch in which *all* members represent the community (Veatch, 1975). In the review model which I propose, members are present as representatives of one or other of the two important concerns in research on human subjects: the concerns of science and the concerns of subjects. Society would fulfil its role by providing a mechanism that balances these two interests and oversees the operation of the system to ensure that it is conducted within these bounds. In other words, while individual members may have a bias, the combined membership of each committee is balanced between the interests of science and subjects.

I have argued that some form of representation of the interests of subjects is necessary. However, it is also recognised that simply to invite lay members to volunteer, or to leave the nomination of lay members to a relevant group, could lead to the presence of members on research ethics committees with views that are extreme in their opposition to research. The 'worst-case scenario' is one in which such members could simply block all research on human subjects. A less extreme situation could be that the presence of 'anti-research' members may polarise the committee and lead to less than adequate review. This is a view that is often put to me by researchers. It has been argued that polarisation could ultimately undermine the system of review by causing the research community to withdraw its support. I do not believe that representation will lead to this outcome. Representation of the various interests is a means for ensuring that all points of view are considered – it does not imply polarisation. As stated in Chapter 4, the experience in Denmark (where committees are balanced between representatives of science and the community) is that members do *not* reach decisions by voting in blocs. I understand that meetings in New Zealand have at times been more animated since the change in the basis of committee membership, but members typically work toward consensus.

Even if polarisation of the views of members on research ethics committees is acknowledged as a possibility, it is still not a strong basis for arguing against representation of the interests of subjects. The rationale for subject representation is well grounded in both democratic theory and the principles of autonomy and justice. The fact that people can use their privileges within a democratic system without compromise and with unswerving commitment to fundamental beliefs is an argument for representation rather than against it. The balance is to be found in a process that allows the holders of varying points of view to have an equal opportunity for expression and control. Democratic representation is an ideal to be aimed at and is an expression of faith in a community's ability to balance the claims of various groups in a manner that leads to harmonious coexistence of differing viewpoints.

The following chapter will outline some of the mechanisms needed to give effect to representation, particularly in relation to the appointment of members, the committee process and the training of committee members.

CHAPTER 9

Giving Effect to Representation: Composition and Functioning of Review Committees

In the previous chapter, I stated that science is well represented on research ethics review committees whereas the interests of subjects are either indirectly represented or not represented at all. The model is paternalistic and protectionist: one in which members of the institution, including researchers, administrators and other staff, meet with one or two community representatives to review proposals for experimentation and endeavour to balance the need for research and the need to protect subjects. In this chapter I consider mechanisms for giving effect to the alternative representative model of research ethics review I have proposed.

COMPOSITION OF COMMITTEES

I am proposing a 'democratic' or 'participatory model' in which representatives of subjects work directly with representatives of researchers to arrive at a consensus between the interests of researchers and the interests of subjects. Given the differences in power and status between lay and expert members there need to be at least as many subject representatives as representatives of science. The situation is similar to that of occupational health and safety committees which have been set up in industries in many countries including Britain, the United States, Canada and Australia. These committees, like the committees proposed in this book, are based on principles of democracy and participation. The issues of power and status between the representatives of management and workers are akin to those between professional and lay members on review committees. On occupational health and safety committees, the number of management representatives must not exceed the number of employee representatives (Wuorinen, 1991). In many countries the chairperson of those committees is also required to be drawn from employees.

For some of the same reasons, those mechanisms could be considered for research ethics committees. There needs to be an equal number of research and subject representatives, and ideally the chairperson would be drawn from the subject representatives.

Appointment of subject and research representatives

I recommend that there be explicit policy for the appointment of both subject and research representatives on research ethics committees.

Research representatives
Finding people with research experience and an interest in ethics to appoint to review committees has not been a major problem for institutions concerned with research. Most commonly, researchers are appointed from the staff of the relevant institutions referring research proposals for review. Although it has been argued that reviewers should be from outside the institution, I am not advocating that for many reasons. Institutional people are 'on the ground' and become aware of research practices within the institution. They are available for informal consultation. I believe they are in a better position to influence the general attitude toward conducting ethical research and they are well placed for a more formal educative role within the institution or region. There may be some advantage in having one research representative from outside the institution (or the region) although I am not suggesting this as a requirement.

However, for research ethics committees established on a regional basis, such as those in France, Britain, and (to some extent) in Australia, there is a more obvious need for guidelines on the appointment of research representatives. A useful model is offered by Danish committees. As was stated in Chapter 4, the Danish Medical Research Council appoints the 'medical/scientific' members from nominations of various medical and scientific bodies in the region (Riis, 1979: 88). I recommend that the regional authority suggest the appropriate bodies who are to nominate research representatives for a regional committee. Whether or not the committee is formed on an institutional basis or a regional basis, I maintain that the policy for research representatives' appointment should be made explicit and subject to approval in the same manner as is suggested for subjects.

Subject representatives

In the previous chapter I advocated that representatives of subjects of research be nominated by a community group and be accountable to the community through that group. There are difficulties in putting suggestions for representation into practice. This is a problem in common with finding adequate representation of any citizens' group (Arnstein, 1969: 217). Spiers, an AIDS activist writing in the broader context of 'community consultation', referred to the 'intransigent problems' of representation. He pointed to the fact that there is 'no one voice that speaks for "the community"; nor is there one singular thought expressed when the concept is invoked' (1991c: 3). This is a problem for subject representation on research ethics committees also.

The nomination of suitable subject representatives is an issue for each committee. It is not one that can easily be resolved at a national level. It depends first on the type of studies considered by the ethics review committee and the pool from which those studies draw their subjects. Secondly, it depends on the availability of a body with an appropriate constituency to represent those subjects. This will be more straightforward for committees where the majority of research proposals draw on subjects from a common pool. A university committee, for example, may consider many research proposals which rely on university students as subjects. The appropriate representatives could be nominated by student associations or student unions in those circumstances. A hospital committee may consider a majority of research that draws on hospital patients. A group representing hospital patients might be the appropriate group to nominate representatives of patients. Similarly, a research ethics committee in an AIDS research institute may look to HIV/AIDS support or activist groups to nominate representatives.

However, many committees consider a variety of studies which draw on subjects from different sources. It may be more appropriate for two or three different bodies to nominate subject representatives to such committees. When no institution with a relevant constituency is available, then health consumers' groups or groups with broad civil rights interests might be asked to nominate representatives. In Australia, a group such as the Consumers Health Forum, or one of their member bodies, could be asked to nominate representatives. I also suggest that the Australian Council of Social Services and its various State branches might be appropriate.

The American 'consensus' document on HIV/AIDS research accepted that in some situations there may be 'no clearly defined community of prospective subjects' or that there may be different groups claiming to represent subjects (Levine, Dubler and Levine, 1991). These are practical difficulties in finding suitable subject representatives. The ideal is that subject representatives be nominated by an appropriate group. However, although this may prove impossible for some committees, it does not remove responsibility from researchers to consult with the relevant community. In the last resort, where there is no group to represent subjects, it may be necessary to nominate individuals. The American 'consensus' document argued that through contacts, 'knowledgeable people' can be identified who can 'serve to represent potential subjects' interests'. I support this view. Even when there is no clearly defined group, suitable individuals can be found to represent the interests of the prospective subjects. I recommend that these individuals should be encouraged to affiliate with a community group that can support them in the role of representative.

In summary then, the basis of membership should be representation of the interests of researchers and subjects. Ideally there will be a body that can nominate suitable representatives. Where in practice this proves difficult, suitable individuals should be identified through discussion with health consumer groups, or with civil rights (or broadly representative) groups, and those members encouraged to act with the support of those groups.

Representatives' roles

Representatives need to be capable of fulfilling their function. The following is an outline of the different roles of research and subject representatives.

Subject representatives' roles

The main function of subject representatives is to understand the likely impact of the proposed research on subjects. Their primary question, from the perspective of the interests of potential subjects, is: 'Should this study go ahead?'. Where necessary, subject representatives should consult with members of the proposed subject population to understand the issues from their point of view. Answering the question will also require working co-operatively with the research representatives to predict, as closely as possible, the likely experience and outcome for subjects. Representatives should be particularly alert to any possibility of unforeseen consequences of entering a study (for example, a loss of options in treatment; the possibility that the study might drag on beyond the nominated completion date; the impact on subjects' privacy; any likely pain, suffering or other discomfort; and potential for loss of earnings). If subject representatives are satisfied that it is not unreasonable to ask subjects to participate, a number of subsidiary issues arise. First of all, the study must be made comprehensible to potential subjects. Subject representatives need to ensure that subjects are provided with information on their rights (such as the right to withdraw at any time) and that participation in the study is optional and will not affect subjects' treatment in any other respect. A summarised description of this role is contained in Table 9.1.

Subject representatives need to talk to subjects about their experience as subjects of research programs. Researchers should allow subject representatives access to their subjects (usually at the

Table 9.1 *The role and responsibilities of subject representatives*

SUBJECT REPRESENTATIVES

RESPONSIBILITIES:
Working with research representatives to identify potential for the study to:
  benefit subjects
  give pain or other discomfort
  jeopardise subjects' privacy
  lead to loss of earnings
  lead to loss of options in treatment
  drag on beyond completion date
Consulting with potential subjects to establish concerns of particular population
  of subjects
Providing information to subjects on their rights
Being available to consult with subjects
Taking part in surveillance of ongoing research
Education of researchers and subjects
Reporting and consulting with nominating organisation

REQUIRED/PREFERRED QUALIFICATIONS:
Experience with subjects or their issues
No other association with research institute
Confident (not unduly deferential)
Capable of identifying inherent conflicts of values
Capable of presenting an argument rationally

completion of their study) for this purpose. I anticipate that researchers may object on the ground that consultation between subject representatives and subjects could interfere with their research. In my view, objections of this sort could be overcome if meetings were conducted at a time and place that did not interfere with research. At the commencement of studies, subjects should be advised of the names and telephone numbers of subject representatives and be encouraged to discuss with them any concerns they may have. In this way subject representatives can function as informal monitors of research. They should also be included in on-site surveillance of ongoing research.

Subject representatives need to be aware of, and familiarise themselves with, the concerns of the particular population of subjects that they are representing. For example, people with HIV or AIDS have particular concerns about the research into their condition, and their representatives need to know what those issues are. The same is true for other populations of subjects – be they children, pregnant women, psychiatric patients, or the elderly. Ideally the representatives will be appointed from people who have this knowledge. Where studies seek to draw on subjects lacking legal capacity for consent, their representatives need to be especially alert to any possible negative consequences and experiences for potential subjects.

To avoid any bias toward researchers' interests, persons nominated as subject representatives should have no other association (past or present) with the relevant research institution(s) nor should they have immediate family members who are, or were, affiliated with the institution(s). I maintain, however, that there is no need to exclude people with knowledge and experience of medical and scientific research work as subject representatives. In a sense, subject representatives need to be experts of a different kind. They need to be primarily expert in representing the interests of subjects and to be very clear that that is their role. This does not exclude the nomination of people who are also knowledgeable about research. Given that people actively engaged in research and medical work may be biased toward the interests of science, however, I think it wise that subject representatives be nominated from people not actively involved in medical or scientific work.[1] The primary

---

1. This is similar to a recommendation on lay members in the National Health and Medical Research Council 'Statement' 1992, Supplementary note 1 (see Appendix 2).

qualification should be their ability to represent the interests of subjects. Some knowledge and experience in research may assist them in this.

It is important that attention be given to finding appropriate people to fulfil this role. Bates and Linder-Pelz (1987: 169) have recommended that lay representatives appointed to regulatory bodies be knowledgeable and assertive. The 1984 Royal College of Physicians guidelines for research ethics committees suggested that lay members be 'persons of responsibility and standing who will not be overawed by medical members'. As stated in Chapter 8, subject representatives, while being respectful of the experts' knowledge, need not be 'unduly deferential'. They do need to be capable of identifying inherent conflicts between researchers' and subjects' interests and representing the interests and values of the subjects.

In our study of research ethics committees in Australia, we found that lay members were not as influential as other members. However, there were some notable exceptions. One lay person was rated as one of the most active and important committee members by the other members of her research ethics committee. In interview she said it was important to speak out and challenge the 'narrow attitudes' of medical and professional 'experts' on the committee and their tendency to support one another. In her view this required the right sort of person. She was a person with previous experience as a representative in other organisations. She also had a particular concern for the welfare of patients and subjects of research as a result of her experience with a disabled family member. In spite of her willingness to be challenging she had a good personal relationship with other committee members who saw her as balanced in outlook and therefore welcomed her views. This example illustrates my point that the choice of an appropriate person as subject representative is more likely to lead to influential and effective representation and to more thorough review.

Consistent with the ideas of accountability already put forward, subject representatives have a responsibility to report back and consult with their nominating organisation. This does not imply that every decision to be taken by a subject representative needs to be ratified by the nominating organisation. There is obviously a practical need for representatives to be able to make decisions independently. However, a responsibility to report back and consult provides an information channel which allows the community group to develop relevant policy. It also provides an additional channel for subjects to make their views known to their representatives.

Research representatives' roles

Appropriate research representatives will be drawn from people with experience in relevant research on human subjects. Although they will be concerned with *all* ethical issues that arise, the research representatives would have particular responsibility for a wide range of issues. These include consideration of scientific validity, the techniques employed by the researchers; the likely impact of the research on the subjects, the adequacy of arrangements for attending to subjects in the event of something untoward happening, the appropriateness of the researchers' predictions and expectations in relation to international literature on the topic, and interpreting and explaining the technical and scientific aspects of the study for the benefit of subject representatives. They should also be prepared to discuss the value of the research in relation to the risk of harm. In addition, research representatives should play a part in surveillance and monitoring of ongoing research. Their names should be given to all researchers and research support staff with the advice that they are the appropriate people with whom to discuss any concerns they may have about the ethical conduct of research. Such discussions would be confidential although the representative would advise that he or she was obliged to report the issue (in confidence) to a sub-committee of the research ethics committee which has been set up for this purpose. Committees need to have developed explicit policy on responding to reports of unethical research practices.

An outline of the research representative's role is contained in Table 9.2. This list of duties makes it obvious that the role is a demanding one, particularly when a wide variety of research is being considered by a committee.

It is my observation that researchers in one discipline are not always able to appreciate the research methods of another. As a non-participating observer of research ethics committees, both in the United States and in Australia, I have been present when social science studies have been rejected. On two occasions the reasons for rejection were based on criticism of accepted psychological methodology rather than shortcomings of the particular proposal under review. Recently, on two separate occasions, Australian professors of economics and sociology (respectively) complained to me that research ethics committees (both composed of a majority of medical-graduate members) had rejected proposals on methodological grounds when, from each of their perspectives, the committees had not understood well-accepted research practices in economics (in the one case) and sociology (in the other). Although I am not aware of any such case, the reverse may also be true – that is, social scientist or economist committee members may be inappropriately critical of medical research methodology.

For this reason, researchers' representatives should present the concerns of researchers from within the relevant discipline. If a proposal being reviewed is from one of the 'social sciences', for example, ethics committee members from other disciplines, such as medicine or the biological sciences, should be careful not to discredit the study because the science does not seem adequate from a biological or medical point of view. The proposition is equally true in reverse. The appropriate criteria are established within the relevant science. It is the research representative's responsibility to consider the methodology from an appropriate perspective.

On most committees, members will require the assistance of outside reviewers to do justice to this task. The committee must be

Table 9.2 *The role and responsibilities of research representatives*

RESEARCH REPRESENTATIVES
RESPONSIBILITIES:
Ensuring that scientific validity has been established
Considering study re. international literature on the topic
Ensuring techniques employed by researchers are reasonable
Explaining scientific jargon to other committee members
Considering the value of the research re. risk of harm
Considering the impact of the research on the subjects
Establishing adequacy of arrangements in event of injury
Taking part in surveillance of ongoing research
Receiving informal reports on ethical conduct of research
Discussion of concerns with staff
Education of other researchers
REQUIRED/PREFERRED QUALIFICATIONS:
Experience in relevant research
Capable of identifying inherent conflicts of values
Capable of presenting case in 'lay' terms
Interest in ethics
Compassion/concern for subjects

empowered to draw on expertise beyond its own members to assist in understanding a study, the methodology, its value and its likely impact on subjects. This is already allowed for in the guidelines and regulations of various countries. In the United States, for example, an institutional review board has the discretion to invite individuals with special expertise to assist the committee, although those individuals may not vote.[2]

As I have argued in Chapter 6, I believe the issue of validity is one that should have been adequately dealt with by a specialist committee or assessors *prior* to the research ethics committee review. The research representatives would nevertheless need to ensure that this prior assessment was adequate. Research representatives would therefore be responsible for marshalling the technical information necessary for an adequate assessment and calling for additional help as necessary.

Nothing I have suggested about the roles of the subject or research representatives should be seen as limiting either group to their prime responsibilities. Appropriate research representatives will still be those people with an interest in research ethics and a compassionate concern for subjects. They should be free to comment on issues such as the clarity of information to be given to subjects. Similarly, subject representatives should be free to raise concerns about technical issues such as the validity of research proposals. However, I recommend that, in any system of primary review in which a subgroup of committee members considers research proposals and makes recommendations to the committee, one research member and one subject representative work together as a team. I also recommend that monitoring, and on-site surveillance of research projects in progress, be conducted by one research representative and one subject representative.

Lawyers, ethicists and ministers of religion

In many countries, research ethics committees include members of the clergy (from various religions) and lawyers. In Australia, a minister of religion and a lawyer are required on all committees. If the basis of membership of research ethics committees is altered

2. US Federal Policy for the Protection of Human Subjects (1991: 28015). A similar provision was made in the guidelines of the UK Department of Health (1991: 8).

to require representation of the interests of science and subjects, a question remains as to whether committees might also include a minister of religion, ethicist or a lawyer. In Australia, the reason given for requiring a minister of religion is that they are seen to be 'privy to the thoughts and concerns of many people from different backgrounds'. It is significant that they are not included because of their religious affiliation or any special training in philosophy or ethics (NHMRC, 1985d: 8). While there is a good argument for including someone with training in bioethics (or applied ethics), it should not be assumed that ministers of religion have this training.

In interviews we found that ministers were often not clear about the reasons for their inclusion and there was a tentativity in their expression of views on committees which was similar to that of lay members (McNeill, Berglund and Webster, 1992b). In my view there is no good basis for assuming that ministers have any more insight into the 'thoughts and concerns of people' than, say, a social worker or journalist. Nor could it be assumed that ministers of religion are impartial – most of the ministers of religion we interviewed were chaplains serving the institution. For these reasons I am of the view that a minister should not be a *required* member of a research ethics committee (see also Kuhse and Singer, 1985: 182; and Muschamp, 1988). This is not to exclude a member of the clergy (with a particular interest in research ethics) from being a member by the same criteria as other subject representatives. There is, however, value in suggesting that a person trained in ethics be included on research ethics committees.

The position of lawyers is somewhat different from that of ministers of religion. On Australian committees, lawyers were seen as important by other committee members some of whom stated that they valued their knowledge of the law. Lawyers typically saw themselves as the 'spokesperson for the lay people' and as a 'lay person with legal training'. Unlike lay members, they were confident in putting their views (McNeill, Berglund and Webster, 1992b). The reasons given by the Australian NHMRC for including lawyers was that law was relevant to some ethical issues. Similar reasons were given for suggesting that lawyers were 'desirable' on Canadian research ethics boards (Medical Research Council of Canada, 1987a: 46). The Australian NHMRC had stressed that a suitable lawyer would be one 'interested in ethical matters and aware of the limitations of the law in many aspects of medical research'

(NHMRC 1985d: 7). We found this to be true of all lawyer members we interviewed. It is my view that lawyers play a useful role on these committees.

Regional authorities in New Zealand are required to consider including members with knowledge and experience in law and ethics. A broad recommendation of this sort is helpful and I recommend that all committees appoint a member with knowledge and experience in law and/or ethics. This member, like the subject representatives, should be independent of the research institute or the regional authority administering the committee. If a practising lawyer is appointed, I recommend he or she should *not* be drawn from lawyers who represent the institution in other matters so as to avoid any possibility of bias.

Size of committees

I believe that research ethics committees are far larger than they need to be. Average numbers on committees in the United States were 14 (with a range of 5 to 55) and in Australia the average was 11 (with a range 4 to 23).[3] The committee at Yale University Medical School (described by Levine, in his widely read book on the ethics of clinical research) had 26 members (Levine, 1986: 328–41). Committees of this size are not warranted by the task and are wasteful of human and material resources (including paper).

Committees tend to be formed either by inviting a representative from each of the various departments that commonly conduct research at that institution or by inviting people involved in the various fields of research under consideration. These are then joined by administrative officers, a lawyer, a minister of religion and one or two community members (see, for example, Levine, 1986: 329). The American regulations appear to support such a committee structure by stating that members should have sufficiently diverse backgrounds 'to promote complete and adequate review of research activities commonly conducted by the institution' (US Federal Policy, 1991: 28014–15). The areas specified as needing to be considered include science; professional conduct and practice; rights and welfare of human subjects; race, gender, cultural issues, and community

3. These figures are from the report and recommendations of the National Commission for the Protection of Human Subjects (1978b: 57) and the survey by McNeill, Berglund and Webster (1990: 290).

attitudes; institutional requirements and regulations; and relevant law. At first reading this suggests a large committee to accommodate the necessary expertise.

In a representational model, however, the relevant expertise does not have to be included within the committee itself. The expertise can be provided in a way that leaves fewer people to make the actual decisions. This could occur through a process of thorough review of the scientific validity of studies prior to ethics evaluation, a greater reliance on referrals to relevant experts prior to committee meetings and invitations to experts to assist the committee on difficult issues. People with expertise in particular areas of research ethics and law could be consulted in the same manner. This approach is not ruled out by guidelines in most countries and is specifically provided for in the United States regulations.

A good model for the size of committees is provided by Danish committees. They have six members: three 'medico-scientific' members and three lay members. Table 9.3 outlines a model for a smaller committee. I recommend that research ethics committees be composed of a minimum of six members and a maximum of eight, with alternative members appointed for those occasions when a primary member is unable to attend. I suggest that there be more than one committee where the volume of work is large. Procedures for expedited review (discussed later in this chapter) should reduce the number of proposals needing consideration by the committee. A committee larger than eight will not be any more efficient in my view.

Table 9.3 *A model research ethics committee*

PROPOSED COMPOSITION
2 or 3 representatives of researchers (nominated by relevant research institution(s))
2 or 3 representatives of subjects (nominated by subject representative groups)
1 administrator from support institution
1 lawyer/ethicist independent of the institution
Total: 6 to 8 members

Two or three of the members would represent researchers and two or three would represent subjects. In addition the committee administrator would be included as a full member and there would be an independent member with knowledge and experience in law and/or ethics. This would give a maximum of eight members. To maintain a balance between the interests of researchers and the interests of subjects, it is suggested that the number of research representatives (together with the administrator) should not exceed the number of subject representatives (together with the lawyer/ethicist). The reason for grouping them in this way is that our research has shown that administrators are influential on committees. Also, they cannot be regarded as independent of the research institution (or regional authority) responsible for the committee. For this reason the administrator has been grouped with the researchers. On the basis that lawyers have been found to be influential and to be an advocate for the subjects' position, a lawyer/ethicist is expected to counterbalance any bias that the administrator may have toward the research institution. For this reason the lawyer/ethicist has been grouped with the subject representatives.

There is a need for a stated quorum. We found that Australian committees were prepared to meet and decide issues in the absence of the non-scientific members (McNeill, Berglund and Webster, 1990). I recommend that *all* members (or, in their absence, individual replacements) should attend each meeting. At the most, there should only be two vacant chairs.

Tenure

There should be a policy on tenure because, without one, it might be assumed that a member holds a position on the committee at the pleasure of the institution (Veatch, 1975). This gives too much influence to the institution.

I consider it wise to limit membership to two terms of three years and to make sure that membership is staggered so that not all subject representatives, nor all research representatives, leave the committee at the same time. A practice suggested by the Medical Research Council of Canada guidelines (1987a: 46) is that potential members should be advised that membership is demanding and that there is an expectation that they should remain on the committee for three years.

Failure to perform the duties required of a committee member should be the only reason for removal. No committee member should be removed for putting positions not approved of by other committee members (Levine, 1986: 329). The grounds and manner of removal ought to be included in an explicit policy statement for the committee.

Payment

Although it is said that members of research ethics committees serve in a voluntary capacity there is a significant difference in this respect between the institutional and non-institutional members, quite apart from their professional status. Veatch (1975: 39) has pointed out that attendance of institutional members at such meetings takes place within their normal institutional duties. As such, their committee work is part of what they are paid for. They may also gain additional advantages from committee membership such as recognition of service that contributes to career advancement. Non-institutional members, however, do not have these advantages from membership and their attendance is clearly voluntary. Some non-institutional members may lose money by attending meetings as they need to take leave without pay from other employment. Non-payment of these members signifies that the institution attributes a lower value to the involvement of the non-institutional members who include (by definition in the Australian context) the non-professional members.

Payment for attendance of research ethics committee meetings is exceptional, however. As far as I am aware, only in New Zealand are members paid for their attendance – although Denmark is apparently considering following suit (Denmark, Ministry of Health, 1989: 70–1, 95). The guidelines for ethics committees in New Zealand (New Zealand Department of Health, 1991) specifically state that members 'are eligible for fees and allowances' although not all committees pay attendance monies in practice. Of those regional authorities in New Zealand that do pay members for attending ethics committee meetings, some pay all members and some pay only their lay members.[4]

At the very least, I recommend that all members who are independent of the institution, including the subject representatives and lawyer/ethicist, be paid for attending meetings. Consideration should also be given to whether research representatives should be paid or whether their service can reasonably be regarded as part of

4. Information from various members of New Zealand ethics committees at the Otago University Bioethics Research Centre Summer School, Dunedin, New Zealand, 10–15 February 1992.

their normal institutional duties. Where all members are paid there should be no difference in the rates paid to individual members – excluding, of course, the administrator who will, in all probability, be paid by salary.

Secretarial and administrative support

Administrative and secretarial support is a vital ingredient in efficient and effective committee review. The importance of adequate administrative and secretarial support is recognised by the American regulations (US Federal Policy, 1991) that require institutions to specify the arrangements made for 'staff to support the IRB's review and recordkeeping duties'. The regulations also refer to the need for 'meeting-space'.

Robert Levine (1986: 328–9), in outlining the staff arrangements for the Institutional Review Board he chaired at Yale–New Haven Medical Center, noted that there was one full-time administrator and part-time secretarial support. The administrator shared responsibility with the chairperson for committee policy issues and communication with members, researchers, funding agencies and others. In addition, the administrator screened projects to determine which required full review, performed most of the expedited reviews, dealt with complaints, administered an informal monitoring system, and organised meetings and educational activities for committee members and staff in the institution. This brief description makes it apparent that the administrative function is demanding and that full-time administrative support is warranted.

In the representational committee scheme I have suggested, administrative and secretarial support should be equally available to subject representatives and research representatives on the committee. Provision for funding of these administrative positions would be made through the institution or the regional authority supporting the research ethics review committee. The institution may consider some system of contribution from funding bodies.

Monitoring of research in progress

In addition to administrative and secretarial support for the committee, there is a need for monitoring of research in progress. The evidence is that members of research ethics committees across the world have *not* been effective in monitoring of research (McNeill, Berglund and Webster, 1990; also Miller, 1989: 517). A study we conducted indicated that on-site monitoring, when it has occurred, has increased researchers' respect for the review process (McNeill, Berglund and Webster, 1992a). These findings give weight to the argument that review committees, or their institutions, should be more active in monitoring and surveillance of research practices and not be solely concerned with plans for research. I recommend therefore that committees be much more active in monitoring of research. Committees could select studies for monitoring that they regard as being high risk or that raise particular concerns (such as studies on those not capable of consent). Some studies may warrant close attention to preliminary results to see whether there are any indications of adverse effects. It may be necessary to require that specialists be engaged to do this analysis. Other studies may warrant visits from committee members (including one research representative and one subject representative). An alternative mechanism is to employ a salaried officer to conduct monitoring of research on behalf of the committee.

Expedited review for projects with minimal risk

The number of research proposals considered by committees worldwide is growing rapidly. It is a common complaint that there are too many proposals to allow adequate review by committee. Much of the research that is proposed has little potential for harm to subjects. Examples of such research include epidemiological studies, questionnaires on issues that are not likely to disturb the participants, and studies on tissues or blood samples that are removed in the ordinary course of treatment. In Chapter 4, Danish committees were reported as dealing with 319 research proposals on average in 1990 and one committee had 711 new research proposals registered with it. However, the only projects actually reviewed by committees in Denmark are those about which the researcher, or any of the committee members, may have doubts, or those in which the researcher seeks to omit informed consent from subjects (Riis, 1983: 127). This is a screening method rather than expedited review and may be too loose in that some studies can be registered without any review. I recommend a system in which projects considered to involve minimal risk be given expedited review.

Discretion can be given to an appropriate person to review, to suggest amendments (as necessary) and approve research projects in which there are only minimal risks of harm to subjects. That person would not be free to reject a study but could refer it to the full committee. The person would be obliged to notify the committee of all studies given approval through expedited review. Committee members may wish to examine expedited approvals from time to time and could choose to limit the exercise of that discretion.

This is, in outline, the expedited review model employed in the United States. The American regulations provide that the chairperson, or an experienced member of the IRB designated by the chairperson, can give expedited approval to research proposals that involve no more than minimal risk. Expedited approval can also be given for minor changes to previously approved research. In terms of the American regulations, research involves no more than minimal risk when

> the probability and magnitude of harm or discomfort anticipated in the research are not greater in and of themselves than those ordinarily encountered in daily life or during the performance of routine physical or psychological examinations or tests. (US Federal Policy, 1991: Section 102(i))

Adoption of expedited review (in these terms) could greatly reduce the workload of individual committee members while still giving them control of the overall process.

FUNCTIONING OF COMMITTEES

Johnson and Johnson, in their book on the dynamics of small groups, distinguish between two aspects of group functioning. The first is achieving the group task and the second is maintaining effective working relationships among members (Johnson and Johnson, 1987: 8, 402). The first is also known as 'goal-orientation' (or as group-task) and the second as 'process' (or as group-maintenance) (Heap, 1977). Most of what is written about committees focusses on the first of these aspects. Yet the second aspect – the relationship between committee members and maintaining effective group process – is also very important. In practice these two aspects work together. Failure to maintain an effective committee process will affect the ability of a committee to achieve its goal.

Functional and dysfunctional committees

There are a number of characteristics that identify a functional committee process: members communicate effectively; there is equality of power, influence and participation of members; and there is trust and group cohesiveness (Johnson and Johnson, 1987). One of the signs of a dysfunctional committee is that power is not shared evenly between members of the committee. As was outlined in Chapter 4, studies in the United States and Australia indicate that in general, power is not shared evenly between members of research ethics committees. The scientific and professional members are more influential, leaving the lay members often feeling peripheral.

These observations are symptomatic of dysfunctional committees. The term 'dysfunctional' is also used of 'family systems'. One of the tendencies of dysfunctional families is to focus all the family problems onto one family member. That person becomes a scapegoat (Satir, 1967). In a similar way, some research ethics committees tend to see lay members as not adequately fulfilling their role and tend to attribute this to a personal inadequacy of the lay member. The problem however is much broader. Lay members on committees, as presently structured, are in a difficult position. Changing the role of the lay person to that of 'representative of subjects' gives the lay member a clear role and function. This (in conjunction with selecting suitable people) will create a more effective committee structure.

Nevertheless, committees composed in this way are likely to experience more difficulties than committees with a homogeneous membership. The views of Foucault (discussed in Chapter 8) support the proposition that there is no simple change to the structure, or conduct of meetings, that will eradicate differences in power and influence. Committees with members drawn from the same institution, having relatively equivalent power and status, will typically function more easily. Members are likely to have pre-established working relationships and there will be less need to be concerned about 'process' or 'group-maintenance'. Committees composed of people with very different status and power, some of whom are from within the institution and some from outside, are likely to be dominated by the powerful unless attention is given to the committee process.

In the context of industrial safety, committees composed of representatives of management and workers have been described as 'joint committees' and special attention is given to leadership and the committee process to make them effective (Wuorinen, 1991). Research ethics committees are also 'joint committees' in that they bring together (or should bring together) representatives of the different interests in research review.

Leadership

A great deal rests on the leader (Auger, 1980; Gilsdorf and Rader, 1981). The most appropriate form of leadership is democratic. By this I mean that every member is encouraged to participate and all views are respected. Skilful leadership can develop a co-operative climate that encourages equal participation of all members. It can also develop group norms that foster the feeling that a member's ideas and views are of real interest to the members, no matter what the perceived status of the member may be.

This is not just the leader's responsibility, however. Committee members can contribute to this also. Nevertheless, the major criterion for appointment of the leader or chairperson should be the ability to lead the committee in a 'consensus manner'. Ideally, the chairperson would be drawn from the subject representatives – indicating that the interests of subjects predominate – and the deputy-chairperson from the research representatives.[5] However, I consider a consensus style of leadership to be more important than the group of representatives from which the leader is drawn. The administrator should never serve as chairperson. This is to minimise the risk of any committee becoming a 'rubber stamp' for executive decisions.

Consensual decision-making

According to the studies previously reported, the majority (77 per cent) of Australian research ethics committees made decisions by consensus, and a high proportion (44 per cent) of IRBs in the United States 'always' or 'often' did so (McNeill, Berglund and Webster, 1990; National Commission for the Protection of Human Subjects, 1978c). It is important, to examine what is meant by 'consensus'. Consensus can be arrived at by a minority of members withholding their contrary point of view in order to maintain harmony and to avoid conflict.

5. Both the New Zealand Department of Health, 'Standard' (1991) and the UK Department of Health guidelines (1991: 8) require that the chairman (or the vice-chairman in the British guidelines) be a lay person.

This is especially so when there is a strong commitment to the notion of consensus expressed by high-status members of a committee. Such a view of consensus can operate oppressively – minority members are reluctant to challenge the consensus and feel a pressure to conform.

In Australia 21 per cent of committees and in the United States 66 per cent of committees decide issues by majority vote. The difficulty with majority voting is that minority views may be simply dismissed. This is another means for avoiding conflict. It is a procedure that may lead quickly to a decision but, because the underlying conflict has not been resolved, it comes at the expense of achieving satisfying and effective group relations. While these approaches avoid conflict, they do not lead to good quality decisions because minority views (often important in achieving a balanced perspective) are not adequately considered.

Although I recommend that decisions be reached by consensus, I have a particular notion of consensual decision-making. Creative and 'quality' decisions come from members being open about differences of view. Differences in ideas and values are necessary for a thorough consideration of an issue. It is the failure to manage conflict effectively, not conflict itself, that is destructive of group process. Conflict between ideas and opinions is to be encouraged, but not conflict between persons. Ideally, consensus is based on all views being taken fully into account and the committee coming to a decision that everyone agrees with. This is a style of working that requires skilful leadership and members committed to reaching well thought-through and balanced decisions. It may also take more time. However, with smaller committees and expedited review of some research, that time is well spent on research proposals which raise ethical concerns.

Training

The foregoing discussion on group process, leadership, and the role of committee members indicates a need for training. In Britain, a report from the King's Fund Institute has recommended that there be co-operation between research ethics committees in the training of their members (Neuberger, 1992). As was suggested in Chapter 6, minimum standards need to be established where there is a large number of committees exercising discretionary powers. Discretion should operate within well-defined limits. Establishing these limits highlights a need for education. Members of research ethics committees need to be trained in substantive issues of research ethics, from broad principles to their application to particular fields. The training program should include the legal and ethical standards already established and should consider how these standards would be applied in particular instances.

In addition there is a need for training in effective committee work. Leaders (or chairpersons) of research ethics committees need instruction and practice in leadership styles that will promote participation. Committee members also need training in their representative roles. Occupational safety committees, comprising management and worker representatives, are in a comparable situation (Wuorinen, 1984). In New South Wales, Australia, four-day training programs are conducted for management and worker members of occupational health and safety committees of one large public facility. Skills training in conducting effective committees is included in these courses together with substantive health and safety issues. The costs associated in conducting these programs are justified by improvements in the committee process and ultimately by improvements in health safety (Colquhoun and Elenor, 1988). I would argue that a similar need exists for research ethics committee members and that the costs would be justified by more effective committees, better working relationships between researchers and subjects, and safer and more equitable conditions for research subjects.

I suggest that this training role be given to a national agency. Educational workshops for committee members are a necessary part of maintaining effective ethical standards in practice. They would help members to be clear about their function and to develop agreed procedures and minimum standards of review. This is a sufficiently important component of ethics review for federal government funding to be sought. It was noted in Chapter 4 that the Norwegian Parliament had allocated 16 million kroner (approximately US$ 2.5 million or A$ 3.3 million) to establish a Centre for Biomedical Ethics for information services, scholarships for training in research ethics, and research in biomedical ethics. I would add the conduct of workshops to this list of activities. I believe there is an equivalent need, in most countries, for the establishment of an educational facility with financial support of this order. One of the 'follow-ons' from educational programs conducted through a national body could be educational activities within research institutions aimed at the wider community of researchers.

A more immediate training need was identified in our interviews with committee members throughout Australia. Many of the lay members had little idea of what their role was and had been given no induction on joining committees. This drew attention to the need for induction for new members to committees – especially for those coming onto the committee from outside the institution. A report from the King's Fund Institute in Britain (referred to above) has made a number of practical suggestions for the induction of new members including the provision of relevant guidelines and copies of articles or academic journals which deal with research ethics (Neuberger, 1992). I recommend that the responsibility for training of new members should be taken by the administrator of individual committees in conjunction with either a research representative or a subjects' representative as appropriate.

Open meetings

The finding in our 1988 survey of Australian research ethics committees was that only 4 per cent of committees were open to the public although 63 per cent were 'open' to invited visitors or to researchers (McNeill, Berglund and Webster, 1990). It has also been found that very few committees in Australia allow access to their records or publish the names of committee members (Caton, 1990a). The 1978 National Commission study in the United States found that 56 per cent of IRBs were open to 'non-members'. Levine (1986: 331-2) states that the IRB at Yale–New Haven Medical Center was open to the public although it met in private on one occasion (to consider a controversial IVF proposal) from fear of disruption of their process by attending journalists.

The reason given by Australian research ethics committees for closed meetings was that research ideas discussed at an early stage of a research program were not protected from plagiarism or commercial exploitation.[6] Australian committee members have expressed the fear that revealing the business of the committee or the names of committee members could expose members to the action of 'cranks' in the same way that animal researchers have been attacked or threatened by extreme anti-vivisectionists. I am not aware

---

6. In Denmark, a patent to protect researchers' ideas has been suggested as a means of overcoming this problem (Denmark, Ministry of Health, 1989: 84).

of any instances of this, however. There was also concern expressed in the United States that allowing journalists to report research plans discussed in research ethics committee meetings would be detrimental to proper scientific investigation and reporting (Christakis and Panner, 1986).

These are the reasons given for confidentiality of committee business and committee membership. However, I suspect that there are also covert reasons for meeting in private. One of these is the concern that if the nature of all research proposals before an ethics committee were revealed publicly, a strong political opposition to some forms of research might develop. This is not a valid reason for secrecy in my view as it circumvents one of the democratic safeguards, namely public accountability.

Publicity itself is a political issue. Restrictions on the press are seen as symptomatic of a non-democratic regime. Yet our supposedly democratic nations have kept secret a great deal of unethical experimentation on human subjects. As discussed in Chapter 1, the secrecy with which the United States treated Japan's experimentation on human subjects meant that there was no opportunity for public reaction. The use by the Australian Department of Defence of mustard gas was kept secret until well after the war and it is only recently that there has been any publicity. Similarly, the secrecy surrounding research on carcinoma *in situ* at the National Women's Hospital in New Zealand meant that there was no opportunity for public reaction. It was only when the case received publicity that any effective changes in review practices were brought about.

Given these instances of abuse, which depended on secrecy, I would argue that committee meetings should be open to the public. For democracy to function effectively, the review process itself (including information on committee review – for example, which studies have been approved) needs to be available to the public. Davis (whose views were also discussed in Chapter 8) argued against secrecy in the exercise of discretion. He stated that 'open plans, open policy statements, and open findings and reasons' were protections against the uncontrolled use of discretionary power. He considered that publishing findings and reasons was more important in the exercise of discretion than it was in judicial hearings (Davis, 1969: 226–7). Other commentators, including Annas (1991) also support open review to protect the rights and welfare of research subjects.

The public interest in holding open meetings is primarily linked to the need to protect the interests of subjects. However, there is also a public interest in protecting researchers. Where there is a particular reason for confidentiality, such as the need to keep material which has potential commercial value from competitors, then confidentiality may be warranted (Christakis and Panner, 1986). This might mean holding part of a meeting in private or withholding some of the documents from public scrutiny, or withholding particular matters from the press. The presumption should be in favour of open meetings although this presumption could be rebutted in specific instances. The committee should decide the relative merits of privacy and openness in relation to each case. This is very similar to the decision that a court makes in deciding whether or not to reveal the name of a person before the court. The committee should be satisfied that there are good reasons for maintaining confidentiality. Many of the ethics committees in New Zealand operate in just this fashion – with most of the agenda being dealt with in open meeting and some parts dealt with in camera.

In practice, adequate consideration for privacy could be offered by notifying researchers that meetings are held in public unless researchers have a good reason for part of the business being dealt with in private. If the researcher requests a hearing in private or requests some documents be treated as confidential, then the committee must be satisfied that there are good reasons which are sufficiently important to outweigh the presumption in favour of open meetings. Otherwise, the committee would be obliged to hold the meeting in public even though the researcher (or others) objected.

Explicit policy

Much of this chapter has focussed on creating structures and working relationships to lead to balanced and equitable review. The structures and policies for reviewing and monitoring research need to be explicit. The review process should be part of a policy for balancing the interests of research and subjects. Committee review should not take the place of a comprehensive policy (Wuorinen, 1991: 54). The research ethics committee can play an important part in developing that policy within an institution. However, when the institution itself takes responsibility for ethical research, the support from the upper echelons is much more likely to generate the necessary support for ethical research practices throughout the institution (or region).

The policy should include a broad statement of principles which could either emanate from the institution itself or be imported from an existing statement of research ethics. The statement would include a description of the research ethics committee and its function. Most of the more specific policy matters would be concerned with the appointment of subject and research representatives on research ethics committees, their tenure, the grounds for removal of committee members, grounds for expedited review, procedures for conducting committee review and reporting to applicants, determining which projects require more than annual review, and reporting proposed changes in approved research.

The policy could also include procedures for monitoring and surveillance of research to ensure that research practices conform to ethical guidelines. Both subject and research representatives have a duty to bring concerns of others or reports of questionable research practices to a meeting as soon as possible. These concerns and reports should be considered confidentially to establish whether there is any basis for concern about the conduct of unethical research – and if so what action to take. As I have already suggested, the committee should have an explicit procedure for dealing with reports of unethical experimentation.

The policy should also include specific guidelines on research in particular areas such as clinical drug trials, research on children, and genetic experimentation. Many countries have substantive guidelines and (where these exist) they can be simply endorsed by the institutional policy. Some countries are yet to develop such guidelines and, until that happens, there may be some advantage in modifying and adopting guidelines from international codes and from other countries. The Australian National Health and Medical Research Council 'Statement on Human Experimentation' is included in Appendix 2 as a possible starting point.

Compensation for subjects and indemnity for committee members

Two other matters, only briefly touched on in this book, are compensation and treatment for injured subjects and protection of liability of committee members. The institution's policy should deal with these issues as they are not adequately dealt with in law or national guidelines in most countries. Both British and Irish requirements are exceptional in providing for indemnity of committee members and compensation for subjects.

The Republic of Ireland, in a 1990 amendment to the Clinical Trials and Drugs legislation, has required that adequate arrangements for compensation of volunteers of drug trials be provided for and it grants immunity from liability to members of research ethics committees (Dooley, 1991). The UK Department of Health guidelines suggest that the relevant authority should indemnify all members of research ethics committees against any costs which may result from an action in law against them – although it was acknowledged that there is very little likelihood of a successful claim. The guidelines also recommend that the relevant authority require that outside funding bodies guarantee compensation for any damages suffered by research subjects in the course of experimentation. The King's Fund Institute report has made similar recommendations for compensation (Neuberger, 1992).

I agree that an explicit indemnity should be offered to committee members, especially to those who may not otherwise be covered by virtue of being employed by the institution. One health authority in New Zealand acceded to the demands of its ethics committee only after the committee had refused to consider any applications until all committee members had been granted an indemnity.[7]

The British guidelines (UK Department of Health, 1991: 8, 14) also recommend that research ethics committees ensure that provisions on compensation (in the event of injury of subjects) be included in every research proposal and negotiated with any outside funding agency, before approval. In Australia, it has been recommended that institutions require sponsors of drug trials to take responsibility for compensation and treatment of subjects injured in the course of a trial (Baume, 1991: 117). Subjects should be advised of the arrangements that have been made for compensation and treatment. These are matters that could also be included in a policy statement.

In the absence of any explicit governmental or national provisions, I recommend that institutions formulate policies along the lines I have suggested. It is open to institutions to give their committees

7. Information given to me by a member of a New Zealand ethics committee during the Otago University Bioethics Research Centre Summer School, Dunedin, New Zealand, 10–15 February 1992.

equivalent representation of science and subjects and to contact appropriate bodies within the area to ask for nominations for subject representatives. The advantages of a clear rationale for committee functioning, the saving of labour in having fewer people in the review process, and the opportunity for working co-operatively with potential populations of subjects, are likely to make these recommendations attractive. However, national guidelines or regulations need to incorporate these proposals and a national agency is needed to put them uniformly into effect.

National agency and regulation

There are a number of reasons for suggesting regulation and overview by a national agency. First, institutions most inclined to adopt improved procedures are typically the ones that are balanced, equitable and thorough in their review. Institutions with the least incentive to change are likely to be the ones most needing to upgrade their review and monitoring procedures. To motivate those institutions, there must be some external enforcement that ensures that their review procedures conform to certain standards. Secondly, the essential element for a representational model of review is an independent process for nominating and appointing subject representatives. In order that subject representatives be independent of the institution, the policy on their nomination and appointment needs validation from outside the institution or regional authority.

My proposal is that the institution (or regional authority) administering a research ethics committee would forward their proposed policy to a national agency. The agency would consider those proposed policies and approve them if they met certain specified criteria. On approval, the policy would be registered with the agency and the research ethics committee would be authorised to function. This proposal is a modification of the United States regulatory system. In addition to this regulatory function, the national agency would be responsible for organising training of committee members as is outlined above.

In the United States, policies for the review of research on human subjects are approved by the relevant government department or agency. Health research institutions seek approval from the Office for Protection from Research Risks (OPRR) within the National Institutes of Health. Institutions are required to provide a 'written assurance' which sets out the institution's policy and terms by which the committee will comply with regulations covering research on human subjects. This 'assurance' has to include a description of the members of the IRB, their qualifications, employment and affiliation with the institution (US Federal Policy, 1991). My proposals for representation could be incorporated in the United States regulations by requiring a statement on the likely subject population of most research conducted within the institutions and the suggested bodies responsible for nominating representatives of subjects to the research ethics committee. A statement would also be made on the procedures for appointing representatives from those nominated. On approval of these procedures by the relevant federal department or agency, representatives would be appointed to the IRB according to that procedure.

I envisage a similar system in other countries. Ideally there would be a national administrative authority similar to the Office for Protection from Research Risks in the United States. The authority should be independent of institutions with a vested interest in research. Where there is no governmental authority, it would still be possible for institutions to ensure independent appointment (and payment) of committee members through a 'no-profit' company or trust as has been done in New Zealand for the appointment of independent patient advocates (as outlined in Chapter 3). Nevertheless, the best solution is for a government authority to be given the role. In most countries, that authority could be linked to a national committee responsible for research ethics. In Australia, the obvious authority for medical research is the Australian Health Ethics Committee. Where there is no national committee there may be another appropriate national body (or bodies). In Britain, the obvious authority for ratifying policies and rules for appointment to committees within the National Health Service is the Department of Health. These systems would ideally be underwritten by legislation or government regulation. In those countries with federal systems, such as Canada and Australia, regulations may need to be written to control research funds and research conducted through federal agencies (as are the regulations in the United States). In other countries that do not have this constitutional difficulty, legislation and regulations can be aimed at the direct control of all research on human subjects.

The advantage of a regulatory system of the sort I have proposed is that it leaves the formulation of policy in the hands of institutions responsible for administering research ethics review committees but ensures that procedures are equitable in terms of representing the two important interests in human experimentation. Society has then fulfilled its role by instituting a mechanism for proper consideration of research which puts the interests of subjects on an equal footing with the interests of researchers. This is more than rhetoric in codes of ethics. These are guidelines which are supported by appropriately qualified people with the training, commitment and support in putting the provisions into practice.

Conclusion

The development of a system of review of human experimentation was a response to unethical research. Chapter 1 sketched a history of unethical experimentation from early times into this century. Revelations of German atrocities committed in the name of science during the Second World War and subsequent revelations of unethical treatment in the United States were significant events in this history. They led to the formulation of national and international codes of ethics for experimentation on human subjects. In Australia, for example, a desire to avoid the possibility of experiments like those of the doctors in 'Nazi' Germany was one of the reasons given by the National Health and Medical Research Council (NHMRC) for adopting guidelines for research.

As well as leading to the formulation of codes of ethics, unethical experimentation prompted the development of review of human experimentation by committee. Research ethics committees (institutional review boards) in the United States were adopted as the direct result of unethical experiments such as the Jewish Chronic Disease Hospital Case (discussed in Chapter 3). Other countries followed the example of the United States and instituted committees as outlined in Chapters 3 and 4. More recently a medical research scandal in New Zealand has illustrated once again that revelations of unethical experimentation can be significant in prompting the development of a system of review by committee. The two countries that have not followed this pattern are Germany and Japan. Various reasons for these exceptions are explored in Chapter 4.

Most Anglo-American and many European countries have placed reliance on research ethics committees to protect subjects of experiments. Some forms of experimentation have been banned by legislation in some countries, but for the most part it has been left to committees to decide whether or not research is ethical. This is

237

a procedural solution rather than a substantive rule-based approach. Confidence is placed on the members of those committees, and on the process of review that they adopt, to ensure that human experimentation is ethical.

To illustrate this point, committees were proposed in the United States before there were any substantive principles or rules (other than a requirement for review). It was only after adopting committee review that the briefest of guidance on consent and evaluation of research was offered. Britain first adopted committee review in 1967 and it was not until 1973 that there was a statement on research ethics (in very broad terms) from the Medical Research Council. In Australia this order of events was reversed. A code of ethics was adopted by the NHMRC in 1966 and committees were formed subsequently in 1973. However, the code was a broad, one page statement on research ethics and it became clear from subsequent 'Statements' that the NHMRC placed its major reliance on committees of review. New Zealand too, in its recently adopted 'Standards', has placed its reliance on committee review with only broad guidelines on consent and scientific validity.

Since the introduction of committee review, some development of principles and rules has occurred. The United States has been the most active in setting rules (through federal regulations) and has elaborated principles of ethics in the Belmont Report (discussed in Chapter 6). Yet the American regulations give a primary position to research ethics committees (IRBs), and the Belmont Report (in which the National Commission set out principles of research ethics) relies implicitly on IRBs for the application of the principles enunciated. Given this emphasis, committees deserve scrutiny to assess whether they are capable of protecting the interests of subjects.

I have taken the view that principles and rules of ethics are in need of further development to reduce reliance on the exercise of discretion by ethics committees. In my analysis of the law on human experimentation in Chapter 5, I argued that legislation was needed to clarify inconsistencies between law and practice and to support *ethical* research. In Chapter 6, I concluded that there was a need for development of principles and rules on what constitutes ethical research. The absence of substantive principles and rules of ethics leaves research ethics committees too wide a discretion. Discretion of this sort can be used wisely but it is open to abuse. With increasing research activity, and increasing commercial involvement in health and drug research, the rules need to be more precisely specified. Otherwise research ethics committees could approve research which most of us would regard as unethical. This was the concern in the 'Baby Fae' case discussed in the Introduction.

However, regardless of how detailed rules of ethics might be, there will still be a need for discretion in the application of those rules. Rules cannot be specified for all situations to which they apply. For this reason, research ethics committees have an important role in applying the principles and rules of ethics to individual research programs. Given this pivotal role, the ability of research ethics committees to act equitably is critical in balancing the interests of science and the interests of subjects in human experimentation.

The difficulty is that those with a vested interest in research still have the balance of power and influence on committees. There are a number of factors which give them greater influence. First, ethics review committees are often based in an institution that has a research function. This setting influences committee members toward the goals of the institution, including those of promoting research.

Second, institutional members and researchers are in the majority on many ethics committees. Given the commitment of those members to the institution and to scientific research, and given the benefits that many of them stand to gain from research, I argue that these members must be regarded as having a bias toward the values of science. In my view, researchers and other institutional members have a conflict of interest in making decisions on the acceptability of research.

Third, researchers possess status and power which arise from their knowledge and expertise. This is a point that was examined in some detail in Chapter 8. Many of the institutional and professional members carry badges of office such as the title of 'doctor' and 'professor' which make their position and status apparent.

Fourth, although it is argued that all members are on committees as individuals, it is not possible for the institutional and expert members to divorce themselves from their professional and institutional perspective. They are effectively representative of an institutional or a scientific perspective even though they might protest otherwise. Members of the community, however, are effectively disempowered by the requirement that they be members of committees as individuals. The potential support that they might gain from a community group is denied to them.

Fifth, the power of appointment and the term of office of the community members is most often in the hands of the institution. This gives institutions the opportunity to appoint 'suitable' members who will be co-operative. Also, the lack of an explicit rule about the term of office of members gives rise to a perception that members are on a committee at the pleasure of the institution. This can further inhibit members in expressing challenging views – especially when those members are from outside the institution.

The final observation on the inequalities between members of committees is that the community members are often unclear about their role and are given little guidance as to what is expected of them.

These factors indicate a lack of clear rationale for either the composition or the purpose of these committees. This is an issue that has been explored at several points in this book and particularly in Chapter 8. The lack of rationale and the mixed membership of these committees manifests itself as a difference in the contributions made by the community members and the professional and institutional members of research ethics committees. My colleagues and I have found that, with the exception of lawyers, the presence of lay members does not appreciably shift the balance of power and that ethics review by research ethics committees remains, in effect, self-regulation by researchers and research institutions.

The basic issue and the reason for review of research ethics by a committee is that a researcher and a research institution faces a conflict between a duty to protect the subjects of experimentation from harm and the need to experiment. This is most apparent in medical research when a treating doctor is also a researcher. In this situation, the doctor has divided loyalties between the need to test new remedies and an ethical duty to give his or her patient optimal treatment (within the resources available). While there are few researchers who would knowingly harm their subjects for the advancement of science, there is some element of risk of harm or potential loss inherent in many research programs. The researcher's conflict of interest means that there needs to be some unbiased overview of the researcher's judgement and treatment of subjects. It is society's responsibility, I believe, to ensure that there is adequate review.

At the outset, I stated that the main issue in the ethics of human experimentation was the need to balance between the interests of science and the interests of subjects. In Chapter 7, these two interests were considered in relation to the role of society. Society was portrayed as having an interest in promoting science and protecting the interests of subjects. What I claimed was needed was a mechanism for finding an equitable balance in particular cases. Ideally, in balancing between two important interests in this society, the decision-makers should have no investment in either interest. Whereas the usual obligation in these circumstances is that decision-makers be impartial, this requirement is difficult to satisfy in evaluation of research. This is because research expertise is needed in the process of judging the ethics of research proposals.

What I have proposed in this book is a rationale and an alternative model based on balancing the two interests in human experimentation. The rationale for research ethics committees is that they are discretionary bodies with the function of applying principles and rules of research ethics to particular research programs so as to balance between the interests of science and the interests of subjects. It follows that their composition should include equal numbers of research representatives and subject representatives. I am suggesting that the two major interests be given adequate representation. Both researcher representatives and subject representatives should have the benefits and the responsibilities of consultation with the people they represent. In other words, both roles require support and should be accountable. Subject representatives ought to be accountable to their constituents: the human participants in experimentation. This view comes in part from a recognition that research representatives are already effectively accountable to their colleagues, at least informally. Equally, both groups of representatives need support. Researchers need the support and need to be able to canvass the views of other researchers and especially researchers in other fields or disciplines. Subject representatives also need the support of a community group and need to be able to canvass the views of subjects of experiments and particular subject populations. To represent subjects of experiments adequately, I believe they should be given access to their 'constituents'. They should be encouraged to visit research sites and discuss subjects' experiences in experiments. They should become familiar with issues and potential problems from subjects' points of view. Committees are then composed of members in equal numbers and with adequate support, representing the two main interests.

These suggestions take into account the inherently political nature of research on human subjects. It cannot be assumed that the interests of science, society and subjects coincide when there is a risk of harm which is borne, in the main, by subjects and there are potential gains which are received, in the main, by researchers and their institutions. Most subjects are naïve about the purposes, methods and possible outcomes of experimentation. Leaving it to researchers and institutions (which have a vested interest in research) to devise and carry out systems of review takes insufficient account of their inherent bias.

It needs to be recognised that commercial and professional groups actively oppose restraints and control on human experimentation. As far back as 1930, a physician speaking for the German National Health Council successfully repudiated suggestions for an official body to regulate research on human subjects (see Chapter 2). In 1938, even after an untested 'elixir' had been found to have fatally poisoned more than a hundred people, business interests in the United States were successful in forcing Congress to dilute proposals for testing and marketing of drugs. My point is that professional, research and commercial interests are well organised and able to respond to proposals that would restrict the interests of science and research. Subjects are not in a similar position and their interests do not have the same political or commercial clout. It is difficult for individual citizens to mount an effective counter to vested interests of this sort.

An analogy is with a construction company that wishes to develop a commercial property adjacent to residential properties. The construction company employs staff who are paid to prepare plans and see them through the process of approval by the relevant authorities. It has financial and political influence through the commercial opportunities that may be generated by its activities. A commercial building can be taxed more and offers the local authority increased revenue.

Those who might oppose these plans are individual citizens who fear intrusions into the enjoyment of their neighbourhood and homes and reductions to the value of their properties. Any opposition that they mount is in their own time and difficult to sustain. Yet these are the people who suffer most by the erosion of their living standards. By banding together in neighbourhood associations they can be effective in developing their arguments and putting their case to relevant authorities. Elected members of municipal authorities can be persuaded to represent the interests of this group. Ideally, this political activity will create the conditions for a balance between commercial development and residential peace and quiet.

In the same way, I argue that the people most affected by human experimentation should be heard. Ideally, research subjects themselves would participate in decisions about research. However, it is not feasible to include actual subjects. For there to be participation of subjects of research in decisions, some form of representation must be found. In Chapter 9, I have made various suggestions about the sorts of groups that might be called on to provide subject representatives. Such groups include consumer health groups and civil rights bodies. People from organisations of this sort could represent subjects, not in the sense of being typical of their constituents, but in the sense of being able to represent their interests. I have also suggested adding an administrator and someone trained and experienced in law or bioethics to assist the deliberations of ethics committees.

In Chapter 9, I made a number of practical suggestions on the appointment of members, the need for administrative support, and the size of committees. I advocated expedited review of studies, involving only minimal risk of harm to subjects, to reduce the workload of committees. My recommendation is for smaller, tighter committees with vigorous support from both research and subject representatives. To enable the committees to remain small, it is important to recognise that their function is to make value judgements. They do not need to encompass all relevant knowledge and expertise within the committee. There should be greater reliance on outside advice – especially for those studies which are physically or psychologically invasive. The committee should consult freely with relevant experts and take advice on individual research proposals that are being considered. Ultimately, however, a *value* judgement has to be made about whether an experiment is justified in terms of the interests it compromises and the potential gains it offers. Where there is any doubt about the balance between these two interests, then the interests of the human subjects should predominate.

The review process should not stop at review of proposals for research, however. There are indications that not all researchers are ethical in their research practices. For example, researchers have played down the experimental nature of suggested procedures in order to fill quotas for research subjects. Others have proceeded with studies that should have been given prior approval by a committee without having sought that approval. For these reasons it is not sufficient to rely on an examination of research proposals. There should be some examination of researchers' practices. Yet there is almost no scrutiny of experimentation in progress. What little monitoring there is relies, in almost every case, on reports written by the researchers themselves.

I advocate that committee members be much more active in monitoring and surveillance of research. These members should expect, as a part of their committee role, to undertake surveillance. I have suggested that they act in pairs (one research and one subject representative) as monitors of research in progress. Studies that present particular risks and studies with subjects who are not fully competent to understand and give consent should be identified as requiring surveillance. Given this expectation, it is reasonable that committee members should be paid. My suggestion for small committees has the added advantage that such payment is less onerous on the relevant institution.

Other forms of monitoring may also be necessary. Trials of new treatments need to be watched closely by analysts who are able to detect early indications that the treatment is having adverse effects. In the case of 'double blind' trials, researcher-monitors (not researchers in contact with subjects) need to be given the responsibility for detecting adverse effects from results as they are received. For some experiments it may be necessary to retain the services of a specialist, other than the researcher, to act as a monitor.

Ethics committees are often expected to decide on the scientific validity of proposed studies. As I argue in Chapter 6, this has the effect of giving pre-eminence to a technical question that can only be resolved by the scientifically qualified members. Non-scientific members are relegated to a powerless position by this agenda. In Chapter 6, I advocated that there should be a separate consideration of scientific validity. Discussion of this issue on ethics review committees has the effect of introjecting scientific and technical issues and shifting the balance of power toward those with scientific and technical expertise. For the same reason, I was critical of the expansion of the role of research ethics committees to include evaluating drug trials (Chapter 4). It is my view that questions concerning the validity of research, which require specialised technical expertise, should be considered prior to an evaluation of the ethics of research.

At various points throughout this book, the need and effectiveness of education for committee members and researchers has been referred to. Members of ethics committees in Australia have noted the importance of education for themselves and for researchers (NHMRC, 1985d: 13). In Britain, Dame Mary Warnock and others have commented on the need for education, as has the President's Commission in the United States.[1] In my discussion of discretion in Chapter 6, I argued that there was a need for maintaining minimum standards through education of committee members and researchers. This training should be in substantive ethical issues of research, principles and rules of ethics and also in committee process and consensual decision-making.

A training role for members of research ethics committees should (ideally) be adopted by a national policy-making body or a national educational facility. Educational workshops for committee members (to help them clarify their function and develop agreed procedures and minimum standards of review) are a necessary part of maintaining effective ethical standards in practice. Researchers, other than committee members, ought also to be included in these workshops. This is a sufficiently important component of ethics review for governments to allocate resources to this function. It was noted in Chapters 4 and 9 that the Norwegian Parliament has allocated a considerable sum to establish a Centre for Biomedical Ethics for information services, scholarships for training in research ethics, and research in biomedical ethics. I would add the conduct of training workshops for members of research ethics committees to this list of activities. One of the 'follow-ons' from educational programs conducted through a national body could be educational activities within individual research institutions aimed at other committee members and researchers. As a part of educational activity within institutions, I believe there needs to be adequate induction of each committee member upon joining a review committee.

One of the issues that I have not explored in any depth in this book is whether research ethics committees should be based within institutions or formed on a regional basis. There are arguments on either side of this issue. Arguments for an institutional base for committees are that members of the committee will be familiar with

---

1. Warnock (1985), Neuberger (1992) and the President's Commission for the Study of Ethical Problems (1983: 135–6).

research staff and come to know about research practices in the institution. It is easier for them to stay in touch with what is happening and they can more easily influence research practices for the better – both informally and by conducting educational activities. Opposing this argument is the view that members of the institution are likely to be biased towards the institution and to have sympathetic relationships that make it difficult for them to act independently. Committees formed on a regional basis are thought to be more independent of the institutions in the area and able to make decisions without undue influence.

However, in my view the important issue is whether both the major parties are represented equally in the review process. Once subjects are given adequate representation, the issue of whether committees are formed on an institutional or regional base becomes less important. One of the purposes for including subject representatives is that their bias towards the interest of subjects acts as a counter to any bias towards research and the institution which other members may bring with them.

Essentially what I am advocating in this book is the democratic right of people to contribute to decisions affecting their lives. Human experimentation raises the issue of adequate protection of the rights and interests of the subjects of experimentation because the influential decision-makers in the committees (as presently constituted) are those with a vested interest in the outcome. This has led me to propose an alternative rationale for committee review and to suggest changes in the model for committee composition and functioning.

The ideal model proposed in this book is based on a committee of six to eight members. However, I am sufficiently pragmatic to recognise that this model will need to be modified according to specific circumstances. Underlying the model is a rationale for committee function and composition. It is the rationale that I would defend more strongly; namely that committees should be balanced between the interests of research and the interests of subjects of experimentation in carrying out their discretionary function.

Each country has its own particular history and issues to deal with. New Zealand, for example, has only recently made major changes to its ethics committees including a requirement that half the committee be community members. I recognise that, given the flux of other changes in the New Zealand health system, another radical change to the basis of committee representation could put at risk the gains that have been achieved. Nevertheless I maintain that in considering the function of research ethics committees worldwide, it is necessary to examine their underlying rationale. Any changes made should be directed toward balancing the two major interests: the interests of science and the interests of subjects. Part of the appeal of these measures is their direct relevance to protection of the interests of researchers and the interests of the human subjects of experimentation. It is the appropriate protection of the values of the researcher and those of the human subject that is the reason for ethics review.

I believe the proposals put forward in this book recommend themselves by their manifest justice. It is my hope that they might be adopted without the need for further revelations of unethical experimentation.

Appendices

Research Ethics Review in Other Countries

For some countries the only available published information is now out of date. For other countries, only brief reports are available or, alternatively, the only material available to me is based on impressions given to me in interviews. Because of the length of Chapter 4, the information on all these countries is presented here as an appendix in the following groupings: 'Other European Countries'; 'India'; and 'Other Countries' (which includes developing countries both in East Asia and in South America).

OTHER EUROPEAN COUNTRIES

In Chapter 4, I reported on research ethics committees in Britain, France, The Netherlands, Belgium, Switzerland, Scandinavia and Germany. In this appendix further reports are presented on European countries including Italy, Spain, Greece, Poland and Hungary. In Europe most of the committees known as ethics committees are committees for the review of research although they occasionally consider clinical ethical issues.

ITALY

In 1987 the Medical Research Council of Canada (1987b: 42) reported that very few Italian institutions had an ethics committee and little information was published on the committees that did exist. One of the few recent reports on Italian committees (contained in the Editorial of the *IME Bulletin* (1988d: 21)) stated that there was a 'worryingly sectarian element' developing between committees which were labelled either Catholic or secular. An exception was a committee in Florence for psychiatric hospitals that included Catholic, Protestant and Jewish members.

SPAIN

Ethics committees are responsible for scientific and ethical evaluation of clinical research projects in Spain. Created by statute, there are 122 of them in hospitals. The Minister of Health announced the formation of a National Ethics Committee in February 1990 (Baudouin, Ouellette and Molinari, 1990: 24).

GREECE

In Greece, in 1978, the Minister of Health required that all applicants for research grants submit evidence of an ethics committee approval. The policy was later abandoned, however. The two principal medical journals now require ethics committee approval before accepting articles reporting research on human subjects. There have been suggestions that the Institute of Medical Ethics may take some action (Editorial, *IME Bulletin*, 1988b: 21).

POLAND

In 1988 the Centre for Biomedical Ethics in Louvain, Belgium, reported that Poland has a number of research ethics committees and a national body.[1] The committees were found in all 11 medical faculties and in 15 central research institutes. These committees had at least five members most of whom were doctors. Some committees have a lawyer or a 'social representative'. The committees review all research projects on human subjects that propose experimentation with a 'known risk element'. They have the power to block research funding and publication of research that has not been approved. The national body, known as the 'Supervisory Committee for Human Experimentation in Medicine', comprised 30 senior scientists and a few additional experts in law and social sciences. This body maintained communication with the research ethics committees. It was responsible for hearing appeals to the decisions of those committees and did so by appointing an *ad hoc* committee of members with the relevant expertise.

HUNGARY

It is not clear, from two separate reports, whether or not there are ethics committees for the review of research in institutions in

---

1. The information contained in this section is drawn exclusively from the Editorial (News), *IME Bulletin* (1988g: 7).

Hungary. Although the *IME Bulletin* (1988f: 7) reported that Hungary appeared to have no research ethics committees, Blasszauer (1988) stated that there were medical ethics committees and institutional ethical councils. Both reports agree that there was a central body which reviewed some proposals. This body was known as the Medical Committee of Research Ethics, a part of the Health Scientific Council, and was responsible for advising the Minister of Health. According to the *IME Bulletin*, that Committee had reviewed only 45 research proposals in 1986. The functions of the Committee were described as providing guidelines, ethical review of research and putting 'forward proposals to permit investigations different from the usual ones, involving tests on human test subjects'. Blasszauer reported that an attempt to produce a national code of medical ethics to guide ethics committees failed due to a lack of support.

INDIA

The information I have on India is based on interviews I conducted in Bombay and New Delhi in January 1990. Previously published information comes from a 1960 report in the *World Medical Journal*.[2] The guidelines current in India were promulgated by the Indian Council of Medical Research in 1980.[3] This statement requires that proposals for research on human subjects be approved by an institutional ethical committee before they can be considered for funding by the Council. It also recommends that other agencies supporting clinical research in India adopt the guidelines or incorporate them into their own assessment of research. Ethics committees were to include clinicians experienced in clinical research, an expert on drugs and 'one or two non-medical persons who could provide guidance to the committee in the matter of ethics and law'. The guidelines recommend that these 'non-medical persons' include a lawyer or a judge. It was suggested that the committee draw some members from other institutions; that committees be kept small (between five and seven members); and that they meet at least once every three months. The guidelines specifically refer to the Nuremberg Code and the Helsinki Declaration and include provisions similar to those contained in the Declaration. There were specific

2. Bassiouni, Baffes, and Evrard (1981: 1647), quoting from Mittra 'Special Report: India', *World Medical Journal* (1960: 84–5). Fluss (1982: 326, 353) without giving any information, also referred to the role of Indian ethics committees.
3. Indian Council of Medical Research, 'Policy Statement', 1980. The guidelines are also mentioned in Editorial (News), *International Digest of Health Legislation*, 1980.

provisions for research on children, the mentally deficient, prisoners, medical students and laboratory personnel.

Although the Policy Statement required the Ethical Committee of the Indian Council of Medical Research to monitor the implementation of the guidelines and check whether the recommendations made by the ethical committees of particular institutions were being followed by investigators, no study or audit of committees had been conducted in India.[4]

A research ethics committee of one large Indian research institution, the All-India Institute of Medical Sciences considers between 40 and 50 research proposals each year.[5] Of these 30 to 40 per cent are approved, 30 to 40 per cent are sent back to the researchers for clarification or modification, and approximately 25 per cent are rejected. The members of this committee are mostly medical graduates. They include five medical graduate members, a retired judge and representatives of two other research organisations. The committee functions in much the same way as in other countries by preview of research proposals by all committee members and subsequent meeting to discuss the proposals. If necessary, researchers are asked to defend their proposals. I was informed that this institution, and other large research institutions in New Delhi and Bombay,[6] are thorough in their review. It was suggested that this was not typical of research review throughout India, however.

I was informed that there are approximately one hundred institutional ethical committees throughout India. Most of these are in medical colleges or research institutions. It is estimated that the average number of members on these committees lies between five and six and that committees consider four or five new proposals for research on human subjects on average each year (Dr B. N. Saxena, personal communication).

OTHER COUNTRIES

The remaining reports of ethics review are sketchy. Very little information is to be found on systems for the review of the ethics

4. From an interview with Dr Badri N. Saxena, Deputy Director of the Indian Council of Medical Research, New Delhi, India (9 January 1990). Dr Saxena was one of the original members of the Committee that proposed the Policy Statement.
5. From an interview with Professor S. D. Seth, secretary/member of the ethics committee of the All-India Institute of Medical Sciences, in New Delhi (9 January 1990).
6. These institutions include the Cancer Research Institute, Bombay; the Institute for Research in Reproduction, Bombay; and the Department of Biotechnology, New Delhi.

of research in developing countries. This probably means that there is little review carried out.

There is, however, concern about the risk of exploitation of research subjects and personnel in developing countries. This occurs largely as the result of externally sponsored research and the lack of any system of research regulation such as committee review. A major difficulty arises where research is of no interest or benefit to the host country and where researchers from foreign countries are insensitive to local issues. There is also a tendency for externally funded research programs to employ the only local people with any medical skills and training and attract them away from other health care or research duties more important to the host country. There is a need for independent review. One commentator suggested this should be independent of the local health authority. The Council for International Organizations of Medical Sciences (CIOMS) has been asked to help by providing external independent opinion. There were often insufficiently trained local people capable of reviewing the project. It is also suggested that medical schools and other health training institutes in developing countries offer teaching programs on research ethics (Ofosu-Amaah, 1982).

Other contributors to a CIOMS Conference in 1981 spoke of the difficulties of cross-cultural research and the way in which principles and practices of research ethics could be culturally specific. The notion of informed consent, for example, was understood in Western countries and related to Western concepts of the autonomy of the individual. However, informed consent may not make much sense in countries in which identity is tied to the community or tribal group (Curran, 1982: 71–3; Ajayi, 1980). This is an issue which has recently been addressed in Australia (NHMRC, 1991a, 1991b) in the context of research on Aboriginal communities.

The reports from 'developing' countries and other countries with limited resources include the Philippines, Korea, Mexico, Argentina and Chile. A commentator from the Philippines (Villadolid, 1982) had been unable to identify any ethics committees in his country in 1981 although he thought there may have been one in the College of Medicine in the West of the Philippines.

A Malaysian commentator (Sinnathuray, 1982) stated that Malaysia, like many developing countries in Southeast Asia and elsewhere, did not have a national medical council to oversee research development and encourage ethical guidelines. Nevertheless, the University of Malaysia Medical Faculty had developed an ethics committee to oversee research. There were three members including the Medical Faculty Chairman, the Director of the University Hospital and a professor from the Law Faculty.

A Korean commentator (Soh, 1982) reported that the 'ethical review system for biomedical research in Korea is still at a very immature stage'. In 1981 there were no formal ethics committees although he claimed some committees established to evaluate and screen research did give some consideration to ethical issues.

No recent report on the development of ethics committees in Argentina has been located. A 1980 report by Pavlovsky (1981) stated that 'it has not become general in Argentinian hospitals, except in a few devoted to research, to have an ethical committee'. The suggestion was that a meeting of a 'national intersectorial' group might lead to a greater number of committees. However, Pavlovsky expressed concern that review could lead to 'troublesome' controls (1981: 121).

Brunser (1981: 126) has reported that hospitals in Santiago had ethics committees that were responsible for overseeing the ethics of drug trials. Their main responsibility, however, was to consider complaints of medical malpractice by doctors in the treatment of their patients. Brunser also gave a detailed report on the ethics committee of the Institute of Nutrition and Food Technology in the University of Chile which was more strictly confined to the ethics of research and which operated with a broad membership including doctors, a biochemist, a sociologist and a lay member.

An order of the General Health Council of Mexico, issued in 1981, requires that a review of biomedical research be conducted by a committee of three – all of whom are to be professional researchers. The duties are to promote, regulate and supervise research and to help research workers. Committees considering research on human subjects are required to report on the ethical aspects of the research (Editorial (News), *International Digest of Health Legislation*, 1984).

There is a report that most experimentation in South Africa is conducted on black patients and that research ethics committees are almost entirely made up of doctors.[7]

7. The report is contained in a book review of G. C. Oosthuizen, H. A. Shapiro, and S. A. Strauss, *Attitudes to Clinical Experimentation in South Africa*, Johannesburg: Hodder and Stoughton, 1985 (in *IME Bulletin*, no. 39, June 1988: 24). A number of requests have been made to the publisher and their agents, but with no success to date.

NHMRC Statement on Human
Experimentation and Supplementary Notes 1992

ETHICS OF MEDICAL RESEARCH ON HUMANS –
EXPLANATORY NOTE

Aware of the Declaration of Helsinki, adopted by the 18th World
Medical Assembly, Helsinki, Finland, 1964, revised by the 29th
World Medical Assembly, Tokyo, Japan, 1975, and the 35th World
Medical Assembly, Venice, Italy, 1983 and of the Proposed International Guidelines for Biomedical Research Involving Human
Subjects published by the World Health Organization and the
Council for International Organizations of Medical Sciences in 1982,
the National Health and Medical Research Council issues the
following statement on human experimentation and associated supplementary notes. These are intended as a guide on ethical matters
bearing on human experimentation, for research workers and
administrators of institutions in which research on humans is
undertaken in Australia.

NHMRC STATEMENT ON HUMAN EXPERIMENTATION
To be read in conjunction with the supplementary notes

The collection of data from planned experimentation on human
beings is necessary for the improvement of human health. Experiments range from those undertaken as a part of patient care to those
undertaken either on patients or on healthy subjects for the purpose
of contributing to knowledge, and include investigations on human
behaviour. Investigators have ethical and legal responsibilities
toward their subjects and should therefore observe the following
principles:

---

* *NHMRC Statement on Human experimentation and Supplementary Notes* is reprinted here
  with the kind permission of the National Health and Medical Research Council.

1. The research must conform to generally accepted moral and scientific principles. To this end institutions in which human experimentation is undertaken should have a committee concerned with ethical aspects and all projects involving human experimentation should be submitted for approval by such a committee[1] (see supplementary note 1 on institutional ethics committees).

2. Protocols of proposed projects should contain a statement by the investigator of the ethical considerations involved.

3. The investigator after careful consideration and appropriate consultation must be satisfied that the possible advantage to be gained from the work justifies any discomfort or risks involved.

4. The research protocol should demonstrate knowledge of the relevant literature and wherever possible be based on prior laboratory and animal experiments.

5. In the conduct of research, the investigator must at all times respect the personality, rights, wishes, beliefs, consent and freedom of the individual subject.

6. Research should be conducted only by suitably qualified persons with appropriate competence, having facilities for the proper conduct of the work; clinical research requires not only clinical competence but also facilities for dealing with any contingencies that may arise.

7. New therapeutic or experimental procedures which are at the stage of early evaluation and which may have long-term effects should not be undertaken unless appropriate provision has been made for long-term care, observation and maintenance of records.

8. Before research is undertaken the free consent of the subject should be obtained. To this end the investigator is responsible for providing the subject at his or her level of comprehension with sufficient information about the purpose, methods, demands, risks, inconveniences and discomforts of the study. Consent should be obtained in writing unless there are good

1. (a) An application to the NHMRC for a research grant involving human experimentation is required to be certified by the ethics committee of the applicant's institution as complying with the *NHMRC Statement on Human Experimentation and the Supplementary Notes* before the application will be considered for funding.
   (b) Persons undertaking human experimentation who are not associated with an institution should ensure that comments on their protocols are sought from an established ethics committee e.g. in a university or hospital.

reasons to the contrary. If consent is not obtained in writing the circumstances under which it is obtained should be recorded.

9. The subject must be free at any time to withdraw consent to further participation.

10. Special care must be taken in relation to consent, and to safeguarding individual rights and welfare where the research involves children, the mentally ill and those in dependant relationships or comparable situations (see supplementary note 2 on research on children, the mentally ill and those in dependant relationships or comparable situations, including unconscious patients).

11. The investigator must stop or modify the research program or experiment if it becomes apparent during the course of it that continuation may be harmful.

12. Subject to maintenance of confidentiality in respect of individual patients, all members of research groups should be fully informed about projects on which they are working.

13. Volunteers may be paid for inconvenience and time spent, but such payment should not be so large as to be an inducement to participate.

NOTES SUPPLEMENTING THE NHMRC STATEMENT ON HUMAN EXPERIMENTATION

These notes are issued by the NHMRC to supplement the *NHMRC Statement on Human Experimentation* and should be read in conjunction with it. They will be reviewed from time to time. The present series (1992) comprise the following –

SUPPLEMENTARY NOTE 1 (1992) –
INSTITUTIONAL ETHICS COMMITTEES

Supplementary note 1 adopted by the Council at its 113th Session June 1992

1. All research projects involving human subjects and relating to health must be considered and approved by a committee constituted in accordance with this supplementary note.
2. Institutions in which such research is undertaken should establish and maintain an institutional ethics committee (IEC) composed and functioning in accordance with this supplementary note.
   Where an institution can not maintain a properly constituted IEC, approval of research proposals should be sought from an IEC established and maintained by another institution.
3. An IEC must ensure that ethical standards are maintained in research projects to protect the interests of the research subjects, the investigator and the institution.

4. *Composition*
   (i) An IEC shall be composed of men and women of different age groups, and include at least one member from each of the following categories:
   - laywoman not associated with the institution
   - layman not associated with the institution
   - minister of religion
   - lawyer
   - medical graduate with research experience.
   (ii) Persons may be appointed to stand-in for members when necesary.
   (iii) An institution may appoint more persons than those specified in 4(i) as members of an IEC.
   (iv) Members and stand-in members shall be appointed by an institution on such terms and conditions as the institution determines and in such manner as to ensure that the committee will fulfil its responsibilities.
   (v) Members shall be appointed as individuals for their expertise and not in a representative capacity.
   (vi) A layperson is one who is not closely involved in medical, scientific or legal work.
   (vii) A minister of religion may be of any faith.

5. *Functions*

    (i) A research project may be approved and may continue only if an IEC is satisfied that:
- the project as set out in the protocol is acceptable on ethical grounds; and
- the project continues to conform to the approved protocol.

   (ii) An IEC shall maintain a record of all proposed research projects including:
- name of responsible institution;
- project identification number;
- principal investigator(s);
- short title of project;
- ethical approval or non-approval with date;
- the relevance of the Privacy Guidelines, which address the use of data from Commonwealth agencies;
- approval or non-approval of any changes to the protocol; and
- action taken by the IEC to monitor the conduct of the research.

The protocols of research projects shall be preserved in the form in which they are approved.

  (iii) The NHMRC accepts the responsibility to communicate with and audit the activities of IECs to ensure compliance with this supplementary note.

An IEC shall accept an obligation to provide information from its records to the NHMRC on request.

6. *Application of functions*

In carrying out these functions, an IEC shall:

    (i) conform with the *NHMRC Statement on Human Experimentation and Supplementary Notes* as published from time to time;

   (ii) while promoting the advance of knowledge by research, ensure that the rights of the subjects of research take precedence over the expected benefits to human knowledge;

  (iii) ensure that, in all projects involving human subjects and relating to health, the free and informed consent of the subjects will be obtained[1];

---

1. Except in accordance with section 7 of supplementary note 6 of the *NHMRC Statement on Human Experimentation and Supplementary Notes.*

      (iv) ensure that no member of the committee adjudicates on projects in which they may be personally involved;

      (v) ensure that research projects take into consideration local cultural and social attitudes;

     (vi) give its own consideration to projects that involve research in more than one institution[1];

    (vii) require the principal investigator to disclose any previous decisions regarding the project made by another IEC and whether the protocol is presently before another IEC; and

   (viii) determine the method of monitoring appropriate to each project.

7. *Meeting procedures*

      (i) Wherever possible, a decision by an IEC shall be made after a person from each of the categories listed in section 4(i) of this supplementary note has had an opportunity to contribute their views during the decision making process;[2]

     (ii) An IEC should seek to reach decisions by general agreement which need not involve unanimity;

    (iii) In the absence of general agreement that a project is ethically acceptable, an IEC shall either establish a procedure to arrive at a decision, for example a simple majority, or inform the principal investigator of necessary amendments to the protocol;

     (iv) An IEC may invite the investigator(s) to be present for discussions of the project; and

     (v) An IEC may seek advice and assistance from experts to assist with consideration of a proposal.

8. *Monitoring*

An IEC shall ensure that there is appropriate monitoring of research projects until their completion. To achieve this a committee shall:

1. An IEC is free to discuss a project with other IECs if it chooses, with due regard to confidentiality.
2. This does not necessarily require the presence of a person from each of the categories at every meeting of an IEC. There are a number of options available to deal with situations where all members cannot be present and these are at the discretion of each IEC. For example, if a member cannot be present at a meeting, their opinion could be communicated in writing or orally and recorded at the meeting.

(i) at regular periods, and not less frequently than annually, require principal investigators to provide reports on matters including:
  - security of records
  - compliance with approved consent procedures and documentation
  - compliance with other special conditions;

(ii) as a condition of approval of the protocol, require that investigators report immediately anything which might affect ethical acceptance of the protocol, including:
  - adverse effects on subjects
  - proposed changes in protocol
  - unforseen events that might affect continued ethical acceptability of the project; and

(iii) establish confidential mechanisms for receiving complaints or reports on the conduct of the project.

SUPPLEMENTARY NOTE 2 – RESEARCH ON CHILDREN, THE MENTALLY ILL, THOSE IN DEPENDANT RELATIONSHIPS OR COMPARABLE SITUATIONS (INCLUDING UNCONSCIOUS PATIENTS)

Revised supplementary note 2 adopted by the Council at its 113th Session June 1992

Ethics of research on children[1]

In these notes the principles and guidelines that are set out largely reflect the 'Report on the Ethics of Research in Children' prepared by the Council of the Australian College of Paediatrics and published in the *Australian Paediatric Journal* 17: 162, 1981.

1. Scientific research is essential to advance knowledge of all aspects of childhood disease. Such research, however, may be performed only when the information sought cannot in practice be obtained by other means.

2. All research must be based on sound scientific concepts and must be planned and conducted in such a fashion as will reasonably ensure that definite conclusions will be reached. Some programs

---

1. In this supplementary note the word 'child' extends to a person from birth until the legal age of majority. Some States and Territories in Australia have special laws applying to the medical treatment of minors.

may offer direct benefit to the individual child, while others may have a broader community purpose. In appropriate circumstances both may be ethical.

3. In all centres undertaking research in children, the following special responsibilities of the institutional ethics committee are emphasized:
    (i) protecting the rights and welfare of children involved in research procedures;
    (ii) determining the acceptability of the risk/benefit relationship of any research study conducted;
    (iii) ensuring that informed consent from parents/guardian and where appropriate the child, is obtained in a manner appropriate to the study;
    (iv) encouraging the performance of necessary and appropriate research; and
    (v) preventing unscientific or unethical research.

4. Consent to research should be obtained from:
    (i) the parents/guardian in all but exceptional circumstances (e.g. emergencies); and
    (ii) the child where he or she is of sufficient maturity and intelligence to make this practicable.

In this context 'consent' means consent following a full and clear explanation of the research planned, its objectives and any risks involved.

5. Risks of research may be considered in terms of:
    (i) therapeutic research (where the procedure may be of some benefit to the child).
    In determining whether there is an acceptable relationship between potential benefit and the risk involved, it is essential to weigh the risk of the proposed research against customary therapeutic measures and the natural hazards of the disease or condition.
    (ii) non-therapeutic research (where the procedure is of no direct benefit to the child).
    The risk to the child should be so minimal as to be little more than the risks run in everyday life.

Risks of research in this context include the risk of causing physical disturbance, discomfort, anxiety, pain or psychological disturbance to the child or the parents rather than the risk of serious harm, which would be unacceptable.

The mentally ill

It is always desirable to obtain informed consent from a person who has the intelligence or capacity to make this practicable. In the case of those who lack legal capacity due to mental illness, consent should also be obtained from the person who stands legally in the position of guardian, next friend, or the like.

Those in dependant relationships or comparable situation

Some people merit special attention before inclusion in a project in order to ensure that consent is both informed and free. It is not possible to define them exhaustively, but in addition to children and the mentally ill they may include the following:

- elderly persons who may have legal capacity but may nonetheless be in a position where they are unable to give a free or comprehending consent;
- wards of state;
- those in doctor and patient and teacher and student relationships;
- prisoners;
- members of the Services; and
- hospital and laboratory staff.

Unconscious and critically ill patients

Unconscious, semi-conscious or critically ill patients from whom or on behalf of whom consent cannot be obtained for treatment or other intervention, because of the urgency of their condition, also merit special attention.

A person might be in such a situation, for example, following a drug overdose or a cardiac arrest. Two kinds of experimental intervention may be envisaged. The first is intended or expected to benefit the person. The second is intended or expected to yield important scientific information but is not intended or expected to benefit the person. (The taking of a sample of blood for studies not directly relevant to the diagnosis or treatment of the patient would be an example of the latter.)

1. Experimental intervention intended or expected to benefit the patient.

    Before approving a research protocol an institutional ethics committee should satisfy itself:

    (i) that the guidelines, other than those bearing on consent, in the statement on human experimentation are followed; and

(ii) that in the light of available knowledge it is reasonable to adopt the experimental intervention as being in the interests of the patient.

2. Experimental intervention is neither intended nor expected to benefit a patient.

Before approving a research protocol, an institutional ethics committee should satisfy itself:

(i) that the guidelines, other than those bearing on consent, in the statement on human experimentation are followed;

(ii) that there are good reasons why the experimental intervention cannot be limited to persons from whom, or on behalf of whom, consent can be obtained.

(iii) that the experimental intervention will be one which will involve no material risks beyond those associated with procedures that are clinically indicated for the patient;

(iv) that the requirements of the research do not influence the procedures that are clinically indicated; and

(v) that the confidentiality of information identifying the patient will be preserved.

SUPPLEMENTARY NOTE 3 – CLINICAL TRIALS

Revised supplementary note 3 adopted by the Council at its 104th Session November 1987

A clinical trial is a study done in humans to find out if a treatment or diagnostic procedure, which it is believed may benefit a patient, actually does so. A clinical trial can involve testing a drug, a surgical or other procedure, or a therapeutic or diagnostic device.

The drug procedure or device may be a new or an old one. It may be under trial in new clinical circumstances, or its conventional use may be under review. It is not always possible to make a clear distinction between ordinary diffusion of clinical knowledge and the medical and surgical circumstances that warrant a formal clinical trial. Clinicians should be aware of the benefits that come from (a) designing and conducting clinical trials, and (b) sharing ethical responsibility for innovation in medical practice.

The *NHMRC Statement on Human Experimentation and Supplementary Notes* are applicable to all clinical trials.

Following are some particular matters concerning the design and conduct of clinical trials that need to be taken into account when ethical aspects are being considered. Clinical trials involving DNA (gene) therapy are subject to additional requirements (see supplementary note 7).

1. Trials should be conducted according to written protocols, which should be approved by institutional ethics committees.
2. When an institutional ethics committee is reviewing a proposal for a clinical trial involving a drug it should be assured:
    (i) that a pharmacologist or clinical pharmacologist has been involved in preparing the protocol;
    (ii) that for trials involving new drugs the protocol includes a full investigational profile[1] of the drug or drugs to be used;
    (iii) that the protocol contains precise information on dosage, formulation, frequency of administration and methods of assessing safety; and
    (iv) that all suspected adverse drug effects observed in the course of a trial will be reported to the Commonwealth Department of Community Services.
3. When an Institutional Ethics Committee is reviewing a proposal for a clinical trial involving a therapeutic or diagnostic device it should be assured:
    (i) that persons suitably qualified to assess the technical and clinical aspects of the device have been involved in preparing the protocol;
    (ii) that the protocol contains adequate information on methods of use, risks and benefits expected; and
    (iii) that the guidelines for investigational use of therapeutic devices prepared by the Commonwealth Department of Health, Housing and Community Services are taken into account[2].
4. The aims of every trial should be precisely stated and important enough to be worth achieving, having in mind the time, effort, cost and possible discomfort that may be involved.
5. The experimental design should be such as to ensure that it will be possible to answer the question asked. In particular institutional ethics committees should be assured of the statistical validity of the design of a proposed trial.

1. The data on formulation would normally be that contained in the National Drug Information Service drug profiles.
2. *Guidelines for the General Marketing or Clinical Investigational use of Designated Therapeutic Devices* are available from the Department of Health, Housing and Community Services, Medical Devices and Dental Products Branch, GPO Box 9848, Canberra ACT 2601.

6. Some trials involve the use of control groups for purposes of comparison. Patients in control groups should receive what is considered to be the best treatment currently available; in some cases this may be simply observation or administration of placebo.
7. When informed consent is being sought, costs which may be incurred by subjects as a result of participation in the trial should be discussed with them.
8. There should be a reasonable expectation that the objectives of a clinical trial will be achieved within a defined period of time. In some circumstances it may be unethical to continue a trial for the full period that was planned. For example, it would be wrong to continue if there were substantial deviations from the trial protocol, or if side effects of unexpected type or frequency were encountered. It would also be wrong to continue if one of several treatments or procedures being compared proved, as the trial progressed, to be so much better, or worse, than other(s) that continued adherence to the trial would disadvantage some of the subjects enrolled.

The progress of a trial should generally, therefore, be monitored. Monitoring should be done by an independent person or small committee. Independence is necessary because it is often important, in order to minimise observer and patient bias, for those conducting a trial to remain unaware of the trends in the results during the study; it may also be hard for them to take a detached view of the merits of continuing a trial already under way. Those conducting the trial should give the monitoring body such information as it may request to enable it to be satisfied that the trial protocol is being followed and that the outcome of treatment, including side effects, is not such as to warrant premature termination of the study.

SUPPLEMENTARY NOTE 4 – IN VITRO FERTILIZATION AND EMBRYO TRANSFER

Supplementary note 4 adopted by the Council at its 94th Session October 1982

In vitro fertilisation (IVF) of human ova with human sperm and transfer of the early embryo to the human uterus (embryo transfer, ET) can be a justifiable means of treating infertility. While IVF and

ET is an established procedure, much research remains to be done and the *NHMRC Statement on Human Experimentation and Supplementary Notes* should continue to apply to all work in this field.

Particular matters that need to be taken into account when ethical aspects are being considered follow.

1. Every centre or institution offering an IVF and ET program should have all aspects of the program approved by an institutional ethics committee. The IEC should ensure that a register is kept of all attempts made at securing pregnancies by these techniques. The register should include details of parentage, the medical aspects of treatment cycles, and a record of success or failure with:
   - ovum recovery;
   - fertilization;
   - cleavage;
   - embryo transfer;
   - pregnancy outcome.

   These institutional registers, as medical records, should be confidential. Summaries for statistical purposes, including details of any congenital abnormalities among offspring, should be available for collation by a national body.

2. Although IVF and ET as techniques have an experimental component, the clinical indications for their use, treatment of infertility within an accepted family relationship, are well established. IVF and ET will normally involve the ova and sperm of the partners.

3. An ovum from a female partner may either be unavailable or unsuitable (e.g. severe genetic disease) for fertilization. In such a situation the following restrictions should apply to ovum donation for embryo transfer to that woman:
   (i) the transfer should be part of treatment within an accepted family relationship;
   (ii) the recipient couple should intend to accept the duties and obligations of parenthood;
   (iii) consent should be obtained from the donor to the recipient couple;
   (iv) there should be no element of commerce between the donor and recipient couple.

4. A woman could produce a child for an infertile couple from ova and sperm derived from that couple. Because of current inability

to determine or define motherhood in this context, this situation is not yet capable of ethical resolution.

5. Research with sperm, ova or fertilized ova has been and remains inseparable from the development of safe and effective IVF and ET; as part of this research other important scientific information concerning human reproductive biology may emerge. However continuation of embryonic development in vitro beyond the stage at which implantation would normally occur is not acceptable.

6. Sperm and ova produced for IVF should be considered to belong to the respective donors. The wishes of the donors regarding the use, storage and ultimate disposal of the sperm, ova and resultant embryos should be ascertained and as far as is possible respected by the institution. In the case of the embryos, the donors' joint directions (or the directions of a single surviving donor) should be observed; in the event of disagreement between the donors, the institution should be in a position to make decisions.

7. Storage of human embryos may carry biological and social risks. Storage for transfer should be restricted to early, undifferentiated embryos. Although it may be possible technically to store such embryos indefinitely, time limits for storage should be set in every case. In defining these time limits, account should be taken both of the wishes of the donors and of a set upper limit, which would be of the order of ten years, but which should not be beyond the time of conventional reproductive need or competence of the female donor.

8. Cloning experiments designed to produce from human tissues viable or potentially viable offspring that are multiple and genetically identical are ethically unacceptable.

9. In this, as in other experimental fields, those who conscientiously object to research projects or therapeutic programs conducted by institutions that employ them should not be obliged to participate in those projects or programs to which they object, nor should they be put at a disadvantage because of their objection.

SUPPLEMENTARY NOTE 5 - THE HUMAN FETUS AND
THE USE OF HUMAN FETAL TISSUE

Supplementary note 5 adopted by the Council at its 96th Session October 1983

Introduction

1. This supplementary note, which should be read in conjunction with the *NHMRC Statement on Human Experimentation and*

Supplementary Notes, is intended as a guide on ethical matters for research involving the human fetus or human fetal tissue. Included in this research is the possible usefulness of transplantation of fetal tissue for the treatment of disease.

2. For the purpose of these guidelines the terms fetus and fetal tissue include respectively the whole or part of what is called the embryo, fetus or neonate, from the time of implantation to the time of complete gestation, whether born alive or dead. The fetal membranes, placenta, umbilical cord and amniotic fluid are regarded as part of the fetus prior to separation; after separation they are also subject to certain guidelines.

The fetus in utero

3. There are two circumstances in which it may be ethical to carry out experiments on the fetus in utero:
    (i) where experiments are consistent with the promotion of life or health of the fetus;
    (ii) where research on antenatal fetal diagnosis provides the mother with information about the health or normality of the fetus and so gives her choices between continuation of the pregnancy, treatment for the fetus, and lawful termination of the pregnancy.

4. There may be risks to both mother and fetus in research on the fetus in utero, and institutional ethics committees (IECs) should carefully consider the risks and benefits to both in every case.

5. It is unethical to administer drugs to, or to carry out any procedure on, the mother with the intention of ascertaining harmful effects that these may have on the fetus, whether in anticipation of induced abortion or otherwise. Some research procedures may be allowable once the physical process of abortion is irrevocably in train.

The separated previable fetus and fetal tissues

6. For the purposes of medical research, a separated previable fetus is at present regarded as one that has not attained a gestational age of 20 weeks and does not exceed 400 g in weight. Adoption of this description will prevent inadvertent withholding of life-sustaining treatment from a separated fetus that may in fact be viable.

7. The following conditions should be observed:

    (i) the fetus should be available for research only as a result of separation by natural processes or by lawful means;

    (ii) dissection of the fetus should not be carried out while a heart beat is still apparent or there are other obvious signs of life;

    (iii) research procedures should not be performed in the immediate area in which clinical procedures are carried out; and

    (iv) those concerned with research involving the use of tissue from a fetus should have no part in the management of either the mother or the fetus, or in deciding if the fetus is previable.

General conditions for research on the fetus and fetal tissue

8. The research must be conducted only in institutions that have a properly constituted ethics committee, and only according to written protocols approved by the ethics committees of all institutions involved.

9. The consent of the mother and, whenever practicable that of the father, should be obtained before research is undertaken. If fetal cells including cells from fetal membranes, placenta, umbilical cord and amniotic fluid are to be stored or propagated in tissue culture, or tissues or cells are to be transplanted into a recipient human, consent for this should be obtained specifically.

10. The decisions (a) whether it is appropriate in a particular instance to approach the mother about the possible use of fetal tissue for research and (b) whether a fetus or its tissue is in a category that may be used for research, must rest with the attending clinician and not with the intending research worker. The obtaining of consent for research should also be through the attending clinician.

11. When an IEC is reviewing a proposal for research it should also take particular account of the following:

    (i) the required information should not be obtainable by other means or by using other species;

    (ii) the investigators should have the necessary special facilities and skills;

    (iii) there should be no element of commerce involved in the transfer of human fetal tissue;

(iv) that the separation of clinical and research responsibilities that is crucial to the ethical basis for research in this area clearly exists; and

(v) a record of all attempts to transplant human fetal tissue, including a description of the outcome, should be maintained by the institution.

12. In this, as in other experimental fields, those who conscientiously object to research projects or therapeutic programs conducted by institutions that employ them should not be obliged to participate in those projects or programs to which they object, nor should they be put at a disadvantage because of their objection.

SUPPLEMENTARY NOTE 6 – EPIDEMIOLOGICAL RESEARCH

Supplementary note 6 adopted by the Council Executive February 1985

1. This supplementary note should be read in conjunction with the *NHMRC Statement on Human Experimentation and Supplementary Notes*. It is intended as a guide on ethical matters arising in medical research using the methods of epidemiology.

2. Epidemiological research is necessary for measuring the frequency and severity of disease in populations, identifying harmful effects from the environment, and establishing the effectiveness and safety of drugs, and other forms of medical and surgical treatment. It is concerned with the improvement of human health; it can provide new knowledge which is unobtainable in any other way.

3. In epidemiological research, medically relevant information about individuals is accumulated so that features of groups of persons may be investigated. These guidelines refer to the use in research of such information whether or not it was originally obtained for research purposes.

4. All epidemiological research should be conducted according to written protocols that state the aims of the study, the data needed and the way in which the data will be collected, used and protected.

5. Protocols for epidemiological research must be approved by properly constituted ethics committees of all the institutions involved in that research. If no institutions with ethics committees are involved, the investigators should secure ethical approval from a properly constituted ethics committee of an

institution that is appropriate to the subjects or community concerned.

6. Access to medical records for research should normally be restricted to medically qualified investigators and research associates responsible to them.

7. Consent of subjects should generally be obtained for the use of their records for medical research, but in certain circumstances an ethics committee may approve the granting of access to records without consent. This course should only be adopted if the procedures required to obtain consent are likely either to cause unnecessary anxiety or to prejudice the scientific value of the research and if, in the opinion of the ethics committee, it will not be to the disadvantage of the subjects.

8. The use in an epidemiological study of confidential or personal information should not be allowed to cause material, emotional or other disadvantage to any individual.

9. Information that is confidential or personal, obtained for research, must not be used for purposes other than those specified in the approved protocol (see para. 5). If the information is to be used for new research, a new protocol must first be approved by an institutional ethics committee.

10. Investigators and their associates must preserve the confidentiality of information about research subjects. The confidentiality of records used in epidemiological research, both in the short and long term, must be at least as secure as it was in the sources from which the records were obtained.

11. Results of research must not be published in a form that permits identification of individual subjects.

12. In epidemiological research consent must be obtained specifically for clinical procedures and these must only be carried out by properly qualified persons and in accordance with the *NHMRC Statement on Human Experimentation and Supplementary Notes*.

13. If in the course of epidemiological research new information of clinical relevance is obtained, or existing treatment is thought to need alteration, the patient and his or her usual medical attendant must be informed.

14. The relationships between subjects and their usual medical attendants must not be adversely affected by the research and confidential relationships between doctors and patients must be preserved.

15. When an IEC is reviewing a proposal for epidemiological research it should also be satisfied that:
    (i)   the research is likely to contribute to the acquisition of knowledge that may improve the health of the community; and
    (ii) the investigators have the necessary skills in epidemiology and facilities for the research.

SUPPLEMENTARY NOTE 7 - SOMATIC CELL GENE THERAPY

Supplementary note 7 adopted by the Council at its 104th Session November 1987

1. Somatic cell gene therapy involves the introduction of pieces of DNA into human somatic (non-reproductive) cells. The aim is to improve the health of people with certain grave inherited diseases. While the development of somatic cell gene therapy is acceptable, the introduction of pieces of DNA into germ (reproductive) cells or fertilised ova for the purpose of gene therapy is not, because there is insufficient knowledge about the possible consequences, hazards, and effects on future generations.[1]

2. All attempts to introduce pieces of DNA into human cells should be considered to be experimental and subject to the *NHMRC Statement on Human Experimentation and Supplementary Notes.*[2]

3. The following particular matters need to be taken into account when protocols for somatic cell gene therapy are being considered by an institutional ethics committee:
    (i)   the therapy should be attempted only in diseases in which the cause is a defect in a single pair of genes. Gene therapy to correct defects in multiple genes should not be attempted; and
    (ii) The choice of diseases for clinical trials is critical. For the present, evidence of hazards associated with the treatment can only be estimated and evaluated from experiments

---

1. There are in addition practical reasons why germ cell manipulation is unlikely to be appropriate for the correction of genetic defects. These reasons are set out in the Medical Research Ethics Committee background paper 'DNA treatment of patients with inherited diseases' cited in footnote 1 overleaf.
2. Supplementary note 3 on clinical trials is particularly relevant.

on animals. Initial trials in patients should therefore be limited:

- to diseases for which there is no effective treatment, and which cause a severe burden of suffering. Diseases causing a lesser burden, when account is taken of currently available treatment, should become candidates for somatic cell gene therapy only after the risks associated with this therapy have been determined by experience in humans over some years[1];
- to diseases in which the effects of treatment can be measured; and
- to patients for whom long-term follow-up is assured.

4. When considering a proposal for somatic cell gene therapy, an institutional ethics committee should also be satisfied:

    (i) that the research team has the necessary depth and breadth of knowledge of, and experience in, molecular genetics;

    (ii) that the purity of the DNA to be inserted and the methods of handling it during its preparation are in accord with current regulations and official guidelines; and

    (iii) that the technique of insertion has been shown by experiments in animals:

- to confine the inserted DNA to the intended somatic cells, without entry into germ cells,
- to achieve adequate function of the relevant gene in a high proportion of attempts; and
- rarely to cause undesirable side effects.

In seeking to satisfy itself on (i), (ii) and (iii) above, and on all technical aspects of any proposal for research on gene therapy, the institutional ethics committee shall consult with the biosafety committee of the institution, which as necessary may consult the official national body concerned with monitoring the safety of innovative genetic manipulation techniques.[2]

---

1. Institutional ethics committees should be guided by the Gene Therapy Committee of the Human Genetics Society of Australasia in deciding whether a disease is appropriate for early trials of gene therapy. Reference should also be made to the Medical Research Ethics Committee background paper 'DNA treatment of patients with inherited diseases' published in *Ethical Aspects of Research On Human Gene Therapy* listed in appendix 1.
2. In 1992 this is the Genetic Manipulation Advisory Committee, previously the Recombinant DNA Monitoring Committee. Enquiries may be directed to GPO Box 2183, Canberra ACT 2601, Ph: (06) 275 3663.

APPENDIX 1

Relevant Reports

The full reports providing background to these documents are as follows:

- *Ethics in Medical Research* Australian Government Publishing Service 1983 – this report concerns supplementary notes 1–4.
- *Ethics in Medical Research Involving the Human Fetus and Human Fetal Tissue* Australian Government Publishing Service 1983 – this report concerns supplementary note 5.
- *Ethics in Epidemiological Research* Australian Government Publishing Service 1985 – this report concerns supplementary note 6.
- *Ethical Aspects of Research on Human Gene Therapy* Australian Government Publishing Service 1988 – this report concerns supplementary note 7.

These reports available free from the Publications Officer, NHMRC, GPO Box 9848, Canberra ACT 2601, Ph: (06) 289 7646.

Legal Citations

Allen v. Voje, 89 N.W. 924 (1902).

Bailey v. Lally, 481 F. Supp. 203 (1979).

Bolam v. Friern Hospital Management Committee [1957] 1 *WLR* 582.

Bonner v. Moran, 126 Fed. Rep. 2nd series, 121-23 (D.C.Cir. 1941). Partial reprint in Katz (1972: 972-74).

Burton v. Brooklyn Doctors Hospital, 452 N.Y.S. 2d 875 (1982).

Carpenter v. Blake, 60 Barb. 488. (New York 1871).

Ellis v. Wallsend District Hospital, (1989) Australian Torts Reports 80,259; On appeal, (1989) NSWLR 553.

F. v. R., (1983) 33 SASR 189.

Fortner v. Koch, 272 Mich. 273 N. 762 (1935).

Halushka v. University of Saskatchewan, (1965) 53 DLR (2d) 436.

Hart v. Herron, (1980) Australian Torts Reports, 67,810.

Hyman v. Jewish Chronic Disease Hospital, 42 Misc. 2d. 427, 248 N.Y.S. 2d. 245 (Sup. Ct. 1964); Reversed: 21 A.D. 2d. 495, 251 N.Y.S. 2d. 818 (1964); Reversed: 15 N.Y. 2d. 317, 206 N.E. 2d. 338 (1965).

Jackson v. Burnham, 39 P. 577, (1895) the Colorado Supreme Court, (reversing *Burnham v. Jackson* 28 P. 250).

Kaimowitz v. Department of Mental Health for the State of Michigan, Civil Action No. 73-19434-AW (Circuit Court, Wayne County, Michigan, July 10, 1973). Unofficial report in *Mental Disability Law Reporter*, pp. 147-154, September–October 1976. Partial reprint in Katz (1972: 9-65) and in Wadlington, Waltz and Dworkin (1980: 973-86).

Merriken v. Cressman, 364 F. Supp. 913 (Pa. 1973).

Mink v. University of Chicago, 460 F. Supp. 713 (1978). Decision affirmed by the appellate court without a published opinion: 727 F. 2d 1112 (7th Cir. 1984).

Moore v. Regents of the University of California, 793 P.2d 479 (Cal 1990).

Needham v. White Laboratories, 76 C 1101 (N.D. Ill. 1976).

Nocton v. Lord Ashburton, [1914] A.C. 932.

Norbis v. Norbis, 161 CLR (1986) 513.

Owens v. McCleary, 281 S.W. 682.

Pierce v. Ortho Pharmaceutical Corp., 84 N.J. 58, 417 A. 2d 505.

Prince v. Massachusetts, 328 U.S. 158, 170; 64 S. Ct. 438, 444 (1944).

R. v. Donovan, [1934] 2 K.B. 498.

Re X (a Minor), [1975] 1 All E.R. 697.

Reibl v. Hughes, (1980) 114 DLR (3d) 1.

Rheingold v. E. R. Squibb & Sons, Inc., 74 Civ. 3420 (S.D.N.Y. 1975).

S. v. S., [1970] 3 All E. R. 107.

Sawdey v. Spokane Falls and N. Ry. Co., 70 P. 972 (1902).

Schloendorff v. Society of New York Hospital, 211 N.Y. 125, 105 N. E. 92 (1914).

Sidaway v. Bethlem Royal Hospital Governors, [1985] 1 All E.R. 643.

Slater v. Baker and Stapleton, English Reports 95, K.B. 860 (Michaelmas Term, 8 Geo III, 1767).

Stammer v. Board of Regents of the University of New York, 29 N.Y.S.2d 38 (1941); decision affirmed: 39 N.E. 2d 913 (1942).

Thomas W. F. Mitchell v. Commonwealth of Australia, Victorian Supreme Court (Reference 1988/1663).

United States v. Karl Brandt, et al, in US Adjutant General's Department, Trials of War Criminals under Control Council Law No. 10 (October 1946–April 1949), vol. 2, The Medical Case, Washington, D.C., US Government Printing Office, 1947.

Valenti v. Prudden, 397 N.Y.S. 2d 181 (1977); Scott v. Casey, 562. Supp. 475 (1983).

Weiss v. Solomon [1989] R.J.Q. 731.

Wellesley v. Duke of Beaufort, (1827) 2 Russ, 1; 38 E.R. 236.

See Index 'court cases' for discussion of some of these cases in the text.

References

Ackerknecht, E. H., 1982. *A Short History of Medicine*, (revised edn), Baltimore and London: Johns Hopkins University Press.

Adams, A. I., 1986. 'The 1984–85 Australian doctors' dispute', *Journal of Public Health Policy*, vol. 7, no. 6, Spring, pp. 93–102.

Ajayi, O., 1980. 'Taboos and clinical research in West Africa', *Journal of Medical Ethics*, vol. 6, pp. 61–3.

Albury, R., 1983. *The Politics of Objectivity*, Victoria, Australia: Deakin University Press.

Alexander, L., 1949. 'Medical science under dictatorship', *New England Journal of Medicine*, vol. 41, no. 2, July, pp. 39–47.

Allen, P. A., Waters, W. E., and McGreen, A. M., 1982. 'Research ethical committees in 1981', *Journal of the Royal College of Physicians of London*, vol. 17, pp. 96–8.

Ambroselli, C., 1984. 'France: A national committee debates the issues', *Hastings Center Report*, vol. 14, no. 6, December, pp. 20–1.

Annas, G. J., 1979. 'All the President's bioethicists', *Hastings Center Report*, vol. 9, February, pp. 14–15.

1980. 'Report on the National Commission: good as gold', *MedicoLegal News*, vol. 8, no. 6, December, pp. 4–7.

1983. 'Consent to the artificial heart: the lion and the crocodiles', *Hastings Center Report*, vol. 13, no. 2, April, pp. 20–2.

1985. 'Baby Fae: the "anything goes" school of human experimentation', *Hastings Center Report*, vol. 15, no. 1, February, pp. 15–17.

1988. *Judging Medicine*, Clifton, New Jersey: Humana Press.

1990. 'Outrageous Fortune: Selling other people's cells', *Hastings Center Report*, vol. 22, no. 6, November/December, pp. 36–9.

1991. 'Mengele's birthmark: the Nuremberg Code in the United States courts', *Journal of Contemporary Health Law and Policy*, vol. 7, Spring, pp. 17–45.

Annas, G. J., and Glantz, L. H., 1987. *Informed Consent in Veterans Administration Cooperative Studies: Legal & Ethical Issues*, published for the Veterans Administrative Coop. Studies Program, January.

Annas, G. J., Glantz, L. H. and Katz, B. F., 1977. *Informed Consent to Human Experimentation: The Subject's Dilemma*, Cambridge, Massachusetts: Ballinger.

Annas, G. J. and Grodin, M. A., 1991. 'Treating the troops: Commentary', *Hastings Center Report*, vol. 21, no. 2, March–April, pp. 24–7.

Appelbaum, P. S., Lidz, C. W. and Meisel, A., 1987. *Informed Consent: Legal Theory and Clinical Practice*, New York and Oxford: Oxford University Press.

Appelbaum, P. S., Roth, L. H. and Lidz, C. W., 1982. 'The therapeutic misconception: informed consent in psychiatric research', *International Journal of Law and Psychiatry*, vol. 5, pp. 319–29.

Appelbaum, P. S., Roth, L. H., Lidz, C. W., Benson, P. and Winslade, W., 1987 'False Hope and Best Data: Consent to research and the therapeutic misconception', *Hastings Center Report*, vol. 17, no. 2, April, pp. 20–4.

Apter, D. E., 1968. 'Notes for a theory of nondemocratic representation', in J. R. Pennock and J. W. Chapman (eds), *Nomos X: Representation, Yearbook of the American Society for Political and Legal Philosophy*, New York: Atherton Press, pp. 28–37.

Areen, J., King, P. A., Goldberg, S. and Capron, A. M. (eds), 1984. *Law, Science and Medicine*, Mineola, New York: Foundation Press.

Arney, W. R., 1982. *Power and the Profession of Obstetrics*, Chicago and London: University of Chicago Press.

Arnstein, S. R., 1969. 'A ladder of citizen participation', *Journal of the American Institute of Planners*, vol. 35, no. 4, July, pp. 216–24.

Asher, A., 1981. 'Consumers' viewpoint', *Medical Journal of Australia*, vol. 1, no. 4, pp. 171–2.

Auckland Women's Health Council, 1989. 'Guidelines for institutions: consumer representation in decision making', Guidelines, no. 11, June.

Auger, B. Y., 1980. 'Care and feeding of a committee', *Manage*, vol. 32, no. 1, January, pp. 2–6.

Australian College of Paediatrics, 1981. 'Report on the ethics of research in children', *Australian Paediatric Journal*, vol. 17, p. 162.

Bailey, F. G., 1977. *Morality and Expediency: The Folklore of Academic Politics*, Oxford: Basil Blackwell.

Bankowski, Z. and Howard-Jones, N. (eds), 1982. *Human Experimentation and Medical Ethics: Proceedings of the XVth CIOMS Round Table Conference Manila, 13–16 September 1981*, Council for International Organizations of Medical Sciences, Geneva.

Barber, B., Lally, J.J., Makarushka, J. L. and Sullivan, D., 1978. *Research on Human Subjects: Problems of Social Control in Medical Experimentation*, New Brunswick: Transaction Books. [Reprint of Russell Sage Foundation, 1973.]

Barber, D., 1988. 'The system has failed', *Sydney Morning Herald*, 13 August, p. 71.

Barnes, B., 1985. *About Science*, Oxford, New York: Basil Blackwell.

Barthelemy, J-E., 1988. 'Ethics Committees flourish in Europe: Belgium' *IME Bulletin*, no. 39, June, pp. 13–14.

Bassiouni, C., Baffes, T. G. and Evrard, J. T., 1981. 'An appraisal of human experimentation in international law and practice: the need for international regulation of human experimentation', *Journal of Criminal Law and Criminology*, vol. 72, no. 4, pp. 1597–666.

Bates, E. and Linder-Pelz, S., 1987. *Health Care Issues*, Sydney, London, and Boston: Allen & Unwin.

Bates, P. W. and Dewdney, J. C. (eds), 1990. *Australian Health & Medical Law Reporter*, NSW Australia: CCH Australia.

Battin, M. P., 1985. 'Non-patient decision-making in medicine: the eclipse of altruism', *Journal of Medicine and Philosophy*, vol. 10, pp. 19–44.

Baudouin, J-L., Ouellette, M. and Molinari, P. A., 1990. 'Toward a Canadian advisory council on biomedical ethics: study paper', Protection of Life Series, Ottawa and Montréal: Law Reform Commission of Canada.

Baume, P., 1991. *A Question of Balance: Report on the Future of Drug Evaluation in Australia*, Canberra: Commonwealth of Australia, July.

Bayer, R., Levine, C. and Murray, T. H., 1984. 'Guidelines for confidentiality in research with AIDS', *IRB: A Review of Human Subjects Research*, vol. 6, no. 6, November/December, pp. 1–7.

Bayer, R., Levine, C. and Wolf, S. M., 1986. 'HIV antibody screening: an ethical framework for evaluating proposed programs', *Journal of the American Medical Association*, vol. 256, no. 13, October, pp. 1768–74.

Beauchamp, T. L. and Childress, J. F., 1989. *Principles of Biomedical Ethics*, (3rd edn), New York and Oxford: Oxford University Press.

Beauchamp, T. L. and Walters, L. (eds), 1982. *Contemporary Issues in Bioethics* (2nd edn), Belmont, California: Wadsworth.

Beecher, H. K., 1966a. 'Ethics and clinical research', *New England Journal of Medicine*, vol. 274, no. 2, June, pp. 1354–60.

1966b. 'Consent in clinical experimentation: myth and reality', *Journal of the American Medical Association*, vol. 195, no. 1, pp. 34–5.

1970. *Research and the Individual*, Boston: Little, Brown and Co.

Benson, P. R., Roth, L. H. and Winslade, W. J., 1985. 'Informed consent in psychiatric research: preliminary findings from an ongoing investigation', *Social Science & Medicine*, vol. 20, no. 12, pp. 1331–41.

Berg, K. and Tranøy, K. E. (eds), 1983. *Research Ethics*, New York: Alan R. Liss.

Bergkamp, L., 1988a. 'Regulation of Medical Experimentation with Human Beings in Western Europe: a comparative legal analysis', Amsterdam: Institute for Social Medicine, University of Amsterdam.

1988b. 'American IRBs and Dutch research ethics committees: how they compare', *IRB: A Review of Human Subjects Research*, vol. 10, no. 5, September/October, pp. 1–6.

1988c. 'Research ethics committees and regulation of medical experimentation with human beings in The Netherlands', *Medicine and Law*, vol. 7, no. 1, pp. 65–72.

Berglund, C. A., 1990. 'Australian standards for privacy and confidentiality of health records in research: implications of the Commonwealth Privacy Act', *Medical Journal of Australia*, vol. 152, 18 June, pp. 664-9.

Berglund, C. A. and McNeill, P. M. 1989. 'Guidelines for research practice in Australia: NHMRC Statement and professional codes', *Community Health Studies*, vol. XIII, no. 2, pp. 121-9.

Bernard, C., 1957. *An Introduction to the Study of Experimental Medicine*, (trans. from the French by Henry Copley Green), New York: Dover Publications.

Blasszauer, B., 1988. 'Professional turmoil in Hungary', *Hastings Center Report*, vol. 18, no. 4, August/September, pp. 2-3.

Bossuyt, M. J., 1987. *Guide to the 'Travaux Preparatoires' of the International Covenant on Civil and Political Rights*, Dordrecht: Martinus Nijhoff Publishers.

Bouchard, D. F. (ed.), 1977. *Language Counter-Memory, Practice: Selected Essays and Interviews by Michel Foucault*, New York: Cornell University Press.

Braithwaite, J., 1984. *Corporate Crime in the Pharmaceutical Industry*, London: Routledge & Kegan Paul.

Brieger, G. H., 1978. 'Human Experimentation: History', in W. T. Reich (ed.), *Encyclopedia of Bioethics*, New York: Free Press, pp. 683-92.

Bromberger, B., 1977. 'Psychosurgery and the Law in the U.S.A., in J. S. Smith and L. G. Kiloh (eds), *Psychosurgery and Society: A Symposium organized by the Neuropsychiatric Institute*, (Sydney, Australia), Oxford and Sydney: Pergamon Press.

1983. 'Patient participation in medical decision-making: are the courts the answer?' *University of New South Wales Law Journal*, vol. 6, pp. 1-23.

1990. 'Clinical Practice', in P. W. Bates and J. C. Dewdney (eds), *Australian Health & Medical Law Reporter*, NSW Australia: CCH Australia, pp. 20,001-21,551, Para 17-700.

Brunser, O., 1981. 'Experience of the protection of the research subject and clinical research in Chile', *Medical Ethics and Medical Education: Proceedings of the XIVth Round Table Conference, Mexico City, Mexico, 1-3 December 1980*, Geneva: Council for International Organizations of Medical Sciences, pp. 124-8.

Burrell, C. C., 1978. 'Report on ethical review committees in New Zealand 1978', prepared for Council for International Organizations of Medical Sciences, unpublished manuscript, December.

1980a. 'Update on 1978 "Report on ethical review committees in New Zealand"', prepared for Council for International Organizations of Medical Sciences, unpublished manuscript, April.

1980b. 'A report on ethical review committees in Australia, 1978', prepared for Council for International Organizations of Medical Sciences, unpublished manuscript, April.

Calabresi, G., 1969. 'Reflections on medical experimentation in humans', *Daedalus*, Spring, pp. 387–405.

Callahan, D., 1984. 'Autonomy: a moral good not a moral obsession', *Hastings Center Report*, vol. 14, no. 5, October, pp. 40–2.

Campbell, J. D. and McEwin, K., 1981. 'The hospital ethics committee', *Medical Journal of Australia*, vol. 174, no. 1, February, pp. 168–9.

Canada Council, 1977. Ethics: Report of the Consultative Group on Ethics, Ottawa: The Canada Council. [Now published by Social Sciences and Humanities Research Council of Canada.]

Capron, A. M., 1972. 'Legal Considerations Affecting Clinical Pharmacological Studies in Children', *Clinical Research*, vol. 21, pp. 141–50.

    1983. 'Prospects for research ethics', in K. Berg and K. E. Tranøy (eds), *Research Ethics*, New York: Alan R. Liss, pp. 389–97.

    1985. 'Legal perspectives on institutional ethics committees', *Journal of College and University Law*, vol. 11, no. 4, Spring, pp. 417–31.

    1986. 'Human Experimentation', in J. F. Childress et al., (eds) *BioLaw: A Legal Reporter on Medicine, Health Care and Bioengineering*, Frederick, Maryland: University Publications of America, vol. 1, pp. 217–52.

Cardon, P. V., Dommel, F. W. and Trumble, R. R., 1976. 'Injuries to research subjects: a survey of investigators', *New England Journal of Medicine*, vol. 295, no. 12, September, pp. 650–4.

Carnerie, F., 1987. 'Crisis and informed consent: analysis of a law-medicine malocclusion', *American Journal of Law and Medicine*, vol. XII, no. 1, Spring, pp. 55–97.

Cartwright, S. R., 1988. *The Report of the Committee of Inquiry into Allegations Concerning the Treatment of Cervical Cancer at National Women's Hospital and Related Matters*, Auckland, New Zealand: Government Printing Office, July.

Cassell, E. J., 1984. 'Life as a work of art', *Hastings Center Report*, vol. 14, no. 5, October, pp. 35–38.

Caton, H., 1990a. 'Confidentiality vs accountability: an ethical conflict within ethics committees', in H. Caton (ed.), *Trends in Biomedical Regulation*, Sydney: Butterworths, pp. 87–92.

    1990b. 'Self-regulation: a study of the ethics committee system', in H. Caton (ed.), *Trends in Biomedical Regulation*, Sydney: Butterworths, pp. 65–86, at pp. 75–8.

    Caton, H. (ed.), 1990c. *Trends in Biomedical Regulation*, Sydney: Butterworths.

Central Scientific-Ethical Committee, 1991. *Report for 1990*, Copenhagen: Minister of Science.

Cheston, W. and McFate, P., 1980. 'Ethics and laboratory safety', *Hastings Center Report*, vol. 10, no. 4, August, pp. 7–8.

Christakis, N. and Panner, M., 1986. 'Baby Fae and the Media: How the law allows appropriate access', *IRB: A Review of Human Subjects Research*, vol. 8, no. 2, March/April, pp. 5–7.

Churchill, L. R., 1980. 'Physician-investigator/patient-subject: exploring the logic and the tension', *Journal of Medicine and Philosophy*, vol. 5, no. 3, pp. 215–24.

Colquhoun, B. and Elenor, C., 1988. 'Program evaluation report: occupational health and safety committees', Sydney: Occupational Health and Safety Unit, Water Board, November.

Coney, S., 1988. *The Unfortunate Experiment: The Full Story Behind the Inquiry into Cervical Cancer Treatment*, Auckland, New Zealand: Penguin.

Consumers Health Forum of Australia, 1990. 'Guidelines for consumer representatives: suggestions for consumer or community representatives working on public committees' (2nd edn), Deakin, Canberra: July.

Costa, L., 1989. 'After Thalidomide', *The Australian Magazine, The Australian*, Saturday 4 and Sunday 5 November, pp. 8–18.

Cowan, D. H., 1975. 'Human experimentation: the review process in practice', *Case Western Reserve Law Review*, vol. 25, no. 3, pp. 533–64.

Cranford, R. E. and Doudera, A. E. (eds), 1984. *Institutional Ethics Committees and Health Care Decision Making*, Ann Arbor, Michigan: Health Administration Press.

Curran, W. J., 1968. 'Current issues in clinical investigation with particular attention to the balance between the rights of the individual and the needs of society', *Psychopharmacology: a Review of Progress 1957-1967*, Washington: US Public Health Service Publication no. 1836, pp. 337–43. [Reprinted in Reiser, Dyck and Curran, 1977, pp. 296–301.]

1969. 'Governmental Regulation of the Use of Human Subjects in Medical Research: The Approach of Two Federal Agencies', *Daedalus: Ethical Aspects of Experimentation with Human Subjects*, Spring, pp. 542–594, at p. 550. [Reprinted in Freund, 1970.]

1982. 'Subject consent requirements in clinical research: and international perspective for industrial and developing countries', in Z. Bankowski and N. Howard-Jones (eds), *Human Experimentation and Medical Ethics: Proceedings of the XVth CIOMS Round Table Conference Manila, 13-16 September 1981*, Council for International Organizations of Medical Sciences, Geneva, pp. 35–79.

Curran, W. J., and Beecher, H. K., 1969. 'Experimentation in children: a reexamination of legal ethical principles', *Journal of the American Medical Association*, vol. 210, no. 1, October, pp. 77–83.

Daniel, T. M., Cherniack, N. S., Douglas, J. G., Kammer, G. M. and Ratnoff, O. D., 1988. 'The ethics of human experimentation', (editorial) *Laboratory and Clinical Medicine*, vol. 112, no. 5, November, pp. 529–30.

Davis, K. C., 1969. *Discretionary Justice: a Preliminary Inquiry*, Baton Rouge: Louisiana State University Press.

de Beaufort, I. D., 1985. 'Ethiek en medische experimenten met mensen', Occasional paper, Instituut Voor Gezondheidsethiek, Assen/Maastricht.

de Souza, D., 1981. 'Ethics of human experimentation', *Medical Journal of Australia*, vol. 1, pp. 163–6.

de Wachter, M., 1988. 'Ethics Committees flourish in Europe: Belgium', *IME Bulletin*, no. 39, June, pp. 17–18.

Delgado, R. and Leskovac, H., 1986. 'Informed consent in human experimentation: bridging the gap between ethical thought and current practice', *UCLA Law Review*, vol. 34, October, pp. 66–130.

Denham, M. J., Foster, A. and Tyrrell, D. A. J., 1979. 'Work of a District Ethical Committee, *British Medical Journal*, vol. 2, pp. 1042–5.

Denmark, Ministry of Health, 1989. *Research Involving Human Subjects: Ethics/Law*, Denmark.

Diggs, B. J., 1968. 'Practical representation', in J. R. Pennock and J. W. Chapman (eds), *Nomos X: Representation, Yearbook of the American Society for Political and Legal Philosophy*, New York: Atherton Press, pp. 28–37.

Dix, A., Errington, M., Nicholson, K. and Powe, R., 1988. *Law for the Medical Profession*, Sydney and London: Butterworths.

Dooley, D., 1991. 'Medical ethics in Ireland: A decade of change', *Hastings Center Report*, vol. 21, no. 1, January–February, pp. 18–21.

Douglas, M., 1985. *Risk Acceptability According to the Social Sciences*, New York: Russell Sage Foundation.

Dresser, R., 1992. 'Wanted: single, white male for medical research', *Hastings Center Report*, vol. 21, no. 1, January–February, pp. 24–9.

Dworkin, G., 1987. 'Law and medical experimentation: of embryos, children and others with limited legal capacity', *Monash University Law Review*, vol. 13, December, pp. 189–208.

Dyck, A. J., 1970. 'Comment on "Philosophical reflections on experimenting with human subjects" ', in P. A. Freund (ed.), *Experimentation with Human Subjects*, New York: George Braziller, pp. 32–8.

Editorial (Special Article), *Annals of Internal Medicine*, 1966. 'Human experimentation: Declaration of Helsinki', vol. 65, pp. 367–8.

Editorial, *Australian Paediatric Journal*, 1981. 'Report on the ethics of research in children', vol. 17, p. 162.

Editorial (News and Political Review), *British Medical Journal*, 1990. 'Monitoring research ethical committees', vol. 300, 13 January, pp. 61–2.

1991. 'Health reforms in New Zealand', vol. 303, no. 6798, 10 August, p. 327.

Editorial (News), *Bulletin of Medical Ethics*, 1989. 'Protecting students in medical research', no. 54, November/December, pp. 10–11.

1990a. 'Points', no. 55, January/February, p. 7.

1990b. 'Bulletin's Norwegian venture', no. 62, October, pp. 8–9.

1991. 'Guidance on RECs published at last', no. 71, September, pp. 3–4.

Editorial (News), *IME Bulletin*, 1988a. 'Making ethics committees work', no. 39, June, pp. 5–6.

1988b. 'Ethics Committees flourish in Europe: Greece', no. 39, June, p. 21.

1988c. 'Ethics Committees flourish in Europe – Switzerland: Guidelines for the organization and work of the Central Committee for Medical Ethics of the Swiss Academy of Medical Sciences', no. 39, June, pp. 20–1.

1988d. 'Ethics Committees flourish in Europe: Italy', no. 39, June, p. 21.

1988e. 'Ethics Committees', no. 50, October, p. 5.

1988f. 'Ethics committees in Eastern Europe: Hungary', no. 43, October, p. 7.

1988g. 'Ethics committees in Eastern Europe: Poland', no. 43, October, p. 7.

1989a. 'French law on medical ethics', no. 49, April, pp. 5–6.

1989b. 'How research ethics committees work', no. 49, April, p. 6

1989c. 'Ethics Committees', no. 50, May, p. 5.

1989d. 'Norway', no. 51, June, p. 6.

1989e. 'France', no. 51, June, p. 7.

1989f. 'More advice to ethics committees', no. 51, June, pp. 10–11.

1989g. 'A surfeit of ethics committees?', no. 52, July/August, pp. 13–15.

Editorial (News), *International Digest of Health Legislation*, 1980. 'Indian Council of Medical Research issues Policy Statement on Ethical Considerations Involving Research on Human Subjects', vol. 31 no. 4, February, pp. 980–6.

1984. 'Ethical issues and professional responsibility', vol. 35, no. 2, pp. 355–8.

Editorial (News), *IRB: A Review of Human Subjects Research*, 1979. 'Illinois law suits resolved by guidelines on research with mentally ill', vol. 1 no. 6, October, p. 8.

Editorial, *Journal of the American Medical Association*, 1937a. 'Deaths following Elixir of Sulfanilamide-Massengill', vol. 109, no. 17, 23 October, p. 1367.

1937b. 'Deaths following Elixir of Sulfanilamide-Massengill: II', vol. 109, no. 18, 30 October, p. 1456.

1937c. 'Elixir of Sulfanilamide-Massengill', vol. 109, no. 19, 6 November, pp. 1531–9.

1937d. 'Deaths following Elixir of Sulfanilamide-Massengill: III', vol. 109, no. 19, 6 November, p. 1544.

1937e. 'Elixir of Sulfanilamide-Massengill: II' vol. 109, no. 21, 20 November, pp. 1724–5.

1937f. 'Deaths following Elixir of Sulfanilamide-Massengill: IV', vol. 109, no. 21, 20 November, p. 1727.

1937g. 'Safeguards proposed to govern distribution of dangerous drugs', vol. 109, no. 21, 4 December, pp. 1911–12.

1938. 'Deaths following Elixir of Sulfanilamide-Massengill: VI', vol. 110, no. 19, 7 May, p. 1727.

Editorial, *Medical Journal of Australia*, 1974. 'Guidelines on Human Experimentation', vol. 1, no. 24, June, pp. 947–8.

1975. 'The Tokyo Assembly of the World Medical Association', vol. 2 no. 19, 8 November, pp. 731–2.

1976. 'Revision of the Declaration of Helsinki', vol. 1, no. 7, February, pp. 179–80.

1978. 'The signicanre [sic] of the Declaration of Helsinki: an interpretative commentary', vol. 2, July, pp. 78-9.

Editorial (News), *New Zealand Medical Journal*, 1990. 'Medicolegal: Medical Council charges Professor Bonham', vol. 103, no. 901, November, pp. 547-9.

1991. 'The Health Commissioners', vol. 104, no. 920, 25 September, p. 409.

Editorial, *World Medical Journal*, 1955. 'Organisational News', vol. 2, no. 1, pp. 12-16.

1957. 'Human experimentation', vol. 4, September, pp. 299-300.

1976. 'The drafting of declarations', vol. 23, no. 2, March/April, p. 27.

Edsall, G., 1969. 'A positive approach to the problem of human experimentation', *Daedalus*, vol. 98, no. 2, Spring, pp. 463-79.

Eisenberg, L., 1977. 'The social imperatives of medical research', *Science*, vol. 198, 16 December, pp. 1105-10. [Reprinted in T. L. Beauchamp and L. Walters (eds), 1982. *Contemporary Issues in Bioethics* (2nd edn), Belmont, California: Wadsworth.]

Epstein, L. C. and Lasagna, L., 1969. 'Obtaining informed consent: form or substance?' *Arch. Internal Medicine*, vol. 123, pp. 682-88.

Ethical Committee, University College Hospital, 1981. 'Experience at a Clinical Research Ethical Review Committee', *British Medical Journal*, vol. 283, pp. 1312-14.

Evans, M. E., 1982. 'The Legal Background of the Institutional Review Board' in Robert A. Greenwald, Mary Kay Ryan and James E. Mulvihill (eds), *Human Subjects Research: A Handbook for Institutional Review Boards*, New York and London: Plenum Press.

Eyer, R. C., 1985. 'Clergy's role on medical ethics committees', *Journal of Pastoral Care*, vol. 34, no. 3, September, pp. 208-12.

Faden R. R. and Beauchamp, T. L., 1980. 'Decision making and informed consent: a study of the impact of disclosed information', *Social Indicators Research*, vol. 7, pp. 314-36.

Faden R. R. and Beauchamp, T. L., 1986. *A History and Theory of Informed Consent*, New York and Oxford: Oxford University Press.

Fagot-Largeault, A., 1987. 'In France: debate and indecision', *Hastings Center Report*, vol. 17, no. 3, June, special supplement, pp. 10-12.

Family Law Council, 1985. 'Report of the Family Law Council Incorporating and Adopting the Asche Committee on Issues relating to AID, IVF, Embryo Transfer and Related Matters, *Creating Children: A Uniform Approach to the Law and Practice of Reproductive Technology in Australia*, Canberra: Australian Government Publishing Service.

Fellner, C. H. and Marshall, J. R., 1970. 'Kidney donors – the myth of informed consent', *American Journal of Psychiatry*, vol. 126, pp. 1245-51.

Fischer, F. W. and Breuer, H., 1979. 'Influences of ethical guidance committees on medical research – a critical reappraisal', in N. Howard-Jones and Z. Bankowski (eds), *Medical Experimentation and the Protection of Human Rights: Proceedings of the XIIth CIOMS Round Table Conference, Cascaus, Portugal, 30 November–1 December 1978*, Geneva: Council for International Organizations of Medical Sciences and Sandoz Institute for Health and Socio-Economic Studies, pp. 65–71.

Fletcher, J. C., 1967. 'Human Experimentation: ethics in the consent situation', *Law and Contemporary Problems*, vol. 32, pp. 620–49.

1983. 'The evolution of the ethics of informed consent', in K. Berg and K. E. Tranøy (eds), *Research Ethics*, New York: Alan R. Liss, pp. 187–228.

Fluss, S. S., 1982. 'The proposed guidelines as reflected in legislation and codes of ethics', in Z. Bankowski and N. Howard-Jones (eds), *Human Experimentation and Medical Ethics: Proceedings of the XVth CIOMS Round Table Conference Manila, 13–16 September 1981*, Geneva: Council for International Organizations of Medical Sciences, pp. 231–4, at pp. 321–66.

Forester, J., 1984. 'Bounded rationality and the politics of muddling through', *Public Administration Review*, vol. 44, no. 1, January/February, pp. 23–31.

Foucault, M., 1979. *Discipline and Punish: The Birth of the Prison*, (translated from the French by A. Sheridan), London: Penguin.

1980. *Power/Knowledge: Selected Interviews and Other Writings 1972–1977*, (ed. C. Gordon), Sussex: Harvester.

1981. *The History of Sexuality: An Introduction*, (translated from the French by R. Hurley), Great Britain: Penguin.

Fox, D. M., 1986. *Health Policies, Health Politics: the British and American Experience, 1911–1965*, Princeton, New Jersey: Princeton University Press.

Fox, R. C., 1960. 'Some social and cultural factors in American society conducive to medical research on human subjects', *Clinical Pharmacology and Therapy*, no. 1, p. 423.

Freedman, B., 1982. 'The validity of ignorant consent to medical research', *IRB: A Review of Human Subjects Research*, vol. 4, no. 2, pp. 1–5.

1987. 'Scientific value and validity as ethical requirements for research: a proposed explication', *IRB: A Review of Human Subjects Research*, vol. 9, no. 6, November/December, pp. 7–10.

Freedman, B. and Glass, K. C., 1990. '*Weiss v. Solomon*: A case study in institutional responsibility for clinical research', *Law, Medicine & Health Care*, vol. 18, no. 4, Winter, pp. 395–403.

Freidson, E., 1970a. *Profession of Medicine: A Study of the Sociology of Applied Knowledge*, New York: Harper & Row.

1970b. *Professional Dominance: The Social Structure of Medical Care*, New York: Atherton Press.

1986. *Professional Powers: A Study of the Institutionalization of Formal Knowledge*, Chicago and London: University of Chicago Press.

Freund, P. A., 1970. *Experimentation with Human Subjects*, New York: George Braziller.

Fried, C., 1978. 'Human experimentation: philosophical aspect', in W. T. Reich (ed.), *Encyclopedia of Bioethics*, New York: Free Press, pp. 699–702.

Giertz, G., 1979. 'Scope of review procedures of ethical review committees', in N. Howard-Jones and Z. Bankowski (eds) *Medical Experimentation and the Protection of Human Rights: Proceedings of the XIIth CIOMS Round Table Conference, Cascaus, Portugal, 30 November–1 December 1978*, Geneva: Council for International Organizations of Medical Sciences, pp. 90–103.

— 1982. 'The work of the ethical committees' [in French], *Medicine et Expérimentation*, Quebec: L'Université Laval.

Gilbert, C., Fulford, K. W. M. and Parker, C., 1989. 'Diversity in the practice of district ethics committees', *British Medical Journal*, vol. 299, 9 December, pp. 1437–9.

Gillespie, R., 1988. 'Research on human subjects: an historical overview', in J. Hudson (ed.), *Proceedings of the Conference: Can Ethics Be Done By a Committee?*, Melbourne: Monash University Centre for Human Bioethics, pp. 3–19. [Reprinted in *Bioethics News*, 1989, Supplement on Ethics Committees, vol. 8, no. 2, January, pp. 4–15.]

Gillett, G. 1989. 'The new ethical committees: their nature and role', *New Zealand Medical Journal*, vol. 102, 28 June, pp. 314–15.

Gilsdorf, J. W. and Rader, M. H., 1981. 'Bringing out the best in committee members', *Supervisory Management*, vol. 26, no. 11, November, pp. 6–11.

Glantz, L. H., 1984. 'Contrasting institutional review boards with institutional ethics committees', in R. E. Cranford and A. E. Doudera (eds), *Institutional Ethics Committees and Health Care Decision Making*, Ann Arbor: Health Administration Press, pp. 129–37.

Gomer, R., Powell, J. W. and Roling, B. V. A., 1981. 'Japan's biological weapons: 1930–1945', *Bulletin of the Atomic Scientists*, October, p. 43.

Goodwin, B., 1989. 'Keen as Mustard', Video, Melbourne: 1989, distributed by Video Education Australasia, Bendigo, Victoria, Australia. Broadcast by the Australian Broadcasting Corporation, 31 August.

Gray, B. H., 1975. *Human Subjects in Medical Experimentation: A Sociological Study of the Conduct and Regulation of Clinical Research*, Malabar. [Reprinted by Robert K. Krieger Publishing, Florida, 1981.]

Greenwald, R. A., Ryan, M. K. and Mulvihill, J. E. (eds), 1982. *Human Subjects Research: A Handbook for Institutional Review Boards*, New York and London: Plenum Press.

Grodin, M. A., 1990. 'The Nuremberg Code and medical research', *Hastings Center Report*, vol. 20, no. 3, May/June, p. 4.

Grodin, M. A., Zaharoff, B. E. and Kaminow, P. V., 1986. 'A 12-Year Audit of IRB decisions', *Quality Review Bulletin: Journal of Quality Assurance*, March, pp. 82–6.

Gruen, L. and Singer, P., 1987. *Animal Liberation: a Graphic Guide*, London: Camden Press.

Harden, V. A., 1986. *Inventing the NIH: Federal Biomedical Research Policy, 1887–1937*, Baltimore and London: Johns Hopkins University Press.

Hartcher, P., 1989. 'Haunting medical holocaust', in 'Spectrum', *Sydney Morning Herald*, Saturday, 19 August, p. 77.

Hayes, R., 1984. 'Epidemiological research and privacy protection', *Medical Journal of Australia*, vol. 141, no. 10, 10 November, pp. 621–4.

Herman, S. S., 1984. 'The non-institutional review board: a case history', *IRB: A Review of Human Subjects Research*, vol. 6 no. 1, January/February, pp. 1–3.

1989. 'A non-institutional review board comes of age', *IRB: A Review of Human Subjects Research*, vol. 11, no. 2, March/April, pp. 1–6.

Hodge, J. V., 1982. 'Ethical Review Procedures in New Zealand', in Z. Bankowski and N. Howard-Jones (eds), *Human Experimentation and Medical Ethics: Proceedings of the XVth CIOMS Round Table Conference Manila, 13–16 September 1981*, Council for International Organizations of Medical Sciences, Geneva, pp. 231–4.

Hodges, R. E. and Bean, W. B., 1967. 'The use of prisoners for medical research', *Journal of the American Medical Association*, vol. 202, no. 6, November, pp. 513–14.

Holman, H., 1975. 'Scientists and citizens', *Hastings Center Report*, vol. 5, no. 3, June, p. 8.

Howard-Jones, N., 1982. 'Human experimentation in historical and ethical perspectives', *Social Science & Medicine*, vol. 16, pp. 1429–48. [Reprinted in Z. Bankowski and N. Howard-Jones (eds), *Human Experimentation and Medical Ethics: Proceedings of the XVth CIOMS Round Table Conference, Manila, 13–16 September 1981*, Council for International Organizations of Medical Sciences, Geneva, pp. 441–95, 1982.]

Iles, N., 1987. 'Curial inconsistencies in the doctor's duty of care', *Adelaide Law Review*, vol. 11, July, pp. 88–106.

Illhardt, F. J., 1988. 'Ethics Committees flourish in Europe: West Germany', *IME Bulletin*, no. 39, June, pp. 19–20.

Illich, I., 1975. *Medical Nemesis: The Exploration of Health*, Great Britain: Lothian.

Indian Council of Medical Research, 1980. Policy Statement on Ethical Considerations Involved in Research on Human Subjects, New Delhi: Indian Council of Medical Research, February.

Ingelfinger, F. J., 1982. 'Informed (but uneducated) consent', *New England Journal of Medicine*, vol. 287, no. 9, August, pp. 465–6.

Isambert, F.-A., 1988. 'Ethics Committees flourish in Europe: France', *IME Bulletin*, no. 39, June, pp. 16–17.

1989. 'Ethics Committees in France', *The Journal of Medicine and Philosophy*, vol. 14, pp. 445–56.

Jain, H. C., 1980. *Worker Participation: Success and Problems*, New York: Praeger.

Japanese Ministry of Health and Welfare, 1989. Pharmaceutical Affairs Bureau, 'Good Clinical Practice for Trials on Drugs (Notification)', Notification no. 874, Pharma Japan Document Translation, 2 October.

Johnson, D. W. and Johnson, F. P., 1987. *Joining Together: Group Theory and Group Skills*, (3rd edn), Englewood Cliffs, New Jersey: Prentice-Hall International.

Johnson, T. J., 1972. *Professions and Power*, London: MacMillan Education.

Jonas, H., 1969. 'Philosophical reflections on experimenting with human subjects', *Daedalus*, vol. 98, no. 2 Spring, pp. 219–47 at p. 236. [Reprinted in Freund, 1970.]

Jones, J. H., 1981. *Bad Blood: The Tuskegee Syphilis Experiment*, New York: Free Press.

Jonsen, A. R. and Yesley, M., 1980. 'Rhetoric and research ethics: an answer to Annas', *MedicoLegal News*, December, pp. 8–14.

Kaimowitz, G., 1980. 'My case against psychosurgery', in E. S. Valenstein (ed.), *The Psychosurgery Debate: Scientific, Legal, and Ethical Perspectives*, San Francisco: W. H. Freeman, pp. 506–19.

Katz, J., 1969. 'The Education of the Physician-Investigator', *Daedalus, Ethical Aspects of Experimentation with Human subjects*, Spring, pp. 480–501.

1972. *Experimentation with Human Beings: The Authority of the Investigator, Subject, Professions, and State in the Human Experimentation Process*, New York: Russell Sage.

1987. 'The regulation of human experimentation in the United States – a personal odyssey', *IRB: A Review of Human Subjects Research*, vol. 9, no. 1, January/February, pp. 1–6.

Ken Heap, 1977. *Group Theory for Social Workers*, Oxford: Pergamon Press.

Kennedy, E., in L. A. Sobel (ed.), 1977. *Medical Science & the Law: The Life & Death Controversy*, New York: Facts on File, at pp. 61–3.

Kimura, R., 1989. 'Ethics committees for "high tech" innovations in Japan', *The Journal of Medicine and Philosophy*, vol. 14, pp. 457–64.

Kliegman, R. M., Mahowald, M. B. and Younger, S. J., 1986. 'In our best interests: experience and workings of an ethics review committee', *Journal of Pediatrics*, vol. 108, no. 2, February, pp. 178–88.

Kuhse, H. and Singer, P., 1985. *Should the Baby Live*, Oxford, New York and Melbourne: Oxford University Press.

LaFollette, M. C., 1988. 'Ethical misconduct in research publication: an annotated bibliography', National Science Foundation: August. [Produced with support from the National Museum of American History, Smithsonian Institute, Washington D.C.]

Lasagna, L., 1969. 'Special subjects in human experimentation', *Daedalus*, vol. 98, no. 2, Spring, pp. 449–462. [Reprinted in Freund, 1970.]

Law Reform Commission of Australia, 1983. Report no. 22, Privacy, Canberra: Australian Government Publishing Service.

Law Reform Commission of Canada, 1989. 'Biomedical experimentation involving human subjects', Working paper 61, Ottawa and Montréal: Law Reform Commission of Canada.

Law Reform Commission of Victoria, the Australian Law Reform Commission and the New South Wales Law Reform Commission, 1989. Joint report and recommendations for legislation in 'Informed Decisions about Medical Procedures', June.

Leake, C. D. (ed.), 1975. *Percival's Medical Ethics*, (2nd edn), Huntington, New York: Robert E. Krieger, pp. 61–205.

Levine, C., 1984. 'Questions and (some very tentative) answers about ethics committees', *Hastings Center Report*, vol. 14, no. 3, June, pp. 9–12.

1988. 'Has AIDS changed the ethics of human subjects research?', *Law, Medicine and Health Care*, vol. 16, no. 3–4, Fall/Winter, pp. 167–73.

Levine, C., Dubler, N. N. and Levine, R. J., 1991. 'Building a new consensus: ethical principles and policies for clinical research on HIV/ AIDS', *IRB: A Review of Human Subjects Research*, vol. 13, nos 1–2, pp. 1–17.

Levine, R. J., 1978. 'The Institutional Review Board' in National Commission for the Protection of Human Subjects of Biomedical and Behavioral Research, *Appendix to Report and Recommendations: Institutional Review Boards*, US Department of Health, DHEW Publication no. (OS) 78–0009, US Government Printer, pp. 4.1–4.73.

1979. 'Clarifying the concepts of research ethics', *Hastings Center Report*, vol. 9, no. 3, June, pp. 21–6.

1981. 'The value and limitations of ethical review committees for clinical research', in Z. Bankowski and J. Corves Bernardelli (eds), *Medical Ethics and Medical Education: Proceedings of the XIVth Round Table Conference, Mexico City, Mexico, 1–3 December 1980*, Geneva: Council for International Organizations of Medical Sciences, pp. 43–61.

1983. 'Informed consent in research and practice', *Arch. Internal Medicine*, vol. 143, June, pp. 1229–31.

1985. 'Institutional review boards and collaborations between academia and industry: some counterproductive policies and practices', *Circulation*, pt. II, vol. 72, no. 2, August, pp. I.48–I.50.

1986. *Ethics and Regulation of Clinical Research*, (2nd edn), Baltimore-Munich: Urban & Schwarzenberg.

1987. 'Commentary: The IRB and the virtuous investigator', *IRB: A Review of Human Subjects Research*, vol. 7, no. 1, January/February, p. 8.

1988. 'Protection of human subjects of biomedical research in the United States: a contrast with recent experience in the United Kingdom', *Annals of the New York Academy of Sciences*, June 15, pp. 133–43.

Lifton, R. J., 1986. *The Nazi Doctors: Medical Killing and the Psychology of Genocide*, New York: Basic Books.

Lock, S., 1990. 'Monitoring research ethical committees', (editorial) *British Medical Journal*, vol. 300, 13 January, pp. 61–2.

Lovell, R. R. H., 1975. 'Forensic aspects of human experimentation', *Australian Journal of Forensic Sciences*, December, pp. 53–7.

1984. 'The role and functions of institutional ethics committees in medical research', in J. N. Santamaria and N. Tonti-Filippini (eds), *Proceedings of the 1984 Conference on Bioethics*, Melbourne: St Vincent's Bioethics Centre, pp. 153–59.

1986. 'Ethics at the growing edge of medicine – the regulatory side of medical research', *Australian Health Review*, vol. 3 no. 9, pp. 239–42.

Lukes, S., 1974. *Power: A Radical View*, London: MacMillan Education.

Mannisto, M. M., 1985. 'Orchestrating an ethics committee: who should be on it, where does it best fit?', *Trustee*, April, pp. 17–20, at p. 19. [Reprinted in Public Responsibility in Medicine and Research (PRIM&R), Educational material for 2-day Conference on 'Ethical decision-making in healthcare: ethics committees and conflict resolution techniques', Boston, Massachusetts, 30 September–1 October 1991.]

March, J. G., 1982. 'Theories of choice and making decisions', *Society*, vol. 20, no. 1, November/December, pp. 29–39.

Markey, E. J., Chairman, US House of Representatives Subcommittee on Energy Conservation and Power of the Committee on Energy and Commerce, 1986. *American Nuclear Guinea Pigs: Three Decades of Radiation Experiments on U. S. Citizens*, 24 October.

Marshall, E., 1986. 'Does the moral philosophy of the Belmont Report rest on a mistake?', *IRB: A Review of Human Subjects Research*, vol. 8, no. 6, November/December, pp. 5–6.

Mason, J. K. and McCall Smith, R. A., 1987. *Law and Medical Ethics*, (2nd edn), London: Butterworths.

May, W., 1974. 'Experimenting on human subjects', *Linacare Quarterly*, vol. 41, November, pp. 238–52.

1977. 'Code and covenant or philanthropy and contract', in S. J. Reiser, A. J. Dyck, and W. J. Curran (eds), *Ethics in Medicine: Historical Perspectives and Contemporary Concerns*, Cambridge, Massachusetts: MIT Press, pp. 65–76.

McCarthy, C. R., 1983. 'Experience with boards and commissions concerned with research ethics in the United States', in K. Berg and K. E. Tranøy (eds), *Research Ethics*, New York: Alan R. Liss, pp. 111–22.

McClelland, J. R., Fitch, J. and Jonas, W. J. A., 1985. *Report of the Royal Commission into British Nuclear Tests in Australia*, Canberra: Australian Government Publishing Service.

McCormick, R. A., 1974. 'Proxy consent in the experimental situation', *Perspectives in Biology and Medicine*, vol. 18, no. 1, Autumn, pp. 2–20.

McDonald, J. C., 1967. 'Why prisoners volunteer to be experimental subjects', *Journal of the American Medical Association*, vol. 202, no. 6, November, pp. 511–12.

McKeown, T., 1979. *The Role of Medicine: Dream, Mirage or Nemesis*, Great Britain: Basil Blackwell.

McNeill, P. M., 1989a. 'Research ethics review in Australia, Europe and North America', *IRB: A Review of Human Subjects Research*, vol. 11, no. 3, May/June, pp. 4-7.

— 1989b. 'The implications for Australia of the New Zealand Report of the Cervical Cancer Inquiry: no cause for complacency', *Medical Journal of Australia*, vol. 150, March, pp. 264-71.

McNeill, P. M., Berglund, C. A. and Webster, I. W., 1990. 'Reviewing the reviewers: a survey of Institutional Ethics Committees in Australia', *Medical Journal of Australia*, vol. 152, no. 6, 19 March, pp. 289-96.

— 1992a. 'Do Australian researchers accept committee review and conduct ethical research?', *Social Science & Medicine*, vol. 35, no. 3, pp. 317-22.

— 1992b. 'The relative influence of various members of research ethics committees', unpublished manuscript.

Mead, M., 1969. 'Research with human beings: a model derived from anthropological field practice', *Daedalus*, vol. 98, no. 2, Spring, pp. 361-86.

Medical Research Council of Canada, 1978. 'Guidelines for the Protection of Humans Subjects in Research', Ottawa: Medical Research Council of Canada.

— 1987a. 'Guidelines on Research Involving Human Subjects', Ottawa: Medical Research Council of Canada, November.

— 1987b. 'Towards an International Ethic for Research with Human Beings', *Proceedings of the International Summit Conference on Bioethics*, Ottawa, Canada, 5-10 April.

Medical Research Council of Great Britain, 1963. 'Responsibility in investigations on human subjects', reprinted from the *Report of the Medical Research Council for 1962-63* (Cmnd. 2382), London: Medical Research Council.

Mellor, D. P., 1958. 'The role of science and industry', in *Australia in the War of 1939-1945*, [Official] *War Histories*, vol. V, series 4, Canberra: Australian War Memorial.

Melmon, K. L., Grossman, M. and Morris, R. C., 1970. 'Emerging assets and liabilities of a committee on human welfare and experimentation', *New England Journal of Medicine*, vol. 282, no. 8, pp. 427-31.

Meyers, K., 1979. 'Power politics and IRB's', Letter to the Editor, *New England Journal of Medicine*, vol. 301, no. 20, 15 November, p. 1129.

Michels, R., 1959. *Political Parties: A Sociological Study of the Oligarchical Tendencies of Modern Democracy*, (translated by E. and C. Paul), New York: Dover Publications.

Mill, J. S., 1962. *Utilitarianism, On Liberty, Essay on Bentham* (edited and with introduction by Mary Warnock), London and Glasgow: Collins/Fontana.

Miller, J., 1988. 'Toward an international ethic for research with human beings', *IRB: A Review of Human Subjects Research*, vol. 10, no. 6, November/December, pp. 9-11.

Miller, J. N., 1989. 'Ethics review in Canada: highlights from a national workshop', Part 1 of 'Current concepts in biomedical ethics', *Annals RCPSC*, vol. 22, no. 7, November, pp. 515–23.

1990. 'Ethics review in Canada: highlights from a national workshop', Part 2 of 'Current concepts in biomedical ethics', *Annals RCPSC*, vol. 23, no. 1, January, pp. 29–33.

Moore, A. P. and Tarr, A. A., 1988. 'Regulatory mechanisms in respect of entrepreneurial medicine', *Australian Business Law Review*, vol. 16, no. 1, pp. 4–44.

Morris, K. N., 1968. 'Compassion, caution and courage', *Medical Journal of Australia*, vol. 1, no. 26, June, pp. 1111–14.

Morris, R. C., 1972. 'Guidelines for accepting volunteers: consent, ethical implications, and the function of a peer review', *Clinical Pharmacology & Therapeutics*, vol. 13, pp. 782–6.

Mouzelis, N. P., 1975. *Organisation and Bureaucracy: An Analysis of Modern Theories*, London: Routledge & Kegan Paul.

Mulford, R. D., 1969. 'Experimentation on human beings', *Stanford Law Review*, vol. 20, pp. 99–117.

Mulkay, M., 1980. 'Interpretation and the use of rules: the case of the norms of science', *Transactions New York Academy of Sciences*, Series II, vol. 39, New York: The New York Academy of Sciences, pp. 111–25.

Muschamp, D., 1988. 'Who should sit on an Institutional Ethics Committee?', in J. Hudson (ed.), *Proceedings of the Conference: Can Ethics be Done by Committee?*, Melbourne: Monash University Centre For Human Bioethics, 15 November, pp. 50–9.

National Commission for the Protection of Human Subjects of Biomedical and Behavioral Research, 1978a. 'Report', Department of Health Education and Welfare, *Federal Register*, Part III, 30 November, pp. 56,183–4.

1978b. *Report and Recommendations: Institutional Review Boards*, DHEW Publication No. (OS) 78-0008, US Government Printer, Washington.

1978c. *Appendix to Report and Recommendations: Institutional Review Boards*, DHEW Publication No. (OS) 78-0009, US Government Printer, Washington.

1978d. *The Belmont Report: Ethical Principles and Guidelines for the Protection of Human Subjects of Research*, DHEW Publication No. (OS) 78-0012, US Government Printer, Washington.

National Council on Bioethics in Human Research (Canada), 1989. 'The National Council on Bioethics in Human Research', Canada: National Council on Bioethics.

National Health and Medical Research Council (NHMRC), 1966. 'Statement on Human Experimentation', endorsed by the NHMRC at its Sixty-second Session in Adelaide, May.

1974. 'National Health and Medical Research Council, Statement on Human Experimentation', *Medical Journal of Australia*, vol. 1, no. 24, June, p. 976.

1976. 'Revised National Health and Medical Research Council, Statement on Human Experimentation', adopted by the Council at its 82nd session, Appendix VIII, Canberra: Australian Government Publishing Service.

1983a. *Ethics in Medical Research*, Report of the National Health and Medical Research Council Working Party on Ethics in Medical Research, adopted by the Council at its 94th Session, October 1982, Canberra: Australian Government Publishing Service.

1983b. NHMRC Working Party on Ethics in Medical Research, 'First report: research on humans', *Medical Journal of Australia*, vol. 1, no. 6, March, pp. 283–4.

1983c. *Ethics in Medical Research Involving the Human Fetus and Human Fetal Tissue*, Report of the National Health and Medical Research Council Medical Research Ethics Committee, Canberra: Australian Government Publishing Service.

1985a. [with Commonwealth Scientific and Industrial Research Organization and the Australian Agricultural Council] *Code of Practice for the Care and Use of Animals for Experimental Purposes*, Canberra: Australian Government Publishing Service.

1985b. Medical Research Ethics Committee, *Embryo Donation by Uterine Flushing: Interim Report on Ethical Considerations*, Canberra: Australian Government Publishing Service. [Adopted by the Council at its Ninety-ninth Session, and published in Appendix V of the Report the 99th Session, June 1985.]

1985c. Medical Research Ethics Committee, *Report on Ethics in Epidemiological Research*, Canberra: Australian Government Publishing Service.

1985d. Medical Ethics Research Committee, *Report on Workshops on the Constitution and Functions of Institutional Ethics Committees in Australia 1984–85*, November.

1985e. *Embryo Donation by Uterine Flushing: Medical Research Ethics Committee Interim Report on Ethical Considerations*, Canberra: Australian Government Publishing Service.

1986a. 'The National Health and Medical Research Council and ethical regulation – a short history', *Australian Health Review*, vol. 9, no. 3, pp. 234–42.

1986b. *Consideration by institutional ethics committees of research protocols involving frozen-thawed human ova*, Canberra: Australian Government Publishing Service.

1986c. Medical Research Ethics Committee, *In Vitro Fertilization Centres in Australia: Their Observance of the National Health and Medical Research Council's Guidelines*, A Report to the National Health and Medical Research Council, August.

1986d. 'Ethics of Fertility Research Conference Report', Report of the 102nd Session of the National Health and Medical Research Council, Canberra, November, p. 10 and Appendix III.

1987a. 'Report of the working group to consider the establishment of a national body on guidelines and research on in vitro fertilisation (IVF)', National Health and Medical Research Council, Report of the 103rd Session, Hobart, June, p. 5 and Appendix I.

1987b. *Ethical Aspects of Research on Human Gene Therapy*, Report to the National Health and Medical Research Council by the Medical Research Ethics Committee, Canberra: Australian Government Publishing Service.

1988a. *NHMRC Statement on Human Experimentation and Supplementary Notes*, Canberra: National Health and Medical Research Council.

1988b. Medical Research Ethics Committee, *Some Advisory Notes on Ethical Matters in Aboriginal Research: including extracts from a Report of the National Workshop of Research in Aboriginal Health*, Canberra: National Health and Medical Research Council, July.

1988c. Medical Ethics Research Committee, *Report on Round Table Conference on Human Gene Therapy*, Canberra: National Health and Medical Research Council, September.

1990. Medical Research Ethics Committee, 'Report from the Aboriginal Health Research Ethics Committee of South Australia', Medical Research Ethics Committee Newsletter, vol. 2, nos 3 and 4, June, pp. 10–11.

1991a. 'Guidelines on ethical matters in Aboriginal and Torres Strait Islander health research', Approved by the 11th Session of the National Health and Medical Research Council, Brisbane, and produced in an interim format pending publication, June.

1991b. Medical Research Ethics Committee, Newsletter, vol. 2, no. 6, June, p. 18.

National Union of Students (UK), 1989. 'The NUS guidelines for students participating in medical research', reported in 'Protecting students in medical research', *Bulletin of Medical Ethics*, no. 54, November/December, pp. 10–11.

Neuberger, J., 1992. *Ethics and Health Care: The Role of Research Ethics Committees in the United Kingdom*, London: King's Fund Institute.

Neutze, J. M., 1990. 'A standard for ethical committees', letter to the Editor, *New Zealand Medical Journal*, vol. 102, 8 March, p. 111.

Neville, R., 1979. 'On the National Commission: a puritan critique of consensus ethics', *Hastings Center Report*, vol. 9, no. 2, April, pp. 22–7.

New Zealand Department of Health, 1988. 'Standard for hospital and health board ethics committees established to review research and treatment protocols', New Zealand: Department of Health, October.

New Zealand Department of Health, 1991. 'Standard for ethics committees established to review research and ethical aspects of health care', New Zealand: Department of Health, December.

Nicholson, R. H., 1986. *Medical Research with Children: Ethics, Law, and Practice*, Oxford: Oxford University Press.

Noach, E. L., 1982. 'Discussion', in Z. Bankowski and N. Howard-Jones (eds), *Human Experimentation and Medical Ethics: Proceedings of the*

XVth CIOMS Round Table Conference Manila, 13–16 September 1981, Council for International Organizations of Medical Sciences, Geneva, pp. 231–4, and pp. 260–1.

Obade, C. C., 1991. 'Whisper down the lane: AIDS, privacy and the hospital grapevine', *Journal of Clinical Ethics*, vol. 2, no. 2, Summer, pp. 133–7.

Office of Science and Technology Privacy and Behavioral Research, 1972. In J. Katz, *Experimentation with Human Beings: The Authority of the Investigator, Subject, Professions, and State in the Human Experimentation Process*, New York: Russell Sage, pp. 728–31.

Ofosu-Amaah, S., 1982. 'Ethical aspects of externally sponsored research in developing countries: an African viewpoint', in Z. Bankowski and N. Howard-Jones (eds), *Human Experimentation and Medical Ethics: Proceedings of the XVth CIOMS Round Table Conference, Manila, 13–16 September 1981*, Council for International Organizations of Medical Sciences, Geneva, pp. 270–5.

Osborne, L., 1981. 'Review of the present situation in Victoria, Australia and overseas', Health Commission of Victoria seminar for members of hospitals ethics committees, Melbourne, unpublished report, 21 August, pp. 10–21.

1982. 'The ethical review committee and medical research', *New Doctor*, no. 24, June, pp. 24–7.

1983a. 'NHMRC Report on Research on Humans: the wrong balance of administration and ethics', *Medical Journal of Australia*, vol. 1, March, pp. 284–5.

1983b. 'Research on human subjects: Australian ethics committees take tentative steps', *Journal of Medical Ethics*, vol. 9, pp. 66–8.

Pappworth, M. H., 1967. *Human Guinea Pigs: Experimentations on Man*, Boston: Beacon.

Parson, W., 1984. 'Uninformed Consent in 1942' (letter to the Editor), *New England Journal of Medicine*, vol. 310, p. 1397.

Parsons, T., 1951. *The Social System*, New York: Free Press of Glencoe.

1969. 'Research with human subjects and the "professional complex"', *Daedalus*, vol. 98, no. 2, Spring, pp. 325–60.

Pateman, C., 1970. *Participation and Democratic Theory*, London and Melbourne: Cambridge University Press.

Paul, C., 1988. 'The New Zealand cervical cancer study: Could it happen again?' *British Medical Journal*, vol. 297, pp. 533–9.

1989. 'A standard for ethical committees' (letter to the Editor), *New Zealand Medical Journal*, vol. 102, 25 January, p. 20.

Paul, C. and Holloway, L., 1990. 'No new evidence on the cervical cancer study', *New Zealand Medical Journal*, vol. 103, no. 903, 12 December, pp. 581–3.

Pavlovsky, S., 1981. 'Clinical research and the protection of the subject in Argentina', *Medical Ethics and Medical Education: Proceedings of the XIVth Round Table Conference, Mexico City, Mexico, 1–3 December*

1980, Geneva: Council for International Organizations of Medical Sciences, pp. 118-23.

Percival, T., 1803. *Medical Ethics*. [Reprinted in C. D. Leake (ed.), 1975. *Percival's Medical Ethics* (2nd edn), Huntington, New York: Robert E. Krieger, pp. 61-205.]

Pernick, M. S., 1982. 'The patient's role in medical decisionmaking: a social history of informed consent', in President's Commission for the Study of Ethical Problems in Medicine and Biomedical Research, *Making Health Care Decisions: The Ethical and Legal Implications of Informed Consent in the Patient-Practitioner Relationship: Volume 3: Appendices Studies on the Foundations of Informed Consent*, Washington DC: Government Printing Office, Library of Congress No. 82-600637, October, pp. 1-35.

Pitkin, H. F., 1967. *The Concept of Representation*, Berkeley and Los Angeles: University of California Press.

1968. 'Commentary: the paradox of representation', in J. R. Pennock and J. W. Chapman (eds), *Nomos X: Representation, Yearbook of the American Society for Political and Legal Philosophy*, New York: Atherton Press, pp. 38-42.

Platt, R., 1966. 'Ethical problems in medical procedures', in G. E. W. Wolstenholme and M. O'Connor (eds), *Ciba Foundation Symposium: Ethics in Medical Progress With Special Reference to Transplantation*, London: J. & A. Churchill, pp. 149-53.

Porter, J. P., 1986. 'What are the ideal characteristics of unaffiliated/nonscientist IRB members?', *IRB: A Review of Human Subjects Research*, vol. 8, no. 3, May/June, pp. 1-6.

1987. 'How unaffiliated/nonscientist members of Institutional Review Boards see their roles', *IRB: A Review of Human Subjects Research*, vol. 9, no. 6, November/December, pp. 1-6.

1991. 'The federal policy for the protection of human subjects', *IRB: A Review of Human Subjects Research*, vol. 13, no. 5, September-October, pp. 8-9.

Powell, J. W., 1981. 'A hidden chapter in history', *Bulletin of the Atomic Scientists*, October, pp. 44-52.

President's Commission for the Study of Ethical Problems in Medicine and Biomedical and Behavioral Research, 1983. *Implementing Human Research Regulations: Second Biennial Report of the Adequacy and Uniformity of Federal Rules and Policies, and of their Implementation, for the Protection of Human Subjects*, Library of Congress No. 83-600 504, Washington: US Government Printing Office.

Pridham, J. A., 1951. 'Founding of the World Medical Association', *World Medical Association Bulletin*, vol. 3, no. 3, July, pp. 207-10.

Ramsey, P., 1970. *The Patient as Person: Explorations in Medical Ethics*, New Haven: Yale University Press. [Extracts reprinted in J. Katz, 1972. *Experimentation with Human Beings: The Authority of the Investigator,*

Subject, Professions, and State in the Human Experimentation Process,
New York: Russell Sage, pp. 589–91.]

1974. 'A reply to Richard McCormick – The enforcement of morals:
nontherapeutic research on children', *Hastings Center Report*, vol. 6,
no. 4, August, pp. 21–30.

Rappoport, S. M., 1979. 'Ethical review practices and protection of human
rights in medicine in the German Democratic Republic', in N.
Howard-Jones and Z. Bankowski (eds), *Medical Experimentation and
the Protection of Human Rights: Proceedings of the XIIth CIOMS Round
Table Conference, Cascaus, Portugal, 30 November–1 December 1978,*
Geneva: Council for International Organizations of Medical Sciences
and Sandoz Institute for Health and Socio-Economic Studies, pp. 65–71.

Reams, B. D. and Gray, C. J., 1985. *Human Experimentation: Federal Laws,
Legislative Histories, Regulations and Related Documents.* [An essay,
which precedes a collection of documents supplied on microfiche or
microfilm.] New York, London and Rome: Oceana Publications.

Regan, T. and Singer, P., 1976. *Animal Rights and Human Obligations,*
Englewood Cliffs, New Jersey: Prentice Hall.

Reiser, S. J., Dyck, A. J. and Curran, W. J. (eds), 1977. *Ethics in Medicine:
Historical Perspectives and Contemporary Concerns,* Cambridge,
Massachusetts: MIT Press.

Richmond, D., 1977. 'Auckland Hospital Ethical Committee: first three
years', *New Zealand Medical Journal*, vol. 86, pp. 10–12.

Riis, P., 1979. 'Composition, authority and influence of ethical review
committees', in N. Howard-Jones and Z. Bankowski (eds), *Medical
Experimentation and the Protection of Human Rights: Proceedings of
the XIIth CIOMS Round Table Conference, Cascaus, Portugal, 30
November–1 December 1978,* Geneva: Council for International
Organizations of Medical Sciences and Sandoz Institute for Health and
Socio-Economic Studies, pp. 85–9.

1983. 'Experience with committees and councils for research ethics in
Scandinavia', in K. Berg and K. E. Tranøy (eds), *Research Ethics*, New
York: Alan R. Liss, pp. 123–9.

1988. 'Ethics Committees flourish in Europe: Denmark', *IME Bulletin,*
no. 39, June, pp. 15–16.

1991. 'English Summary', in Central Scientific-Ethical Committee,
Report for 1990, Copenhagen: Minister of Science.

Robertson, A., 1986. 'What price the human alternative?', *Alternatives to
Laboratory Animals*, vol. 14, pp. 93–5.

Robertson, J. A., 1984. 'Committees as decision makers: alternative struc-
tures and responsibilities', in R. E. Cranford and A. E. Doudera (eds),
Institutional Ethics Committees and Health Care Decision Making, Ann
Arbor, Michigan: Health Administration Press, pp. 85–95.

Rose, H. and Rose, S., 1971. *Science and Society*, Harmondsworth: Penguin
Books.

Ross, W. D., 1930. *The Right and the Good*, Oxford: Clarendon Press. [Reprinted 1961.]

Roth, L. H., Appelbaum, P. S., Lidz, C. W. and Benson, P., 1987. 'Informed consent to psychiatric research', *Rutgers Law Review*, vol. 39, pp. 425–41.

Rothman, D. J., 1987. 'Ethics and human experimentation: Henry Beecher revisited', *New England Journal of Medicine*, vol. 317, no. 19, pp. 1195–9.

Routley, T. C., 1949. 'Aims and objects of the World Medical Association', *World Medical Association Bulletin*, vol. 1, no. 1, April, pp. 18–19.

Royal College of Physicians, 1967. Report of the Committee Appointed by the Royal College, 'Supervision of the ethics of clinical investigations in institutions', *British Medical Journal*, vol. 3, 12 August, pp. 429–30.

1984. *Guidelines on the Practice of Ethics Committees in Medical Research*, London: Royal College of Physicians, September.

1990a. *Guidelines on the Practice of Ethics Committees in Medical Research involving Human Subjects* (2nd edn), London: Royal College of Physicians.

1990b. *Research Involving Patients*, London: Royal College of Physicians.

Rutnam, R., 1988. 'Ethics in medical research: Australian developments', *Community Health Studies*, vol. 12, no. 2, pp. 127–33.

Rutstein, D. D., 1969. 'The ethical design of experiments', *Daedalus*, vol. 98, no. 2, Spring, pp. 523–41.

Sackville, R., 1980. 'Professions under scrutiny: observations on the regulation of doctors and lawyers', *Current Affairs Bulletin*, vol. 56, pp. 16–26.

Sass, H-M., 1983. 'Reichsrundschreiben 1931: pre-Nuremberg German regulations concerning new therapy and human experimentation', *The Journal of Medicine and Philosophy*, vol. 8, pp. 99–111.

1989. 'Blue-ribbon commissions and political ethics in the Federal Republic of Germany', *The Journal of Medicine and Philosophy*, vol. 14, pp. 465–72.

Satir, V., 1967. *Conjoint Family Therapy: A Guide to Theory and Technique*, Palo Alto, California: Condor.

Savitt, T. L., 1982. 'The use of blacks for medical experimentation and demonstration in the Old South', *Journal of Southern History*, vol. 68, no. 3, August, pp. 331–48.

Schafer, A., 1983. 'Experimentation with human subjects: a critique of the views of Hans Jonas', *Journal of Medical Ethics*, vol. 9, pp. 76–9.

Schöne-Seifert, B. and Rippe, K-P., 1991. 'Silencing the Singer: Antibioethics in Germany', *Hastings Center Report*, vol. 21, no. 6, November–December, pp. 20–7.

Schultz, A. L., Pardee, G. P. and Ensinck, J. W., 1975. 'Are research subjects really informed?' *West Journal of Medicine*, vol. 123, pp. 76–80.

Scutt, J. A. (ed.), 1988. *The Baby Machine: Commercialisation of Motherhood*, Carlton, Australia: McCulloch Press.

Shannon, T. A. and Ockene, I. S., 1985. 'Approving high risk, rejecting low risk: the case of two cases', *IRB: A Review of Human Subjects Research*, vol. 7, no. 1, January/February, pp. 6–8.

Sharma, I. C., 1965. *Ethical Philosophies of India* (edited and revised by S. M. Daugert), New York: Harper Torchbooks.

Singer, P., 1977. *Animal Liberation: A New Ethics for our Treatment of Animals*, London: Jonathan Cape. [Also published as *Animal Liberation: Towards an End to Man's Inhumanity to Animals*, 1977. Paladin, Granada Publishing.]

1979. *Practical Ethics*, London: Cambridge University Press.

(ed.) 1985. *In Defence of Animals*, Oxford: Basil Blackwell.

1989. 'Rats, patients and people: issues in the ethical regulation of research', Annual Lecture, published as a monograph by the Academy of the Social Sciences in Australia.

1990. 'Bioethics and academic freedom', *Bioethics*, vol. 4, no. 1, January, pp. 33–44.

Sinnathuray, A., 1982. 'Ethical review procedures in Malaysia', in Z. Bankowski and N. Howard-Jones (eds), *Human Experimentation and Medical Ethics: Proceedings of the XVth CIOMS Round Table Conference Manila, 13–16 September 1981*, Council for International Organizations of Medical Sciences, Geneva, pp. 235–8.

Skegg, C. G., 1986. 'Cervical screening' (letter to the Editor), *New Zealand Medical Journal*, vol. 99, 22 January, pp. 26–7.

Smith, J. S. and Kiloh L. G. (eds), 1977. *Psychosurgery and Society: A Symposium organized by the Neuropsychiatric Institute* (Sydney), Oxford and Sydney: Pergamon Press.

Smith, S. F., 1984. 'Some recent cases on informed consent', *Adelaide Law Review*, vol. 9, no. 3, September, pp. 413–25.

Sobel, L. A. (ed.), 1977. *Medical Science & the Law: The Life & Death Controversy*, New York: Facts on File.

Soh, C-T., 1982. 'National drug regulations and ethical review procedures in Korea', in Z. Bankowski and N. Howard-Jones (eds), *Human Experimentation and Medical Ethics: Proceedings of the XVth CIOMS Round Table Conference Manila, 13–16 September 1981*, Council for International Organizations of Medical Sciences, Geneva, pp. 239–41.

Spiers, H. R., 1991a. 'Community consultation and AIDS clinical trials: Part I', *IRB: A Review of Human Subjects Research*, vol. 13, no. 5, May–June, pp. 7–10.

1991b. 'Community consultation and AIDS clinical trials: Part II', *IRB: A Review of Human Subjects Research*, vol. 13, no. 4, July–August.

1991c. 'Community consultation and AIDS clinical trials: Part III', *IRB: A Review of Human Subjects Research*, vol. 13, no. 5, September–October, pp. 3–7.

Sprigge, T. L. S., 1987. *The Rational Foundation of Ethics*, London and New York: Routledge & Kegan Paul.

Stewart, R. B., 1975. 'The reformation of American administrative law', *Harvard Law Journal*, vol. 88, no. 8, June, pp. 1667–813.

Swain, D. C., 1962. 'The rise of a research empire: NIH, 1930 to 1950', *Science*, vol. 138, no. 3546, December, pp. 1233–7.

Swazey, J. P., 1978. 'Protecting the "animal of necessity": limits to inquiry in clinical investigation', *Daedalus*, vol. 107, pp. 129–45.

Teff, J. H. and Munro, C., 1976. *Thalidomide, the Legal Aftermath*, Farnborough, Hants: Saxon House.

Thompson, I. E., French, K., Melia, K. M., Boyd, K .M., Templeton, A. A. and Potter, B., 1981. 'Research Ethical Committees in Scotland', *British Medical Journal*, vol. 282, pp. 718–20.

Toulmin, S., 1977. 'The meaning of professionalism: doctors' ethics and biomedical science', in H. T. Englehardt Jr and D. Callahan, (eds), *Knowledge, Value and Belief*, Hastings-on-Hudson, New York: Institute of Society, Ethics and Life Sciences.

1981. 'The tyranny of principles', *Hastings Center Report*, vol. 11, no. 6, December, pp. 31–9.

1982. 'How medicine saved the life of ethics', *Perspectives in Biology and Medicine*, vol. 24, no. 4, Summer, pp. 736–50.

United Kingdom, Department of Health, 1991. 'Local Research Ethics Committees', London: Departments of Health and Social Security, April.

US Federal Policy for the Protection of Human Subjects; Notices and Rules, 1991. *Federal Register*, Part II, vol. 56, no. 117, 18 June, pp. 28002–32.

Veatch, R. M., 1975. 'Human experimentation committees: professional or representative?', *Hastings Center Report*, October, pp. 31–40.

1979. 'The National Commission on IRBs: an evolutionary approach', *Hastings Center Report*, vol. 9, no. 1, February, pp. 22–8.

1984. 'Autonomy's temporary triumph', *Hastings Center Report*, vol. 14, no. 5, October, pp. 38–40.

Veressayev, V., 1916. *The Memoirs of a Physician* (translated from the Russian version of 1901 by Simeon Linden), New York: Alfred A. Knopf. [Excerpts reprinted in Katz, 1972. pp. 284–91.]

Villadolid, L. S., 1982. 'Discussion', in Z. Bankowski and N. Howard-Jones (eds), *Human Experimentation and Medical Ethics: Proceedings of the XVth CIOMS Round Table Conference Manila, 13–16 September 1981*, Council for International Organizations of Medical Sciences, Geneva, pp. 252–3.

Voluntary Licensing Authority (UK), 1989. *The Fourth Report of the Voluntary Licensing Authority For Human In Vitro Fertilisation and Embryology*, London: Voluntary Licensing Authority, April.

Wadlington, W., Waltz, J .R. and Dworkin, R. B., 1980. *Cases and Materials on Law and Medicine*, Mineoloa, New York: Foundation Press.

Walker, J., 1970. 'Normative consequences of democratic theory', in H. S. Kariel (ed.), *Frontiers of Democratic Theory*, New York: Random House, pp. 227–47.

Walters, W. A. W., 1986. 'Institutional Ethics Committees', unpublished paper presented at Bioethics Course conducted by Monash University Centre for Human Bioethics, Warburton, 8-12 December.

Warnock, M., 1985. *A Question of Life: The Warnock Report on Human Fertilisation and Embryology*, Oxford: Basil Blackwell.

1988. 'A national ethics committee: to meet the growing public demand for candour', *British Medical Journal*, vol. 297, 24-31 December, pp. 1626-7.

Weber, M., 1978. *Economy and Society: an Outline of Interpretive Sociology*, vol. 2 (edited by G. Roth and C. Wittich), Berkeley: University of California Press.

Weeramantry, C. G. and Di Giantomasso, D. F., 1983. Consent to the Medical Treatment of Minors and Intellectually Handicapped Persons, occasional paper, Monash, Victoria: Faculty of Law, Monash University, June.

Weisbard, A. J., 1987. 'On not compensating for bad outcomes to biomedical innovations: a response and modest proposal', *Cardozo Law Review*, vol. 8, pp. 1161-88.

Werko, L., 1982. 'Ethical aspects of externally sponsored research', in Z. Bankowski and N. Howard-Jones (eds), *Human Experimentation and Medical Ethics: Proceedings of the XVth CIOMS Round Table Conference Manila, 13-16 September 1981*, Council for International Organizations of Medical Sciences, Geneva, pp. 231-4, pp. 291-3.

Williams, P. and Wallace, D., 1989. *Unit 731: Japan's Secret Biological Warfare in World War II*, New York: Free Press.

Willis, E., 1983. *Medical Dominance: The Division of Labour in Australian Health Care*, Sydney: George Allen & Unwin.

Winton, R., 1976. 'Revision of the Declaration of Helsinki', (editorial) *Medical Journal of Australia*, vol. 1, no. 7, February, pp. 179-80.

1978. 'The significanre [sic] of the Declaration of Helsinki: an interpretive commentary', (editorial) *Medical Journal of Australia*, vol. 2, July, pp. 78-9. [Reprinted in *World Medical Journal*, 1978, vol. 25, July/August, pp. 58-59.]

Wittgenstein, L., 1953. *Philosophical Investigations*, (translated by G. E. M. Anscombe), Oxford: Blackwell.

Woltjen, M., 1986. 'Regulation of informed consent to human experimentation', *Loyola University Law Journal*, vol. 17, pp. 507-32.

Woodward, W. E., 1979. 'Informed consent of volunteers: a direct measurement of comprehension and retention of information', *Clinical Research*, vol. 27, pp. 248-52.

Wootton, A. J., 1977. 'Some notes on the organization of talk in a therapeutic community', *Sociology*, vol. 11, no. 2, pp. 333-50.

Working Party of the Maternity Services Task Force, 1989. 'Consumer/community representation and participation in maternity services', New Zealand, December.

World Health Organization, 1987. Information Document of the Health Legislation Unit of the World Health Organization (WHO), 'Human Experimentation: a concise overview of international instruments and legislation, guidelines, ethical codes, etc. in the seven Summit Countries', *Report of the Summit Conference on Bioethics*, Ottawa, prepared by Judith Miller, Medical Research Council of Canada, April, pp. 232–69.

World Health Organization and Council for International Organizations of Medical Sciences, 1982. *Proposed International Guidelines for Biomedical Research Involving Human Subjects*, Geneva: CIOMS.

World Medical Association, 1964. Declaration of Helsinki: Recommendations Guiding Medical Doctors in Biomedical Research involving Human Subjects, *New England Journal of Medicine*, vol. 271, p. 473.

1975. As revised by the 29th World Medical Assembly, Tokyo, Japan.

1983. As revised by the 35th World Medical Assembly, Venice, Italy.

Wuorinen, V., 1984. 'Check-list and guidelines for joint occupational health and safety committees: organizational factors', Hamilton, Ontario: Canadian Centre for Occupational Health and Safety.

1991. 'Managing joint committees', *Occupational Health and Safety Canada*, vol. 7, no. 2, March/April, pp. 48–54.

Yesley, M. S., 1980. *Hastings Center Report*, vol. 10, no. 5, October, pp. 5–9.

Zarkrzewski, W., 1968. 'The mechanism of popular activity in the exercise of state authority in people's Poland', in *Nomos X: Representation, Yearbook of the American Society for Political and Legal Philosophy*, New York: Atherton Press.

Zetterstrom, R., 1982. 'Ethical aspects of clinical design in Sweden', in Z. Bankowski and N. Howard-Jones (eds), *Human Experimentation and Medical Ethics: Proceedings of the XVth CIOMS Round Table Conference Manila, 13–16 September 1981*, Council for International Organizations of Medical Sciences, Geneva, pp. 231–4.

Zimmerman, D. H., 1971. 'The practicalities of rule use', in J. D. Douglas (ed.), *Understanding Everyday Life: Toward the Reconstruction of Sociological Knowledge*, London: Routledge & Kegan Paul, pp. 221–38.

Index